RACE, RACISM
SOCIAL WO

Contemporary issues and debates

Edited by Michael Lavalette and Laura Penketh

First published in Great Britain in 2014 by

Policy Press
University of Bristol
1-9 Old Park Hill
Bristol BS2 8BB
UK
t: +44 (0)117 954 5940
e: pp-info@bristol.ac.uk
www.policypress.co.uk

North American office:
Policy Press
c/o The University of Chicago Press
1427 East 60th Street
Chicago, IL 60637, USA
t: +1 773 702 7700
f: +1 773-702-9756
e:sales@press.uchicago.edu
www.press.uchicago.edu

Reprinted 2015

British Library Cataloguing in Publication Data
A catalogue record for this book is available from the British Library

Library of Congress Cataloging-in-Publication Data
A catalog record for this book has been requested

ISBN 978 1 44730 707 5 paperback
ISBN 978 1 44730 708 2 hardcover

Cover design by Qube Design Associates, Bristol
Front cover image: www.istock.com
Printed and bound in Great Britain by CMP, Poole

Woodland CARBON
www.woodlandcarbon.co.uk
CMP (UK) LTD
Printed on Carbon Captured paper

Contents

Notes on contributors

Beverley Burke is a senior lecturer in social work at Liverpool John Moores University, UK.

Liz Fekete is executive director of the Institute of Race Relations and author of *A suitable enemy: Racism, migration and Islamophobia in Europe* (Pluto 2009).

Susan Gillett is an experienced frontline social work practitioner. She specialises in work with young people, including unaccompanied asylum seeking children.

Joe Greener is a lecturer in social policy at Liverpool Hope University.

Philomena Harrison is a senior lecturer in social work at Liverpool Hope University.

Gareth Jenkins has recently retired from London South Bank University.

Michael Lavalette is professor of social work at Liverpool Hope University and national co-ordinator of the Social Work Action Network. He is co-editor of the new journal *Critical and Radical Social Work.*

Barrie Levine is a senior lecturer in social work at Glasgow Caledonian University. He is on the national steering committee of the Social Work Action Network.

Rhetta Moran works and campaigns alongside ayslum seekers and refugees. She initiated www.rapar.org.uk in 2001 and co-edited the book *Doing research with refugees* (2006) published by Policy Press.

Judith Orr is a journalist and a member of the executive committee of Abortion Rights.

Laura Penketh is a senior lecturer in social work and social policy at Liverpool Hope University. She is the author of *Tackling institutional racism* (Policy Press 2000).

Gurnam Singh is principal lecturer in social work at Coventry University.

Dave Stamp is a frontline worker in Birmingham.

Špela Urh is a lecturer in social work at Ljubljana University.

Charlotte Williams is professor of social work at RMIT, Melbourne.

Acknowledgements

Working within higher education (HE) is becoming more intense by the year; the marketisation of higher education means there is greater pressure on lecturers to publish more, teach more, market courses, 'sell' universities, and carry out increased levels of administration. A recent survey by the lecturers' union, UCU, found that levels of stress and anxiety within academia were higher than in any comparable profession.

Given these unpalatable truths, we would like to thank all our contributors for finding the time and space to complete their chapters for us. We hope we have not added to their stress burdens too much!

The idea for this book came out of a number of debates and conferences organised by the Social Work Action Network over the last few years. We would like to take this opportunity to thank our friends and colleagues for providing, within SWAN, an open 'public space' where debates can be aired and solutions – practical and theoretical – 'tried out'.

The danger of naming people is that we will forget someone vitally important to our recent political and philosophical trajectory. Nevertheless, we would like to thank our friends, colleagues and comrades at Liverpool Hope University and within SWAN, who have supported us while we were putting this project together. In particular, we'd like to thank Chris Jones, Vassilis Ioakimidis, Rich Moth and Iain Ferguson.

Karen Bowler at Policy Press was supportive of the book proposal from the very beginning. Karen has now moved on to other projects with her new family, and we wish her well. Isobel Bainton has taken the project over since Karen's departure and has ensured that we have worked to a tight (and entirely appropriate) time schedule. We would like to thank Isobel and her team for their support.

At our shared home, putting the book together was often at the expense of spending time with our children. Although our daughters are now at an age where they don't want to spend too much time with us, we would like to thank Saskia and Olivia for their patience! Finally, in the middle of writing and organising this book, Sheila Lavalette, mum, mum-in-law and friend, passed away suddenly. Despite our great loss we are sustained, in part, by the knowledge that Sheila was always appalled by all injustices and discrimination. We dedicate this book, with love, to her memory.

In memoriam

Sheila Lavalette

(1942–2012)

Some terms and definitions

'Race'

'Race' is a social construct and not a scientifically valid reality. The science of genetics has demonstrated that there is more statistically significant genetic diversity within population groups than between them, and that the physiological differences associated with 'race' have no more significance than hair or eye colour. However, most people think that 'races' exist and as a concept it continues to shape patterns of discrimination and disadvantage.

Racism

Racism is a relatively modern phenomenon that grew up with the development and expansion of capitalism, reflected in the racism of slavery, the racism of Empire and the racism of post-war migration. In each period, racist ideologies were constructed based on the view that white 'races' were superior to black 'races' to justify segregation, discrimination and exploitation.

The concept of 'race' continues to motivate 'action', behaviour and discrimination that we can understand as racism. This occurs when a group of people is discriminated against on the basis of characteristics that are held to be inherent in them as a group. In short, although biologically discrete 'races' do not exist, racism certainly does, and millions of people's lives are blighted by racist discrimination.

Structural/institutional racism

Structural analyses see notions of natural inferiority and superiority arising in the conditions of capitalism, and institutional racism describes the systematic discrimination that minority ethnic communities experience, in, for example, the labour market, the criminal justice system, and in relation to housing and education. In short, racism is an institutional feature integrated into the history and social, economic, political and ideological fabric of British society. Institutional racism gained public and political significance in the UK as a result of the MacPherson Report, which published the findings of the investigation into the murder of Stephen Lawrence in 1993. The Report concluded that racism is deeply ingrained in all organisations and institutions, with a specific focus on police racism in Britain.

Anti-racist social work practice

Anti-racist social work practice emphasises the importance of structural and institutional disadvantage in understanding the experiences of minority ethnic individuals and communities, and highlights the need to consider the disadvantage and racism that they encounter. In doing so it directs attention away from individual and cultural explanations and focuses on deficient material resources, racist policies, procedures and practices within organisations, and dominant ideologies of the state. Anti-racism has been highly contested in the field of social work education and training, and despite attempts by the Central Council for Education and Training in Social Work (CCETSW) to implement anti-racist policies and procedures in the early 1990s, it has become marginalised within the field.

Oppression/anti-oppressive practice

Oppression refers to systematic social practices that result in inhumane, degrading and unequal treatment of individuals or groups in society, and with injustices linked to the dominance of particular groups over others. Oppression is 'socially constructed'. It may make reference to supposed biological categories, but it reflects a series of social practices that have developed within particular historical circumstances. Oppression can take place on the basis of class, 'race', gender, disability, age and sexuality. Anti-oppressive practice is underpinned by a requirement that social workers understand the nature of oppression in society and how it affects service user groups, and that they act to counter it in their intervention.

Ethnicity

Ethnicity is used to describe a group possessing some degree of coherence and solidarity, and who share common origins and interests. So, an ethnic group is not a mere aggregate of people, but a self-conscious collection of people united, or closely related, by shared experiences. Ethnicity defines the salient feature of a group that regards itself as in some sense, distinct, and can be passed from one generation to the next. However, ethnicity may weaken as successive generations question its validity. For example, original migrants may have found the maintenance of their culture highly important, whereas their sons and daughters find it irrelevant. Yet, ethnic affiliation is not always easily dismissed, as it can be deeply embedded in the consciousness through years of socialisation within an ethnic group.

Prejudice

Prejudice can be defined as learned beliefs and values that lead an individual or group of individuals to be biased for, or against, members of particular groups prior to actual experience of those groups. Holding negative values and beliefs about a particular group bears a strong influence on how behaviour towards that group will be organised. Minority ethnic communities can suffer if individuals with prejudicial beliefs implement them in discriminatory ways.

Multiculturalism

Multicultural perspectives are based on the notion that learning about other peoples' cultures will reduce prejudice and discrimination in society. They incorporate the belief that contact with other cultural lifestyles will reduce the ignorance and prejudice of the white population. However, multiculturalism has not always been embraced by politicians and the general public. For example, in Britain during the 1970s and 1980s, key political figures worried about the country being 'culturally swamped', and since then there has been an increased focus on the national allegiances of migrant communities. More recently, the tendency to link migration with cohesion and social order reflects and resonates with much older debates that question the willingness of migrants to integrate, and focus on their preferential access to limited labour market opportunities and public resources such as healthcare and social housing. These discourses have been effective, and have led to increasing attacks on migrant populations across Europe, made worse by declining economic opportunities and austerity measures. As a result, a commitment to multiculturalism has been undermined.

Cultural identity/difference

Cultural identity defines a junction between how a culture defines subjects and how they imagine themselves. It can represent a stable consistent feature that unifies people, particularly in periods of struggle, and in terms of oppression it can act as a form of solidarity and resistance. Alternatively, as well as the multiple similarities that unite people, there are also significant differences that shape people's lives and experiences. In this respect, the ruptures that fragment populations are as important as the common experiences that unite them. Identity then is not an unchanging experience, but is fashioned by history, by circumstance, and by the mode of thinking that prevails in any collectivity. Difference persists in and alongside continuity, and the boundaries of difference are also continually being repositioned in relation to different points of reference. In this respect, differences are as much as part of cultural identities as similarities.

Islamophobia

Islamophobia is a modern form of racism that has gained increased significance in the context of 9/11 and the 'war on terror', and that has allowed 'the West' to construct Islam as the new enemy based on a 'clash of civilisations' thesis. It reflects negative and damaging stereotypes and assumptions that portray Islam as irrational, barbaric and sexist, and as inferior to Western culture. In this context anti-Muslim hostility becomes 'normalised' and is used to justify discriminatory policies and practices. The European Monitoring Centre on Racism and Xenophobia has found increasing evidence of Islamophobia in the form of physical and verbal abuse, and attacks on property across its member-states. This has been exacerbated by the increased activities of far-right and neo-Nazi groups and their attempts to target Muslims as scapegoats.

Antisemitism

Broadly, antisemitism is related to an adherence to views, attitudes or actions directed against the interests, legal rights, religious practices or lives of Jews. However, it is a fiercely debated and contested concept that has had its meanings and uses changed by circumstances. Anti-Semitism has been viewed in terms of both religion and race. The most virulent expression of the latter is clearly the Holocaust of World War Two, which was intended to eliminate European Jewry.

Xeno-racism

Xeno-racism is not just directed at those with darker skins from the former colonial territories, but at the newer categories of the displaced and dispossessed who are entering Europe. Although it is a form of racism that is not based purely on colour it nevertheless bears the marks of the old racism. It has been fully incorporated into domestic asylum policy across Europe, and is evident in rising levels of direct and political violence against asylum seekers/refugees and migrant communities. Xeno–racism has had impacts on policy developments across Europe that include criminalising asylum seekers, placing them in detention centres and removing their entitlement to welfare services.

Asylum seeker

In terms of international refugee law, an asylum seeker is a person who is attempting to obtain official status as a refugee in a country by meeting the requirements of the asylum law obtaining there. Although the substantive content of asylum law varies by country, the 1951 United Nations Convention Relating to the Status of Refugees and its 1967 protocol, provide minimally accepted international standards for such laws. Concern over asylum issues has gained increased political significance across Europe, and is linked to a rise in xeno-racism.

Refugee

A refugee is a person who seeks refuge outside their country of origin on grounds of persecution, and this may be based on factors such as race, religion, culture or political/sexual orientation. The 1951 Convention Relating to the Status of Refugees specifies that people who have sought refugee status should not be forcibly returned to a country where they fear persecution. The task of the host country is to determine whether the applicant is entitled to the status of refugee. Economic migrants are not covered by the 1951 Convention.

Intersectionality

Race and ethnicity are not the only causal factors in explaining and generating patterns of social inequality and exclusion, as social and economic status, locality and geography, education status, migration and residency status, religion, age and gender all intersect and interact with race and ethnicity. For example, in the fields of health, education, employment and policing there have been significant differences in the experiences and outcomes between and within diverse ethnic populations. Taking education as an example, while better-off pupils are more successful academically, the increasing achievements of Bengali pupils, who are among the most socially and economically deprived population groups, has to be accounted for. So, too, do the higher rates of school exclusions for African-Caribbean boys, despite their average social and economic position. Social and economic factors will also be shaped by education, status, locality, religion, age and gender. Thus it is important to reflect on the ways in which race and culture intersect with other lines of social division and impact on social relationships and social practices.

Cultural competence

Cultural competency is, broadly speaking, an approach in which policy makers and welfare providers integrate an awareness of, and sensitivity to, cultural diversity in relation to policy formation and practice, and are able to provide relevant and effective services to an increasingly diverse and multi-ethnic population. Cultural competence integrates a sociological recognition of structural factors, and combines this with a broader level of culture, placing an emphasis on self-reflection, communication and research. In the UK, it has been overwhelmingly located in the health-care sector, becoming part of the everyday policy and practice discourse, but has also become a feature of social work education, training and practice.

INTRODUCTION

Race, racism and social work

Michael Lavalette and Laura Penketh

This book explores issues of 'race', racism and anti-racist social work practice – with a particular focus on modern Britain. The dominant message from the media and politicians regarding social work is that it is dominated by 'political correctness' and focuses disproportionately on issues of class, 'race' and gender. In the training of social workers there is too much emphasis on what one Conservative minister in the 1990s termed 'isms' and 'ologies' (Castle 1992).

This view of social work resurfaced towards the end of November 2012 in a range of stories, where politicians and media commentators attacked social workers for removing three children of East European origin from foster carers who were members of the anti-immigration, anti-EU UKIP party – a party who have explicit policies against 'multiculturalism' (see Jenkins, Chapter Seven, this volume). *The Observer* quoted the Conservative Education Secretary Michael Gove as saying that social workers had made 'the wrong decision in the wrong way for the wrong reasons' (McVeigh 2012). *The Sun* claimed the decision had provoked 'fury' (Prynne 2012); while *The Sunday Mirror* quoted the UKIP party leader as saying that 'heads must roll' for the decision (Moss 2012). However, the complexities of any particular case are rarely considered – and, in this instance, there was no real debate regarding the suitability of members of an anti-immigration, anti-European, anti-multiculturalism party, to foster children from a migrant East European background.

On the same day *The Mail on Sunday* ran two further stories attacking 'politically correct' social workers who, in the first instance, the paper alleged, had 'tried to prevent [a foster mum] ... from adopting a black baby they placed in her care – because she was white' (Douglas 2012), while in the second it was claimed that social workers at the voluntary sector organisation Barnardo's had prohibited a former UKIP party election candidate and district nurse from having a role with children leaving the care system because of her party's views on multiculturalism (Carlin et al 2012). Earlier in September 2012 social workers were attacked in the media for not addressing adequately the issue of Asian men's role in 'grooming' and sexual abuse cases (see Orr, Chapter Ten, this volume), with *The Daily Mail* apparently incredulous that 'not a single social worker' would be sacked for their 'political correct' failings (Doyle 2012a; 2012b).

The case made in the media and by some politicians, therefore, is that there is too much focus on issues such as 'race', ethnicity and discrimination within social work. Yet, in many ways, these issues are far less prominent than they once were within social work education and research. For example, an examination of the content of a range of social work journals available for academics and students reveals the relative absence of debates regarding racism and the impact of such discrimination on the lives of black and Asian service users (with the possible exception of work with asylum seekers (see, for example, Hayes 2012). It would seem that the phrase 'anti-racist social work' has almost completely disappeared from the social work lexicon – if we were to make a judgement on the basis of titles of articles in *The British Journal of Social Work*. Similarly, there have been very few books that have focused on 'anti-racist social work' over the past 10 to 15 years (with the notable exception of Bhatti-Sinclair 2011). There is now relatively little discussion about the nature of structural racism in modern societies and its impact on minority communities, and the focus has shifted to concern about diversity, difference, equality and rights (see Singh, Chapter One, this volume).

Whatever the reasons for this (see below), there is ample evidence of the way that racism continues to blight the lives of Britain's black and minority ethnic (BME) communities, which points to a real need for social workers to understand the nature of structural discrimination.

Racism and discrimination in Britain today

The Equality and Human Rights Commission's (EHRC) report *How fair is Britain?* (EHRC 2011) provides immense detail of the levels of poverty and disadvantage among Britain's BME communities. The main thrust of the report examines 'fairness' and looks at a whole range of inequalities within Britain. It provides concrete evidence of inequalities in the labour market that discriminate against black and Asian populations, and outlines how these groups have unequal access to social and welfare provision. The Report also examines how aspects of policing, particularly 'stop and search', reflect increasing levels of harassment against non-white groups. As such, the Report's findings are worth discussing at some length.

The EHRC Report starts by looking at levels of poverty and unemployment. In relation to poverty, the figures reveal that one in five of the black and Asian population live in households with less than 60% of median income (after housing costs), and that this rises to nearly one in three for Bangladeshi-headed households. Disturbingly, nearly three-quarters of Bangladeshi children and half of black African children are growing up in poverty. As the Report notes:

> People of Indian origin are more likely to have low household income than White people, despite the fact that a low proportion of Indians earn low hourly wages and they have higher than average educational attainments. More than half of Pakistani and Bangladeshi adults live in poverty and are also much less likely than average to a have a current account or home contents insurance. Just over a quarter of Pakistani and Bangladeshi adults have formal savings, compared to two-thirds of White people. Asian and Black households are also several times more likely than White British households to live in overcrowded or substandard homes. (EHRC 2011: 460)

Similarly the Institute of Race Relations (IRR) notes that:

> Nearly three-quarters of 7-year-old Pakistani and Bangladeshi children and just over half of those black children of the same age are living in poverty. About one in four white 7-year-olds are classed as living in poverty. (IRR 2012)

While, in a report by Reuters into wealth and assets it is claimed that:

> The UK's Department of Work and Pensions has found that 60 percent of black and Asian households have no savings at all, compared to 33 percent of white households. The UK's first Wealth and Assets Survey in 2009 reported that while the average white household had £221,000 ... in assets, Black Caribbean households had £76,000, Bangladeshi households £21,000 and Black African households £15,000. (Reuters 2011)

These figures reflect the unequal status of the black population in the labour market and the disproportionate levels of unemployment that they experience. For example, black people in their early twenties are nearly twice as likely not to be in employment, education and training as their white counterparts, and Muslims have the lowest rate of employment of any religious group, with only 47% of men and 24% of women in employment (EHRC 2011: 401–3). As Ball et al (2012) note:

> The youth unemployment rate for black people has increased at almost twice the rate for white 16- to 24-year-olds since the start of the recession in 2008. ... Unemployment among young black men has doubled in three years, rising from 28.8% in 2008 to 55.9% in the last three months of 2011.

Living in poverty also affects health, education and housing status. As the IRR note:

> BME groups as a whole are more likely to report ill health, and experience ill health earlier than white British people. Some health variations are linked to poverty and wider social inequalities, although there are a range of inter-linked and overlapping factors. (IRR 2012)

There is a clear correlation between poverty, and mortality and morbidity rates. Pakistani and Bangladeshi communities have the shortest life expectancy rates in the UK (EHRC 2011: 80). Black Caribbean and Pakistani babies are twice as likely to die in the first year of life as white babies, while overall, Pakistani and Bangladeshi communities are more likely to report 'poor health' and disability (EHRC 2011: 81). They also find it more difficult to access and communicate with their GPs than other groups. When religion is the defining category, Muslims tend to report worse health than average.

The EHRC report also discusses rates of mental illness (2011: 271, 276–8). Here, evidence reveals that Gypsies, Travellers and asylum seekers have the highest rate of mental illness; this is not surprising considering that, as well as being vulnerable to poverty and inequality, they also face high levels of hostility and victimisation in today's society. Nearly twice as many Bangladeshi men than white men suffer mental health problems (EHRC 2011: 644). As Mind report, a disproportionate number of people admitted as inpatients in mental health services come from BME groups; in 2010, 23% of inpatient admissions were from a BME background (Mind 2011). Further, people from BME groups are more likely, than white British people, to be detained or put in seclusion. In 2010, people from BME groups were between 25% and

38% more likely, than white British people, to be compulsorily detained under mental-health legislation and up to 99% more likely to be put in seclusion (Brindle 2011).

Education is a key determinant of life chances, but within poor black communities there are glaring inequalities. Male pupils from some black groups who are eligible for free school meals are performing less well than white groups as early as age five (EHRC 2011: 645), and astonishingly the report reveals that being black and male appears to have a greater impact on levels of numeracy than being learning disabled. The worst affected group are Gypsy and Traveller children, whose performance is actually declining, with less than one in six obtaining at least five good GCSEs (EHRC 2011: 306).

Discrimination is also present when it comes to school exclusions. In 2010 there were a phenomenal 8,000 permanent exclusions and 380,000 fixed-term exclusions. These figures cover a wide range of working class pupils 'but black pupils remain three times more likely to be excluded than white ... and face stiffer sanctions' (Muir 2010).

In terms of university education, while more black students are studying for degrees, they are much less likely to attend the 'top' Russell Group institutions. Whereas a quarter of white students attend the most elite universities, less than 10% of black Britons do (EHRC 2011: 339, 344–5).

In relation to housing, poverty has an impact on access to decent housing, revealed in figures that show that Asian and black households are several times more likely than white British households to live in overcrowded conditions. The report notes that across all housing tenancies:

> Just over 9% of all Asian (including Asian British) households are overcrowded ... while almost 15% of all Black (including Black British) households are overcrowded. ... In contrast, fewer than 2% of all White British households are overcrowded. (EHRC 2011: 501)

In the social rented sector the figures are worse: '4% of all White British households in the social rented sector are overcrowded, whereas 14% of all ethnic minority households are' (EHRC 2011: 502).

The EHRC report also provides evidence of ways in which black groups are still experiencing racism within the criminal justice system. Black people are seven times more likely, than white people, to be stopped and searched, and on average, five times as many black people, than white people, are imprisoned (EHRC 2011: 134, 643). It notes that:

> Black people in England experienced around 145,000 excess stop and searches in 2007/08 – Asian people, around 43,000: the disproportionality ratio was 6.5 for Black people, and 1.9 for Asian people in that year ... some Gypsies and Travellers have experienced blanket raids of their sites on the basis of unfounded allegations by local communities. (EHRC 2011: 135, 136)

For Harker (2011) racism is worse today than it was in the 1980s, with black people seven times more likely to be stopped and searched than white people. Townsend (2010) discusses the ways in which police increasingly use Section 60 of the Criminal Justice and Public Order Act (1994) to harass black youngsters. Section 60 was originally introduced to deal with football 'hooligans' where there was a 'threat' of serious violence. It allows the police to search anyone in a designated area without specific grounds for suspicion. Analysis by the London School of Economics and the Open Society Justice Initiative found that there were 41 section 60 searches for every 1,000 black people, yet only 1.6 for every 1,000 white people. These are figures that provide the widest 'race-gap' in stop and search that have been found anywhere internationally. Ministry of Justice figures (2008/09) reveal that Asian people are also 6.3 times more likely to be stopped and searched than white people. Townsend cites a quote by Ben Bowling, Professor of Criminal Justice at Kings College, London, who states:

> The police are making greater use of a power that was only ever meant to be used in exceptional circumstances and lacks effective safeguards. This leaves room for increased stereotyping which is likely to alienate those communities which are most affected. (Townsend 2010)

Only a small proportion of people subject to 'stop and search' are ever charged or imprisoned. But:

> On average, five times more Black people than White people in England and Wales are imprisoned. ... This has caused the proportion of ethnic minority prisoners to rise to around 25% of the prison population (while they make up 11% of the population in England and Wales). (EHRC 2011: 171–2)

The Muslim population currently makes up 12% of the prison population in England and Wales: 'The percentage of Muslim prisoners in England and Wales almost tripled from 3,681 in March 1997 to 9,975 in December 2008' (EHRC 2011: 174).

In April 2012, the Metropolitan police chief was summoned to parliament to give evidence about these and related figures, and mounting claims of prejudiced behaviour, including reports of racially motivated abuse, assaults and bullying by police officers. At the time, 10 cases involving alleged racism were referred to the Independent Police Complaints Commission. Eight police officers were suspended and a further three were placed on restricted duties.

Incidents included a police officer who was recorded on a mobile phone allegedly racially abusing a black suspect inside a police van after the riots in the summer of 2011. In another case, a black fire-fighter, who tried to assist police officers while off duty, claimed he was targeted because of his skin colour. The fire-fighter, who also trained as a police constable, saw a young man hurl a rock at a police van and approached officers to pass the information on. However, when he did, officers behaved like '"wild animals": swearing at him, dragging him from his car, subjecting him to a "violent" attack, and eventually shooting him with a stun gun' (Lewis 2012). He was then locked up for hours and prosecuted for a crime he had not committed.

Racist abuse has also been documented within the immigration services, in particular, within companies awarded government contracts to deport foreign nationals and refused asylum seekers. In October 2010, three G4S guards were arrested on suspicion of possible manslaughter when a 46-year-old Angolan deportee died while being forcibly restrained on a flight from Heathrow. Further reported examples include a 35-year-old Ugandan deportee who was repeatedly punched and kicked by guards in two separate attacks in February 2012: one assault took place as the plane was on the runway at Heathrow, and the other at the airport in Ethiopia while he was waiting for a connecting flight. In September 2011, a female Nigerian asylum seeker claims she was assaulted in front of her three young children on a plane bound for Italy. She said 'The escorts beat me on the chest and legs, pulled my hair, twisted my left hand and put their hands around my neck' (Grandjean et al 2012).

Allegations of racist abuse have also been made with regard to the treatment of asylum seekers at the main asylum application processing centre in Cardiff, Wales. A former employee has spoken publicly about racist attitudes and practices, alleging that workers used a stuffed gorilla as a 'badge of shame' whenever an employee approved an asylum application, and that one method used to determine the authenticity of an asylum seeker claiming to be from North Korea was to ask whether the person ate chop suey. She also states that on her first day a manager said that if it was up to her asylum seekers would be shepherded outside and shot. Kate Smart, director of policy and advocacy at the Welsh Refugee Council, said it was appalling that vulnerable people, many of whom had been tortured and seen relatives killed, may have been treated so badly (Taylor and Muir 2010).

There are other groups in Britain who are also bearing the brunt of racist attacks. Research by the IRR (2011) has revealed that East European migrant workers face significant threats of racial violence, with the highest recorded number of incidents involving Polish workers. Attacks have risen since the expansion of the European Union (2004/2007), when 12 new countries were incorporated, including Hungary, Estonia and Poland. In one incident, a Polish male was racially abused and then stabbed to death in Wrexham in 2007, and in another, a Polish worker was robbed and beaten to death in Northern Ireland in 2009. Other cases have seen individuals left fighting for their lives and/or with permanent disabilities. In one particularly violent occurrence in Hull in 2010, two Polish nationals were foraging in the bins of a fast food restaurant, when a white male drove by and told them to 'get a job', before deliberately driving his 3-tonne van into one of them, breaking his ribs and the vertebrae in his back, as well as shattering his collar bone. The driver then got out of the van and knocked the other Pole unconscious. Other research by Human Rights First documented an incident in Belfast in 2009, when around one hundred Romanians were forced to take shelter in a church after a systematic campaign of racist violence against them.

Gypsies and Travellers are also subject to high levels of racist abuse, evident in abusive media coverage and overtly racist statements from local and national politicians. In 2004, Trevor Phillips, now Chair of the Equality and Human Rights Commission, compared the situation of Gypsies and Travellers living in Great Britain, to that of black people living in the Deep South in the 1950s. The IRR, which records all deaths with a (known or suspected) racial element, has found that since the death of Stephen Lawrence in 1993 at least 96 people have died in such attacks (IRR 2011).

Overall, the EHRC report reveals disturbing evidence of the ways in which structural inequality still blights the lives of Britain's black community, and the negative and discriminatory impact it has on lives, experiences and opportunities.

These appalling levels of racist abuse, violence and discrimination do not exist in a vacuum. They have grown and festered in a climate of economic recession and austerity where media, politicians and the far-right have agitated against, and found a convenient scapegoat in, minority populations. The most recent evidence emphasises the extent of discrimination faced by Britain's BME communities and the impact racism has had on their lives.

Anti-racist social work

Anti-racist approaches within social work had their roots in the social movements against racism in the 1970s and early 1980s in Britain. These movements included a wide array of campaigns against racism and racist political violence (such as the campaign around the New Cross fire where 13 young party goers were killed in a fire started by racists), against the Far-right (for example, Rock Against Racism, Anti-Nazi League, Campaign Against Racism and Fascism), against police harassment and racist immigration controls. These movements were also shaped by the inner city uprisings that exploded in various parts of Britain in 1981, particularly in Bristol, Brixton (London), Chapeltown (Leeds), Handsworth (Birmingham) and Toxteth (Liverpool) (see Harman 1981; Widgery 1986; Sivanandan 1990; Gilroy 1987; LA Rose 2011; and Renton 2006).

These were all primarily movements of the streets, but they started to have a 'reflection' within parts of the social work community, a process that sped up during the 1980s as many former movement activists (from a range of campaigns) started to join and work with (or for) the Labour Party in national and local government.

In this context, anti-racist perspectives began to emerge, which went beyond a concern with individual prejudice and culture in order to expose the structural and institutional nature of racism in society. The emergence of anti-racism was informed by increasing evidence of the inferior economic status of black people in Britain, and the negative consequences for health, welfare, housing and education. Anti-racist perspectives offered a much more radical interpretation of discrimination within society and pointed to the ways in which racism was built into the structures and institutions of capitalist society. They were also critical of the supposed neutrality or independence of the state under capitalism, which was seen to reflect dominant and political interests, and to benefit from racism that divided people along racial lines.

Much of our understanding of 'race' and racism within social work theorisation at this time developed out of the work of sociologists such as Miles (1982), Sivanadan (1982), Fryer (1984), Ramdin (1987), Solomos (1988) and Hiro (1992). These writers emphasised that racism had not always existed but became embedded within society with the development of capitalism (it was 'socially constructed' but within concrete historical circumstances); that it had gone through various phases of development (most notably Fryer's account of the ways in which modern racism developed through the racism of 'slavery', 'empire' and 'migration'); and that racism operated at different 'levels' through individual prejudice, through societies institutions and being embedded within the very structure of advanced capitalism.

Although for most people the concept of institutional racism is linked to the findings of the Stephen Lawrence Inquiry as outlined in the MacPherson Report (1999), it was during the 1980s, and in the field of social work education and training, that the approach was first acknowledged and taken seriously within a state institution. Pressure was put on the Central Council for Education and Training in Social Work (CCETSW) to tackle institutional racism, and to incorporate anti-racist learning requirements into the Diploma in Social Work. The impetus for this development was an increasing recognition and concern that the black population were under-represented as professionals and service users in social work agencies (Cheetham 1987; also both Williams, Chapter Three, and Singh, Chapter One, in this volume), and that the needs and demands of black service users were being ignored in social service agencies.

CCETSW's anti-racist initiative was influenced by discussions that took place among black and white social work academics and professionals who were concerned about racism in the field of social work. The concerns they raised in workshops and at conferences put pressure on CCETSW, and in 1989 they introduced the Rules and Regulations for the Diploma in Social Work (Paper 30), which made it a compulsory requirement for social work students to address issues of 'race' and racism, and to demonstrate competence in anti-racist practice. As a result, university courses and social work agencies were required to facilitate anti-racist education and training, with the aim that eventually social workers in the field would be conscious of the structural and institutional nature of racism in Britain and would be able to support service users affected by discrimination.

In many ways this was a remarkable initiative, which represented a radical step forward in the field. It emanated from a government agency and contained within its remit a recognition that institutional racism was a feature of British society, and that social work education and training should be structured by anti-racist concerns and principles. This was reflected in CCETSW's anti-racist policy, which was formally adopted in 1988 and that stated:

> CCETSW believes that racism is endemic in the values, attitudes and structures of British society, including that of social services and social work education. CCETSW recognises that the effects of racism on black people are incompatible with the values of social work and therefore seeks to combat racist practices in all areas of its responsibilities. (CCETSW 1991: 6)

The Diploma in Social Work further stipulated learning requirements in relation to anti-racist social work, which included:

> Recognising the implications of political, economic, racial, social and cultural factors upon service delivery, financing services and resources delivery.
>
> Developing an awareness of the inter-relationships of the processes of structural oppression, race, class and gender. (CCETSW 1991: 6)

Those providing courses, such as universities, were also expected to implement and monitor anti-racist policies and practices.

So, how can we explain the demise of anti-racism in the field of social work in the context of these profound and wide-ranging commitments from CCETSW during the late 1980s and early 1990s? This requires an understanding of how the successful implementation of the anti-racist initiative was seriously impaired by a political and professional backlash, which denied the structural and institutional nature of racism, and accused CCETSW of being taken over by groups of obsessed zealots whose major concern was to express rigid 'politically correct' values. This view was articulated by Professor Robert Pinker, who was particularly vociferous in his condemnation of the development. He was critical of radical elements taking over CCETSW and of social workers being 'brainwashed'. Those involved in developing anti-racist approaches were accused of believing that 'oppression and discrimination are everywhere to be found in British society, even when they seemed "invisible"' (Pinker 1999: 18–19).

Such internal criticism was matched by politicians who, throughout the 1990s, decried social work's focus on the 'isms', when what was required, according to John Major in the aftermath of the James Bulger murder, was the 'needs to condemn a little more and understand a little less' (MacIntyre 1993).

The attack on social work – from within the profession and from politicians and media outside – led to moves to undermine the relevance and importance of anti-racist recommendations, reinforced by the views of the then chair of CCETSW, Jeffrey Greenwood, who, in Autumn 1993, publicly committed himself to 'rooting out politically correct nonsense' (*The Independent*, 28 August 1993). He ordered a review of anti-discriminatory policies, and as a result, the Diploma in Social Work was published with the formal commitment to anti-racism dropped.

Postmodern turn

Under such pressure a commitment to anti-racist social work was watered down. However, this process was also justified in intellectual terms by the belated 'postmodern turn' within social work. Postmodern ideas swept through the academy in the late 1980s and gradually gained some hold within social work. Postmodernism rails against 'metanarratives' and any attempt to try and understand the world as a 'totality'. It denies that there are any 'truths' but instead emphasises the partial nature of human knowledge and fluidity of social categories (Rojek et al 1989).

Callinicos (1989) has argued that postmodern ideas particularly took hold among a layer of former activists, who had moved into academia and witnessed their hopes for a different world disappear as the movements of the 1960s went into decline. The harsh political atmosphere of Britain in the 1980s was a further fillip to ideas that suggested that both history and progress were (to misquote Henry Ford) 'bunk'. And, of course, the People's Revolutions of 1989 were also used to 'prove' that we had reached the 'end of history' (Fukyama 1992) or that talk of revolution and a systemic alternative to capitalism was a dangerous myth.

Postmodernism came to social work, not in its 'pure form' but often in an inconsistent way (Ferguson and Lavalette 1999) that attempted to marry a politics of difference and diversity, with notions of economic globalisation and welfare restructuring (Leonard 1997). In these terms postmodernism was promoted as a set of ideas that broke free of ideological monoliths, and instead promoted a diverse politics of engagement, a focus on individual rights, a democratic promotion of service-user voice, and in place of a concern on structural inequalities based on class, race or gender, an emphasis on service-user diversity.

However, these trends have led us to a place where social work focuses on a range of differences, with little emphasis on inter-sectionality and the structural impediments that form the terrain upon which so many service users live their lives.

One immediate consequence of this is that social work theorisation has not kept up with the fast-shifting 'politics' of race and racism in Britain and Europe, where much racism is coded in terms of supposed 'cultural incompatibility' (Fekete, Chapter Two, this volume).

As *The Guardian* journalist Gary Younge argues, the last decade has witnessed a sharp regression, as 'the shift in emphasis from race to religion and from colour to creed and culture' has grafted 'old views on to new scapegoats' (Younge 2009b). The roots of this shift towards culture were traced by Barker and Beezer (1983) and had their historic roots in the speeches of Enoch Powell and the infamous 'swamping speech' of Margaret Thatcher in 1978. However, there has been an important and notable 'quickening' in the transformations of racist discourse and targets in recent years. Racism now increasingly focuses on creed and culture and on nationality and citizenship – concepts that do not neatly correspond to older ideas of race concerned with biology and skin colour. The targets of anti-immigrant hostility are not necessarily black, and those engaged in racism towards Muslims are not automatically hostile to all black Britons. Many of those vilifying Muslims – like the English Defence League – will earnestly explain that they hold no brief for racists, and that they only intend to defend human rights or 'British values' from a culture that violates them.

The 'war on terror' is a proximate cause of much of this racism. However, the temptation to reduce the question of Islamophobia to a sub-narrative of the 'war on terror' is one that must be avoided. Racism towards Muslims pre-dates 9/11 and is not necessarily tied to pro-war opinion. It has far more to do with domestic social processes than a singular focus on the 'war on terror' would allow.

Nor does cultural chauvinism towards Muslims stop at the boundaries of Islam. The emergence of Islamophobia – the demonisation of Muslim communities – has allowed older forms of racism to once again emerge in mainstream culture. Segments of liberal opinion have adopted the New Right's agenda on race relations, often swallowing wholesale the culturalist arguments on immigration and citizenship that were crafted in opposition to multiculturalism. This has all too often led to a prosecutorial attitude to Muslims, the rationale being that 'Britishness' includes respect for feminism, human rights and 'Enlightenment values', all of which are supposedly at odds with Islam, or at least with immoderate manifestations of it.

Within social work there has been a clear concern with diversity and this has led to the promotion of 'cultural competencies' as a means of working with minority communities (see Harrison and Burke, Chapter Four, this volume). However, there has been less focus on the ways that culture has been used as a cover to justify racist policies and procedures. There has been little discussion, within social work journals, of the impact of this 'new racism' on minority communities – and specifically, its impact on Muslim communities, as Islamophobia has become the most vicious and pernicious form of racism across much of the West since the 1990s (Barker and Beezer 1983; see also Singh (Chapter One), Jenkins (Chapter Seven), Penketh (Chapter Eight) and Lavalette (Chapter Nine) in this volume).

At present, social work education in Britain is being redrawn in line with the new Professional Capabilities Framework (PCF). The PCF has established nine overlapping domains, each with nine levels that reflect the increasing complexity of understanding and practice that would be expected of more experienced and strategic staff. Domains two, three and four require social workers to be aware of appropriate social work values and ethics, aware of the diverse communities and groups they will work with, and be concerned with appropriate rights and concepts of justice in their work. In each of these domains anti-racist understandings and practices are central. However, equally importantly, domains six (knowledge) and eight (contexts and organisations) emphasise that 'social contexts and social constructs' are important. Working in this domain requires recognition that we live in a socio-political world where debates and issues take different forms and issues appear in different ways at different times and periods. This is of particular relevance because of the shifting language of policy formation and the coded language of 'race'. Let's give three examples to emphasise the meaning.

Over the last 20 years there has been a tendency for 'reform' language to be colonised by advocates of the New Right. Thus concepts such as 'empowerment' and 'resilience' have shifted their meaning. 'Empowerment' was initially a word that was derived from the service-user movements and meant a collective assertion of service-user rights. However, now it is increasingly reduced to mean 'to be empowered as a consumer' within the care market. 'Resilience', as those forced to attend benefit assessments attest, is something that is now 'expected' and 'enforced' upon vulnerable people by government agencies and their representatives. Thus policy-language changes in different contexts.

A second example comes from the linguistic demonisation of sections of the poor in modern Britain. The media have trivialised and castigated 'chavs' (Jones 2011), while politicians have sought to draw a distinction between supposed 'strivers' and 'skivers' or 'workers' and 'shirkers'. Behind these phrases lurks a vicious policy-turn that cuts benefits, threatens mass evictions of families from social rented accommodation and pits people against each other.

Our third example relates directly to the coded language of 'race'. Political and media debate is rarely framed in explicitly racist terms about any problematic black or Asian presence. However, debate about our 'soft touch' benefit system, about 'swarms' of asylum seekers attempting to enter Britain, about Britain being 'swamped' by alternative cultures, about the 'failings of multiculturalism' and the 'incompatibility' of Western and non-Western cultures are relatively common.

These examples emphasise that social workers – through each of the nine levels of the PCF – need to adopt a critical gaze towards the shifting political debates that shape our world. They need to reject simplistic, superficial and commonsense explanations that blame minority and marginalised groups and instead dig beneath the surface to uncover the real relationships that are shaping our unequal social world. This requires engaging constantly with political and social debates about a range of issues that create and recreate the world within which social work operates, and that creates the 'public causes' of so much of the 'private pain' that affects the lives of social work service users.

In the chapters that follow we present a range of voices from academics, practitioners and activists who are concerned about the impact of racism on the lives of minority communities within Britain, how this affects service delivery and how it is posing questions for workers in the field.

There are three broad types of essays in the book. Chapters One to Six focus on issues of race, racism and anti-racist social work theory. This includes discussion and debate over the present nature of racism today and its impact on social work (Fekete, Singh); over the 'problem' of black leadership (Williams); over the competing claims of 'cultural competency' and antiracist social work (Harrison and Burke); and two chapters that address issues that have not featured as much as they should have within anti-racist social work debates: anti-Roma racism (Urh) and antisemitism (Levine).

Chapters Seven to Ten look broadly at aspects of Islamophobia. As has been noted the PCF requires social work students and practitioners to be aware of the shifting contexts within which policy and practice takes place. These debates are important as they impact on commonsense understandings of issues and social problems amplifying and targeting particular groups within the community. Chapter Seven (Jenkins) looks at the recent attacks on multiculturalism by various national political figures – and, in particular, unpicks the argument that suggests that the present 'crisis of immigration' is a result of post-war multiculturalism that failed to 'assimilate' minority communities into supposed British cultural values. Chapter Eight (Penketh) presents findings of research undertaken with second and third generation Muslim women and its implications for work with Muslim communities. Chapter Nine (Lavalette) looks at the 'Prevent Agenda', first brought in by New Labour and tied to issues of social inclusion, but more recently clearly set out as a counter-terror mechanism for dealing with 'Muslim extremism'. While in Chapter Ten (Orr) looks at the way in which the recent scandal of child grooming was racialised within the media and portrayed as a crime associated with men of Pakistani origin; a recent example of what social work academic/criminologist Stan Cohen called a 'moral panic'.

Finally Chapters Eleven to Thirteen look at some practice-related issues. Chapter Eleven (Stamp) looks at how austerity cuts are targeting services for minority communities and asks what social workers should do when faced with such issues. Chapter Twelve (Moran and Gillett) looks at debates over the age assessment of asylum-seeking children and once again poses the question: what should practitioners do when faced with this new form of eugenics? Chapter Thirteen looks at the social care workforce and the use of poorly paid, migrant workers in this growing sector within the privatised care market.

The aim of these chapters collectively is to promote thinking, and stimulate debate on these important topics. Together we hope that the volume resparks debate and research in the various ways that racism blights the lives of service users and workers within social services in Britain, and re-opens debate about the necessity for a social work practice that is fully committed to the principles of anti-racism.

ONE

Rethinking anti-racist social work in a neoliberal age

Gurnam Singh

In this chapter Singh looks back at the development of anti-racist social work and traces the intellectual journey it has been through over the last 20 years. The Professional Capabilities Framework (PCF) domain 8 requires social workers to be aware of the changing contexts within which social work takes place, and social work and social care organizations operate and function. The chapter looks back at the recent history of anti-racist social work and 'sets the scene' for many of the debates that follow. Singh argues that we need to rethink our understandings of anti-racism in the context of shifting politics and race, difference and diversity.

Introduction

In the face of significant shifts in 'race' equality policies and discourses within social welfare, from those rooted in neo-Marxist critiques of post-colonial Western capitalist societies to ones based on neoliberal market models, this chapter sets out an argument for the need for a new reinvigorated anti-racist social work project. The chapter does not seek to offer a detailed step-by-step 'how to do guide', but rather it offers an account of the historical, ideological and political contexts within which ideas associated with anti-racist social work have developed over the past 35 years. It begins by highlighting the emergence of municipal anti-racist social work, which was born out of broader anti-racist social movements of the late 1970s and 1980s. It then goes on show how anti-racist social work morphed into individualised 'anti-oppressive' and 'anti-discriminatory' practice and 'diversity awareness' from the 1990s to the present period. In doing so, the chapter seeks to argue that a series of political and ideological factors have led to a significant weakening of anti-racism within public welfare in general and social work in particular. At the policy level, we have seen a displacing of anti-racism by notions of managing diversity and anti-discriminatory practice. At the community level there has been a fragmentation of old anti-racist collectivities built upon race/class solidarity and, at the same time, an assertion of ethno-religious-communal identity-based politics. At the professional level anti-racist social work has been unable to evolve models to reflect the shifting discourses of 'race' and the emergence of new or 'xeno-racism' that is not necessarily built on black/white racial binaries (Sivanandan 2006; see also Fekete, Chapter Two, this volume). And, at the theoretical level, there has been the legacy of the turn to postmodernism and, by some, the repudiation of Marxism as the basis for understanding the relationship between lived experience, history and oppression.

The chapter begins with a brief summary of the short history of the emergence of anti-racist social work in the 1980s. This is followed by a broader discussion of the ways in which different theoretical and political perspectives on anti-racism and anti-racist social work have emerged. Following this the discussion then focuses upon the impact of neoliberalism. The chapter ends by offering a new vision of anti-racist social work that is based on critical understanding of culture and difference. This is a vision that avoids both an outdated Marxist rejection of culture as displaced or false consciousness, and a postmodernist valorisation or blind pursuit of difference. Finally, to avoid any confusion, the term 'black' is deployed in this chapter to refer to all groups that in the UK historical and cultural context have been and continue to be constructed as 'other' to the assumed white European norm.

The birth of anti-racist social work

In the aftermath of widespread rioting in Brixton and many other inner cities throughout the UK in the summer of 1981 and a subsequent independent judicial enquiry, Lord Scarman issued a report on 'race' and policing in the UK. The report raised a series of issues concerning relations between the state and Britain's black communities. Most significantly, Scarman introduced into public discourse the notion of institutionalised racism, hitherto a concept that was confined to the academic lexicon. Social work education and practice became one of the most active and well-publicised sites for the struggle against institutionalised racism (Penketh 2000).

Among other things, the policy changes following Scarman opened up the social work profession to black people. However, the employment of black social workers, rather than leading to the eradication of racism, resulted in the uncovering of previously unacknowledged and virulent forms, as well as creating new antagonisms centred on concerns about the mistreatment of black service users, care workers and professionals (Stubbs 1985; Husband 1991; C. Williams 1999; Penketh 2000). One of the specific contentions of early anti-racist social work was the inherent Eurocentricism of social work, which was not confined to practice alone; social work education became an important site of struggle (CCETSW 1991a and 1991b; Humphries et al. 1993; Singh 1996).

While racism persisted, anti-racist social work of the time secured important concessions in such areas as the employment of black staff, facilitating policy development, funding, raising consciousness, black activism and the development of black perspectives. Most importantly this period in the development of anti-racist social work was born out of a much wider political struggle of black and white activists against all forms of racist oppression on a number of fronts from, for instance, defending back communities against racial attacks and harassment, through to tackling the British state in terms of racist policing, immigration policy, schooling and housing policies (F. Williams 1996). Inevitably, this linking of anti-racist social work to wider black political struggles and social movements resulted in new and exiting forms of theorising based on critiques of the stereotyping and pathologisation of black families and communities (Singh 1996; Keating 2000).

However, in seeking to displace negative racialised conceptions of black people, one consequence of an uncritical mobilisation of 'race' categories, albeit in a strategic manner, was that advocates of anti-racism ended up adopting postures that appeared to legitimise or reinforce the very same race thinking that they were seeking to eradicate (Bonnett 2000). For instance, one can see in the literature an uncritical use of racialised categories. For example, by drawing on the work of African-American psychologist, W. E. Cross, Maximé (1986) offers a rationale for, and solution to, the psychological trauma faced by black children brought up in primarily white care-settings. By adopting a therapeutic method involving the gradual exposure of the 'black child' to their 'racial origin' thus engendering 'racial pride', one can create the conditions for 'psychological nigrescence', or the process of becoming black (Maximé 1986; Robinson 1997).

Such essentialist notions of 'racial pride' and 'racial origin' feature in much of the anti-racist social work literature, the cumulative effect of which is the blurring of the rationale underpinning racist and anti-racist sentiment. Gilroy (1990), for instance, expressed deep reservations about the emergence of anti-racist orthodoxy in social work that became characterised by an 'idealisation' of 'black family forms', which were seen as the only effective basis upon which black children could acquire the necessary psychological skills to thrive in a racist world. For Gilroy, by demanding 'same "race" placement' policies, anti-racist social workers simply ended up inverting the very pathological imagery they were seeking to confront. Apart from the nature of the critique, most significantly the symbolic aspect of Gilroy's intervention had far-reaching implications. Given that 'same "race" placement' policies constituted a key demand in anti-racist social work in the 1990s (Pennie and Best 1990), the fact that one of the foremost black anti-racist scholars was suggesting that this policy was underpinned by racist ideology was of seismic significance. Perhaps the most insightful aspect of Gilroy's critique was the questioning of the premise that black social work professionals and black clients shared a commonality of experience. Indeed, he argued that the proponents of 'municipal anti-racism' were becoming disconnected from the lived realities of the vast majority of black people.

Resonating with some of the points outlined above, Fiona Williams (1996), another staunch anti-racist activist, recognised four key critiques of anti-racist social work, namely, it had become formulaic, as exemplified in the polarised nature of debates about the placement needs of black children; it tended to neglect the reality of lived experience that is structured through a complex meshing of 'race', gender, class and other oppressions; it was overly obsessed with ideological concerns at the expense of developing reflexive practice and practical solutions to the needs of service users; and it tended to reduce the totality of black experience to a response to white racism, thereby conferring a 'victim status' on black people. Fiona Williams (1996) went on to suggest that anti-racist social work's apparent inability for self-critique was left in a vulnerable position. So, if such critiques highlighted some perceived shortfalls of anti-racist social work, they also acted as a reminder that questions of how best to develop policies to eradicate racism were and remain contested. In the following section, some of the broad spectrum of approaches are summarised.

Multiculturalism

Emerging in the 1970s as a antidote to the failing of the hitherto policy of 'assimilation' of migrants from the former British colonies, of all the approaches, perhaps multiculturalism is one that has stood the test of time and continues to influence much of social policy. This approach lies at the core of the idea that most people are not racist but lack appropriate awareness of cultural differences. The goal then is to develop 'cultural competence' in order to maximise communication and understanding. Politically, liberal multiculturalism began as an 'enlightenment' strategy which, in its early stages, resonated with universal ideals. However, as its focus shifted toward the promotion of ethnic and 'cultural' particularity, it increasingly appealed to cultural relativism rather than universality. This appeal to relativism represents an impasse for multiculturalist discourse, leaving it on the one hand unable to counter the charge of being an accomplice, for example, to religious extremism, but on the other, unable to provide the ground from which one might challenge contemporary reassertions of 'racialised' national identity (see Singh and Cowden 2011).

Cosmopolitan-humanism

Although not widely acknowledged, this is an emergent approach that is primarily identified with theorists such as Paul Gilroy and Jason Hill. This approach is distinctive from multiculturalism in one fundamental way because it emphasises the importance of human sameness as opposed to human difference, and with an insistence that the rejection of the division of human beings according to arbitrary conceptions of 'race', religion and ethnicity. This is exemplified in Paul Gilroy's argument for 'Planetary Humanism' (2000) and Jason Hill's argument that becoming a 'cosmopolitan' involves moving beyond 'blood identities' (2009). While operating primarily at a philosophical level, the cosmopolitan-humanist approach is appealing for the way it places the possibility for transcending racial identities. However, its weakness lies in the gap between such utopian impulses and any discussion of a social or professional practice through which these concepts might be articulated or realised – how, in other words, does one move from the brutal reality of the racialised subject and inequalities, to this cosmopolitan 'state of grace'? Moreover, it exposes itself to those on the political Right who seek to undermine 'race'-equality policy strategies for motives altogether different. A good example of this is the way that current Conservative/Lib Dem government has castigated anti-racist social workers for placing too much emphasis on 'ethnic matching' in the search for suitable substitute families for children trapped in the care system (Muir 2012). Nonetheless, as a utopian project, cosmopolitan-humanism, in reminding us of our 'essential' humanity, offers real possibilities for confronting racialised discourses and practices that one might unwittingly be advocating.

Postmodernism

Both within anti-racist and social work literature more generally, from the early 1990s postmodernism developed a significant influence. Although there are many conceptions of postmodernism, the one that appeared to be of particular appeal was a conception with an apparently magical capacity to address issues of power, knowledge, difference and subjectivity (Fawcett and Featherstone 1995). For those concerned with the welfare of minorities and the voice of the oppressed and silenced under the conditions of capitalism and post-colonialism, postmodernism seem to answer all their questions. For black activists, particularly those concerned with the need to address the long-term impact that slavery and colonialism was having on the continuing racialisation of black people as the 'other', inferior, exotic, mad or dangerous, by extolling the virtues of 'anti-essentialism' and the politics of difference, postmodernism appeared to resonate with demands made by them for respect of difference and alternative epistemological standpoints, such as those proffered by 'Afrocentricity' (Graham 1999 and 2000). However, if postmodernism was successful in providing important insights into the complex relationship between discourse and power, it was relatively ineffective in forming a material basis for alternative politics or practice (Ferguson and Lavalette 1999). Moreover, while adherents to postmodernism argued for progressive liberating social work, as Mullaly (2001: 316) points out, at the same time they were busy deconstructing 'such meta-narratives as feminism, Marxism, socialism and other critical perspectives to the point where reconstruction becomes impossible' .

Marxist race–class synthesis

If postmodernism revealed itself to be politically impotent, that accusation could not be aimed at Marxist analysis of racism. Growing out of the work of Ambalvaneer Sivanandan and the Institute of Race Relations (IRR), as well as the earlier work of Stuart Hall, this perspective is essentially concerned with the relationship between 'race', class and the critique of capitalism. In his most well-known work, *Policing the Crisis*, Hall suggested that through the construction of a moral panic centred on Black youth and the street crime of mugging, the government was able to deflect public attention away from the government's policies and role within the deepening economic and social crisis (Hall et al 1978). In doing so, Hall argued that 'race' needed to be understood essentially as 'modality' of class. This position was eclipsed in the late 1980s with the decline of Marxism and concurrent rise of postmodernism, however, it has been powerfully restated recently by Carter and Virdee who argue that if sociology is to 'provide a more relevant account of the phenomena of racism and ethnicity' it needs to bring 'an emancipatory working class subject (one that is "white" but also increasingly "black" and "brown" in the core of the capitalist world economy) back into their accounts of racism and anti-racism' (2008: 675–6).

This rejection of the old black/white binary in the configuration of anti-racism can be seen also in the emergence of an analysis of what has become known as 'new' or *xeno-racism* (Sivanandan 2002 and 2006). Sivanandan suggests that old racisms, which drew heavily on old colonial theories of race, have now evolved to incorporate the new 'others' constructed around moral panics associated with terrorism and new flows of asylum seekers and migrant labourers. Even though these new 'others' may look no different to the dominant class, like old racisms, hatred and fear of the 'other' enables them to be racialised as a discrete category of human:

> The racism meted out to asylum seekers and migrants, even when they are white, for instance – which is passed off as xenophobia, the (natural) fear of strangers. But the other side of the 'fear or hatred of strangers' is the preservation and defence of 'our people', 'our culture', our race – nativism. If it is xenophobia, it is, in the way it denigrates and reifies people before segregating and/or deporting them, a xenophobia that bears all the marks of the old racism, except that it is not colour coded. It is racism in substance, though xeno in form. It is xenoracism, a racism of global capital. (Sivanandan 2006: 2)

Neoliberalism and anti-racist social work

If the above accounts help us to locate some of the complex philosophical and theoretical challenges and antagonisms associated with the development of a coherent anti-racist project, it is also necessary to be mindful of the impact of unfolding political contexts. And in this regard, the key question that one needs to ask is, given the continued existence of racist oppression, why has anti-racist social work apparently fallen off the radar? If not among activists, certainly the language of anti-racism, so apparent throughout the 1980s and 1990s, has gradually been exorcised from much of the social work literature and has increasingly become submerged into a discourse of anti-oppressive practice, anti-discriminatory practice and the promotion and management of diversity (Okitikpi and Aymer 2010; Thompson 2011). While clearly, some of the erasure of anti-racism can be attributed to the influence of postmodernism discussed earlier, there can be no doubt that the forces of neoliberalism have affected social work and, by association, anti-racism in very specific and corrosive ways.

Firstly, we have seen the massive growth of a phenomenon called 'neoliberal managerialism', which, as Harris (2003) suggests, has wrestled power away from professionals into the hands of managers, employers and private providers. Secondly, on the economic front, we have seen the acceleration of the twin tracks of privatisation of, and cuts in, public welfare services. Thirdly, we have seen the acceleration of a perverse economic theory that seeks to assert that income inequalities are virtuous for they provide incentives for people to do well and that we all benefit from the so-called trickle down effect! As Harvey (2005: 2) notes, neoliberalism seeks to create and preserve an institutional framework 'required to secure private property rights and to guarantee, by force if need be, the proper functioning of markets. Furthermore, if markets do not exist (in areas such as land, water, education, healthcare, social security, or environmental pollution) then they must be created, by state action if necessary.'

Advocates of neoliberalism certainly would reject any accusation that they are racist in any way at all. Indeed, they would argue that their approach is totally colour-blind and empowering in that it seeks to establish a basis for services to be responsive to the needs of all 'customers', black or white. However, persuasive evidence indicates neoliberal policies have, and are, having a devastating impact on the most vulnerable in society. As John Rapley (2004) in his book *Globalization and Inequality: Neoliberalism's Downward Spiral* argues, while neoliberal policies may have had the effect of raising aggregate incomes globally, inequalities in wealth and income in all societies have increased. A report by the Save the Children (2012: vii) points out that 'the distribution of poverty within the world has fundamentally changed in the last two decades.' In 1990, the vast majority – 93% – of people in poverty in the world lived in low-income countries. Today, despite the fact that inequalities between countries remain high, more than 70% of the world's poorest people – up to a billion – live in middle-income countries.

Neoliberalism is not only just about what is 'out there', in the economy, but in fact it is also about the phenomena that are able to influence the minutiae of our personal and professional existence, our sense of being and the sense of despair and powerlessness, indeed fatalism, that this can engender. This is a condition that Fisher (2009), in his book *Capitalist Realism,* argues reflects reality in that we are led to believe we now live in a world of no alternatives and, therefore, to imagine a different future is itself a futile activity. In this sense, neoliberalism is as much a politics of 'no hope' as it is an economic project aimed at serving the interests of late capitalism in very particular ways. It is clearly the case that the kinds of idealism and optimism that accompanied anti-racist social work in the 1980s and 1990s have been lost. Indeed, in some senses, this lack of political imagination makes it easier for social workers to align themselves with the rather anodyne notions of anti-discriminatory practice than the more politically challenging ideas associated with anti-racism.

In contrast to the earlier outright denigration of anti-racist social work by the New Right in the guise of 'Thatcherism' (see Hall and Jacques 1991) – so graphically displayed in the rewriting of CCETSW Paper 30 and the expunging of all references to 'anti-racism' (Jones 1993; Singh 1994; F. Williams 1996) – the New Labour position was less clear. While embracing the general proposition of the existence of 'institutional and endemic racism' following the publication in 1999 of the Macpherson Report into the racist murder of Stephen Lawrence, there developed a general apathy towards an overtly political anti-racist project. However, Macpherson, in a way that Scarman did not, was able to articulate in a much more precise way the complex functioning of institutionalised racism. In contrast to Scarman's emphasis on individual prejudiced behaviour of some police officers, Macpherson rightly placed the responsibility on 'The collective failure of an organisation to provide an appropriate and professional service to people because of their colour, culture, or ethnic origin' (Macpherson 1999: 28).

In interrogating not only the experiences of black people but also the workings of the Metropolitan Police Force, Macpherson found that while experiencing racism can be very brutal its workings are very often extremely subtle, hidden, and more pervasive and endemic than was ever imagined by Scarman. Moreover, in recommending that the public bodies should be subject to the equality legislation, clearly Macpherson presented policy makers and practitioners with an unprecedented challenge. Paradoxically, this admission of 'guilt' by the state led, if anything, to a decline in a politicised anti-racist project. Anti-racism morphed from a distinctly political project to a managerial task. This view is founded on the belief that in the wake of new social movements, we all now live in 'enlightened times', and that the issue is no longer one of political struggle but the logistics of working in partnership to promote social justice and community cohesion (Cantle 2001). In the broadest sense, the thrust of New Labour led to promotion of a consensual view of the world, thereby concealing a conflict of social interests. In the process, the historic struggles for human emancipation became reduced to the struggle over management and administration.

Throughout the New Labour period and continuing into the more recent Conservative/Lib Dem coalition government, anti-racism has been gradually pushed to the margins for the reasons outlined above. A new agenda of 'promoting and managing diversity' and increasingly, in the name of neoliberal education reforms, the creation of faith-based schools, has not only led to the undermining of secular anti-racist projects but also, most worryingly, the encouragement of a new sectarian-based politics (Singh and Cowden 2011). Lentin (2004) is similarly skeptical of models that seek to give equal importance to the struggle for justice and rights on the one hand, and cultural differences on the other. For her, policies that promote cultural differences run the danger of reifying group identity, which may result in the possibilities for political solidarity being undermined, which is a critical ingredient of anti-racist collectivities (see also Lentin and Titley 2011).

Clearly, a genuine plural society in which difference is not only tolerated but also celebrated, where service provision is built on difference being seen as a norm not a problem, is a prize to be treasured. Yet, as Malik (1998: 3) points out, given that identities and constructions of difference are themselves often formed in and out of an experience of racism, an uncritical acceptance of difference may simply end up 'celebrating the differences imposed by a racist society, not identities freely chosen by those communities'. At best, then, celebrating difference merely enables us to accept a status quo, society as it is.

Reconstructing anti-racism in social work

So far the chapter has focused on some of the challenges, both from within and without, associated with what could be termed an 'old' anti-racist social work project. We now need to look at a way forward to enable us to build a new project: one that needs to face up to the ongoing onslaught of neoliberalism, the fragmentation of old communities of resistance, the emergence of xeno-racism and the declining morale of social work itself in the face of managerialism.

On a theoretical level, a newly reconstructed anti-racism will need to develop an altogether new and critical relationship to culture and difference, one that avoids an outdated Marxist rejection of culture as displaced or false consciousness, and a postmodernist valorisation or blind pursuit of difference (Malik 1998). Most analyses of anti-racist social work have been conducted largely across ideological lines, often leading to passionate debates about the relative merits of different theoretical and political perspectives. While this has served an important purpose, at times there has been a tendency to lose sight of the fact that anti-racist social work came about out of a lived experience, a praxis whereby individuals sought to identify with each other's experience in order to build a common cause. In other words, it began as a social movement born out of black demands for justice and equality (Sivanandan 1991; F. Williams 1996), the clearest manifestation of this being the 1981 riots. Much of the subsequent work was undertaken at a time of great uncertainty and an increasingly oppressive political context. Specifically, in relation to social work, as mentioned earlier, we saw this attack most dramatically displayed in the highly symbolic expunging of Paper 30 (CCETSW 1991a) and its 'anti-racist' content, and the unceremonious dismantling of the CCETSW's Black Perspectives Committee.

Nevertheless, it would be wrong to characterise anti-racist social work as 'defeated'; many positive things have happened, not least the emergence of a powerful black presence in social work practice and education. Much of the mainstream literature in social work is structured around many of the demands that anti-racists made: of not assuming cultural homogeneity; of attending to the issues of power; of involving users in the development and delivery of services; and in working towards a diverse workforce where there is some degree of congruence with the providers and recipients of services. Indeed, a cursory scan of the literature in allied professions of health and education will highlight the wider influence that anti-racist social work has had on shaping professional values.

Still, there can be no denying that the politicised conceptions of anti-racist social work of the 1980s and early 1990s reflected particularly the work of the Northern Curriculum Development Project (CCETSW 1991a and 1991b) and this has been largely displaced by a managerialist discourse of equality, diversity and cultural competence in more recent times. While there are undoubtedly some positive aspects of this shift, particularly in the way that a critical approach to diversity has the potential to open up the possibility 'to legitimate and validate other world views, such as Afrocentricity' (Graham 2000: 434) and in problematising essentialism, there are real dangers in moving towards approaches that become disconnected from political questions and universal ideals (Singh and Cowden 2011). This would result in falling prey to a particularly romanticised and uncritical view of culture, of tradition or the past. All cultures, communities and identities are products of material and historical circumstances, and both dimensions need to be understood simultaneously. For example, to understand British Asian culture requires not only an appreciation of the traditions of the Indian subcontinent but also of the impact of the caste system, of colonialism and capitalism, of the migrant experience and the forms of political and cultural resistance that emerge from this.

Following on from the important insights into xeno-racism, a new anti-racist social work project will need to be much more nimble at building alliances with different groups of workers, citizens and service users. At the individual level this will mean that practitioners will become much more agile at linking theory, politics and action in dynamic ways. This may appear to be a little daunting but, most importantly, the new anti-racist practitioners will need to develop different forms of praxis for ways of 'being' and 'doing', to act and think about what one is acting for and against, to transform and be transformed and, ultimately, to realise that emancipatory change does, and will always, involve taking sides, even if the utopian dream is to construct a society in which all members work together. Such a project must transcend ontologies of '*self*' and '*other*', or put another way, of '*me*' and '*we*'. As hooks (1989) states:

> To begin revisioning, we must acknowledge the need to examine the self from a new, critical standpoint. Such a perspective, while it would assist on the self as a site for politicisation, would equally insist that simply describing one's experience of exploitation or oppression is not to become politicised. (hooks 1989: 107)

She goes onto argue that only by connecting this critical self-awareness to an understanding of the structures of domination can we begin to develop the necessary collective imaginary and strategies for change. Specifically, in relation to structural racism and the state, F. Williams suggests that one of the lessons that those concerned with tackling racism can learn from past experience is of the risks involved in 'putting anti-racist social work in the hands of state agencies' (Williams 1996: 218). Indeed, at a historic moment where the welfare state, and by association social work itself, is being subject to privatisation and fragmentation, increasingly anti-racist social work will need to re-establish its roots within old and new communities of resistance. Communities that transcend old distinctions of race and ethnicity and ones that share a common understanding that, in part, their oppression is a product of the inhumane and oppressive neoliberal system of capitalism, and a common belief in forging alliances to fight for an alternative.

Conclusion

This chapter has not sought to uncover a list of 'competencies' required to be an 'anti-racist' social worker, nor suggest how social workers might work with black and minority ethnic families. Though there is a place for such literature, however, one needs at the same time to be aware that without a theoretical and historical analysis of the political nature of racism and anti-racism, such prescriptions become reduced to myopic behavioural responses more aimed at satisfying a managerialist imperative to tick a box than becoming a morally active anti-racist practitioner (Husband 1995).

As long as there is racism, there will be a need for anti-racism. What form this will take depends largely on the way racism reproduces itself, what new antagonisms surface, who loses and who benefits. While there is no disputing that the ideas of anti-oppressive and anti-discriminatory practices have their functions, the historic struggle against racism must not be lost in the important task of connecting oppressions. Opposition struggles, such as anti-racism, are always borne out of a critical praxis, moments in history where a few individuals are prepared to develop a common cause and act. Racism is a weapon that often targets its victims with accuracy and stealth. It is elusive and slippery and just when one thinks it is cornered, it re-emerges somewhere else, preying on old and new victims. What anti-racism and other movements against oppression have done is to establish an agenda, a discourse to name and confront oppression. However, a sustainable project against the structures of oppression can only be one that manages to build structures of anti-oppression. If variants of Marxist analysis enabled us to understand the material and ideological antecedents of racism, then perhaps postmodernism has enabled us to understand, more completely, the *modus operandi* of racism, to unravel the genome of racism and lay bare its DNA sequence. Armed with this knowledge, there is every possibility that a newly reconstituted anti-racist social work will emerge in due course.

On the surface the social work profession appears a beacon of light when it comes to ethnic diversity and equality. From being an almost totally white profession in the mid-1970s the evidence suggests that social workers from minority ethnic communities are now well represented. And perhaps, most notable of all, is the apparent transformation of social work education, once criticised for its biased Eurocentric rendering of black people, where non-white minorities were either ignored or constructed as inherently pathological, we now see a wide body of literature on questions of culture, race, diversity, anti-discriminatory and anti-oppressive practice. However, as has been argued in this chapter, the continued ascendency of racism both old and new demands a more expansive anti-racist project. It must be a project that is capable of recognising how 'race', far from being consigned to the dustbin of ideological history, has re-emerged in new virulent forms that are no longer reliant on skin colour or other such external biological features for the demonisation of 'the other'. This is the racism that is projected against anybody that fits the stereotype of Muslim, asylum seekers, migrant labourer and, as Owen Jones (2011) in his book *Chavs: The Demonisation of the Working Class,* people belonging to white working-class communities.

Racism amounts to the reduction of complexity, to the creation of illicit explanatory shortcuts that pave the way for domination and exploitation of differences. In the final analysis, perhaps the question is not how can social work professionals be anti-racist but what are the consequences for those professionals and professions that are incapable of being so? This is particularly relevant in societies such as ours, where the 'national economic interest' is increasingly being used to justify the oppression of the most vulnerable sections of the population.

The key challenge now confronting anti-racists, in general, and anti-racist social workers, in particular, is how to develop a project that is at once capable of confronting racist oppression, in all its guises, and has an inbuilt reflexivity that avoids fixing people, black or white into racialising social practices. Specifically, there is a need to acknowledge the pain and anger caused by racism, whether that is directed towards workers or service users. While evidence-based remedies constitute an important tool in the armoury for anti-racists, one should not underestimate the importance of subjectivity and emotion, for these elements are critical for motivating the self and others to act. However, as hooks points out, a renewed anti-racist project will need to mobilise this legitimate anger in very particular ways, moving 'it beyond fruitless scapegoating of any group, linking it instead to a passion for freedom and justice that illuminates, heals, and makes redemptive struggle possible' (hooks 1995: 20). If anti-racist social work is to have a future, it will need to respond to the changing social and political context of the global economic crisis and continued ascendancy of neoliberalism. In some senses, the worst is yet to come. As the economic crisis deepens and governments seek to impose even more draconian economic measures, it is likely to lead to greater flows of economic migrants and refugees and intensification of hate crimes against targeted minorities. If this chapter has managed to clarify some of the theoretical, political and practical challenges that undertaking such a task might entail, then it has achieved its purpose.

Suggested further reading

Patel, N. (2002) 'The campaign against anti-racism in social work', in D.R. Tomlinson and W. Trew (eds) *Equalising opportunities, minimising oppression: a critical review of anti-discriminatory policies in health and social welfare,* London: Routledge.

Singh, G. (2006) *Anti-racist social work and postmodernism.* In Teaching 'Race' in Social Sciences – New Contexts, New Approaches. Ed. by Todd, M., and Farrar, M. Birmingham. C-SAP/ HEA.

Sivanandan, A. (1990) *Communities of resistance,* London: Verso.

TWO

The growth of xeno-racism and Islamophobia in Britain

Liz Fekete

In this chapter Fekete looks at the growth of 'xeno-racism' – a 'non-colour-coded' racism that is based on conceptions of immigration status, culture and religion. Racism is not a static concept. Within social work understandings of 'race' and racism we have often utilised Peter Fryer's (1984) important three-fold distinction of the racisms of slavery, empire and post-war migration. Martin Barker (1981) in the early 1980s was already arguing that there was clear evidence of a 'new' racism that focused on culture (and was exemplified by Thatcher's infamous 'swamping speech' in the run up to the 1979 UK general election). Fekete argues this process has continued and deepened as a result of political and economic changes over the last 25 years. It is exemplified in media debates, in policy frameworks around asylum seeking and in state-controlling frameworks for so-called 'problem communities'. The relevance for social workers is obvious: the victims of racism may be black and Asian men or women, or they could be Polish or Romanian workers, or people from Roma communities or perhaps, most demonised of all, people from Muslim communities from anywhere across the globe. In our practice, and in our understandings of the world, we need to be aware of the structural and institutional barriers that social workers, social care workers and social work service users from these racialised groups will face. The Professional Capabilities Framework (PCF) domain 6 requires social workers to keep up to date with current social science knowledge bases, and in the field of 'race' and racism Fekete's discussion of xeno-racism is an important concept for social workers to grasp and engage with.

Introduction

The recognition of institutionalised racism[1] by Sir William Macpherson, in his 1999 report into the death of Stephen Lawrence, was a watershed. But even as one form of racism was acknowledged and, to a limited extent, addressed,[2] new forms of racism were emerging, based less on colour than immigration status, culture and/or religion. Already in the 1990s, a new form of non-colour-coded racism was giving rise to a discriminatory approach towards asylum seekers and refugees, who were excluded from the welfare state and demonised as illegal immigrants and asylum shoppers from 'over-populated' and 'socially insecure countries with weaker economies'.[3] The anti-Muslim racism that has taken hold since 9/11 and the implementation of the 'war on terror' is, similarly, based on demonisation, threat and exclusion, but this time not in terms of welfare but in terms of the law. Both racisms are institutional and structured – rooted as they are in discriminatory systems in welfare and in criminal justice. However, more and more, and particularly since the 'riots' of 2011, it has become clear that the institutionalised racism recognised by Sir William Macpherson has never gone away. Once again, the way in which the police and the criminal justice system discriminate against young people, from African-Caribbean, Asian, Gypsy, Traveller and other minority ethnic backgrounds, is becoming a matter for concern, as is the way the media hold black and minority ethnic (BME) cultures and lifestyles to be the causes of poverty and underachievement.

The aim of this chapter is to examine the key features of global and domestic systems that are shaping the lives of BME communities in Britain today – communities that have a different profile and demographic from those in the earlier period of post-war settlement and struggle (Sivanandan 2008). Understanding how institutionalised racism operates now involves identifying the strains of popular racism in media frameworks and the speeches of politicians that camouflage the structural elements of racism and discrimination. However, first we need to step back and examine how xeno-racism and cultural racism, linked to Islamophobia, took root, and the specific processes through which new racisms came to be institutionalised. Both racisms owe a lot to developments across Europe, particularly the EU harmonisation of asylum and immigration policies (see Fekete 2009).

The parameters of xeno-racism

In the 1990s, as far-right and nativist movements, such as the Front National in France and the Danish People's Party, began to make significant political breakthroughs in Europe, Europe's press began to mirror the extremists' view that asylum seekers and refugees were bogus, and 'welfare scroungers'. The term 'asylum shopper' (a reference to the myth that those seeking asylum pass through several European countries before settling in the country with the most generous welfare system) came into fashion – as did phrases like 'the boat is full' and the 'onslaught of the poor'.

When in 1996 the burden of housing and supporting asylum-seekers in the UK began to shift from the central to the local state (mostly in London), local authorities responded by dispersing asylum seekers to other parts of the country, such as the Kent coast, where they were placed in the cheapest possible accommodation. This was a time when many of the dispersed asylum seekers were Roma from Eastern Europe and the Balkans, who had been displaced following the break-up of the former Soviet Union and had experienced subsequent horrendous levels of racial violence. The local newspapers, *The Dover Express* and *The Folkestone Express* were not impressed. A *Dover Express* editorial in October 1998 ran the headline 'We want to wash dross down the drain', then continued in similar vein: 'Illegal immigrants, asylum-seekers, bootleggers ... and scum of the earth drug smugglers have targeted our beloved coastline ... we are left with the backdraft of a nation's human sewage and no cash to wash it down the drain' (Kundnani 2007: 80).

The Dover Express editorial may have been the media at its most extreme, as were the ludicrous stories that appeared in newspapers like *The Sun* and *The Daily Mail* claiming that asylum seekers were poaching the Queen's swans in order to barbecue them, or eating donkeys. However, headlines such as 'Britain, bogus asylum seekers, enough is enough' and editorials that focused on the inroads asylum seekers were making into the housing budget, the NHS or social security systems, were more the order of the day. This, in turn, created an environment in which politicians felt that appeals to anti-immigrant sentiment would not be construed as playing the 'race card'. By the time of the Conservative Party conference at Harrogate, held in the run-up to the 2001 general election, Tory leader William Hague warned that if Labour won the election, Britain would be turned into a 'foreign land'. (Hague used the phrase 'We will give you back your country' eight times, during this speech.)

Appealing to such sentiment is now commonplace in British politics – witness Gordon Brown's 'British jobs for British workers' speech at the 2007 Labour Party conference – as is passing off myth as facts and, for instance, Home Secretary Theresa May's 2011 speech to the Conservative Party conference, in which she wrongly claimed that a liberal judge had refused to deport an illegal immigrant because he had a pet cat. Australians have a name for such speech making. They call it 'dog whistle' politics.[4] Just as only dogs, not humans, hear the high pitch of the dog whistle, politicians use a coded language that avoids overtly racist terminology while tapping into the prejudices of key voters who fully understand the unstated idea expressed.

In fact, the myth that Europe was threatened by 'mass immigration', which began to take hold in the late 1990s, came as the EU was militarising its borders and introducing a whole range of measures to manage migration. The 1951 UN Convention on Refugees (Geneva Convention) and other instruments of humanitarian law hold that it is not a crime to cross international borders, even if that means evading immigration controls, if your purpose is to seek asylum and as long as you do so with good cause and present yourself promptly to the authorities. However, refugees were no longer being discussed within the humanitarian framework of the Geneva Convention, but within the criminological framework of anti-trafficking laws. A range of anti-trafficking and anti-smuggling initiatives were leading to the criminalisation of so-called illegal entry (see Morrison 2000 for the definitive account of this process). And the public arguments surrounding the new anti-trafficking legislation blurred the line between trafficker and trafficked, treating all parties as complicit in the act of 'illegal migration'.

This situating of the refugee within criminological frameworks at an EU (and international) policy level, lent credence to the popular discourse that treated those seeking asylum not as people from many different countries, with many different experiences and each with an individual story to tell, but as a homogeneous and undifferentiated mass. Hence the fascination, from the 1990s onwards, among politicians and press, with flat statistical projections of asylum flows; hence the offensive language in which migratory movements of displaced people are described in terms of environmental catastrophe.

It was this dehumanisation of a people that Europe sought to exclude that signalled the emergence of what Sivanandan first described as 'xeno-racism':

> It is a racism that is not just directed at those with darker skins, from the former colonial territories, but at the newer categories of the displaced, the dispossessed and the uprooted, who are beating at western Europe's doors, the Europe that helped to displace them in the first place. It is a racism, that is, that cannot be colour-coded, directed as it is at poor whites as well, and is therefore passed off as xenophobia, a 'natural' fear of strangers. But in the way it denigrates and reifies people before segregating and/or

> expelling them, it is a xenophobia that bears all the marks of the old racism.

Thus, from the 1990s onwards, both centre-right and centre-left parties in Europe began to implement legal, structural and institutional mechanisms that set that foreign-ness *in situ*, criminalising asylum seekers (through compulsory fingerprinting of all claimants, for instance), or isolating them from the rest of society, by removing them from the welfare state and/or placing them in detention centres, prior to removal. In the UK, it was after the election of a New Labour government, in 1997 that xeno-racism became fully incorporated into domestic asylum policy. For many decades, campaigners in the UK had fought against the racism of the British state as epitomised in discriminatory laws. The Commonwealth Immigrants Act of 1962 had, for the first time, limited the entry of (black) British subjects, imposing on them the requirement of work vouchers, and by 1971, primary immigration was all but abolished for black people. The 1999 Immigration and Asylum Act (the passage of which coincided with the EU's harmonisation of asylum and immigration policy at Tampere) meant that responsibility for the housing and welfare of destitute asylum seekers passed from the Department of Social Security (welfare benefits) and the Department of Environment, Transport and the Regions (housing benefits) to the Home Office. In other words, the housing and social care of asylum seekers was no longer considered an issue of social welfare but one of immigration control. Furthermore, having stripped asylum seekers of their former eligibility to council housing, and security of tenure provisions under housing legislation, an entirely new administrative body, the Home Office's National Asylum Support Service (NASS) was established in the Home Office's Immigration and Nationality Department to oversee the new control mechanisms.

This was not a uniquely British model for dealing with asylum seekers: the institutionalisation of compulsory dispersal represented the transfer to the UK of the continental 'designated accommodation system'. Also brought to Britain was a system, already practised in Germany and Switzerland, of withdrawing cash benefits from asylum seekers and replacing them with payment in kind or vouchers. A mass campaign against the voucher system, which was viewed as degrading and stigmatising, seemingly led to its abolition. In fact, the 2002 Nationality Immigration and Asylum Act introduced new benefits-related legislation, with some categories of asylum seekers removed from even the meagre support offered by NASS, while others (as well as 'failed' asylum seekers who could not be removed) re-entered the voucher system, and remain there to this day. Thus the overall system was merely refined, with the principle – of using benefits removal as part of a politics of deterring asylum seekers from making claims – remaining firmly in place. Under NHS regulations introduced in 2004, free NHS hospital treatment was removed from failed asylum seekers (except in emergency), leaving cancer sufferers unable to afford radiotherapy and newly diagnosed HIV/AIDS patients unable to access hospital out-patient treatment or anti-retrovirals, and pregnant women refused antenatal care and forced to give birth at home.

It is still possible to remember a time – prior to 1998 – when asylum seekers had the same social rights as other members of society, when they were not subjected to what, to all extents and purposes, is a modern version of the aliens' legislation of the early twentieth century. Over the last fifteen years, a *cordon sanitaire* has been erected around asylum seekers (and others without documents), which excludes them from social rights and even suggests that human rights – like the right to shelter or the right to life – should be limited to citizens. This brings to mind Hannah Arendt's observation after the Second World War that 'the moment human beings lacked their own governments and had to fall back upon their minimum rights, no authority was left to protect them and no institution was willing to guarantee them' (Arendt 1985: 292). A system specifically designed to grind down asylum seekers and stigmatise them as the undeserving (foreign) poor has now been combined with ever-more complex and exclusionary immigration and citizenship provisions, to create untold misery – and untold injustice, particularly for future generations.

They are children too

For the injustices created by this system, as experienced by children and young adults, are now catching up with us and demanding political solution. We are living in a country where a significant number of children in inner-city schools do not have passports. They are no different from any other British child or teenager, they share the same experiences and they grow up with other young people who do not segregate friendships along the lines of 'native' and 'non-native'. In other words, even though the state withholds social rights from them on account of their lack of citizenship or residence status, they are totally integrated and even a *Sun* journalist with a nose for foreigners would be hard-pressed to distinguish them from their 'native' counterparts. While some of these children, if their parents are asylum seekers, will eventually gain refugee status, and others may have citizenship rights (even if their parents, or a parent, does not), their first experience of Britain will be of a country that treated their parents as 'non-people'[5] and condemned their families to a life of hardship lacking in food, clothing and basic dignity. Many of these children will have spent periods in the cold, inhuman and sometimes violent climate of a detention centre, which is no place for a child. Others will have seen their families – some of whom may have citizenship, others not - split up in a deportation operation. These can end tragically, as occurred in the case of Jimmy Mubenga, who died in October 2010 after being forcibly restrained during a deportation flight to Angola, leaving behind a wife and five children, some of whom have citizenship status, while others, including Mrs Mubenga, do not.[6]

Some children, whose parents have no papers, only find out that they are not British citizens when they reach the age of 18 and apply for a passport. Young people, particularly from Somalia, Sudan and Rwanda, who arrived in the UK as unaccompanied minors or separated children,[7] are particularly vulnerable. A number of these young people lost family members in circumstances of the utmost brutality, but may not have come into contact with social services in their formative years; their emotional and behavioural problems may not have identified them as 'youth at risk' and opportunities may have been lost that would give them a sense of belonging in British society. Parentless and forgotten, they may find an alternative family on the streets, or drift into gangs. But should they commit a criminal offence, they could well end up in a segregated prison earmarked for foreign national prisoners pending deportation. And a system based on segregation and preparing prisoners for deportation, undermines the rehabilitative purpose of prison as well as carrying fewer rights (Fekete and Webber 2010).

Section 72 of the 2002 Nationality, Immigration and Asylum Act, defining when refugees can be deported, deemed a 'particularly serious crime' any offence attracting a punishment of two years' imprisonment or more, or any offence specified in Home Office regulations. However, the courts have, on occasion, overruled Home Office decisions to deport young adults for minor criminal offences, as well as issuing legal rulings against the Home Office's attempts to strip young adults of their refugee status if found guilty of one of a whole range of offences. (We have yet to see how many of those children and young adults convicted during the 2011 summer 'riots' come from communities of the 'non-native' and how many received the ultimate punishment of a deportation order.)

To recap: the language that began to emerge in the 1990s, when asylum seekers were described in terms of an environmental catastrophe, as a 'mass', 'horde', 'influx', 'swarm', has been matched by policies of a crass brutality that extends even to children. Of course there is nothing uniquely British in the creation of a deportation machine, armour-plated against corrosion from any sense of compassion or responsibility. Today, the scale and pace of deportations is accelerating rapidly in every country of Europe. Even as the number of arrivals decline, a speedier system of removal has been accompanied by the increased use of force, as well as measures that both deny asylum seekers access to justice and limit the ability of non-governmental organisations (NGOs) and professionals to scrutinise the system and provide independent oversight. Young people are often regarded as the most resilient among the displaced, but in 2009–10, for the first time since the IRR started documenting deaths in the asylum process, two teenagers committed suicide (in Sweden) and countless others self-harmed, including 18-year-old Lorraine Thulambo, who tried to hang herself in Bedfordshire's Yarl's Wood Immigration Removal Centre (IRR 2010). Despite the 'every child matters' mantra, the Home Office does not record suicide attempts of young people in detention,[8] and records of self-harm incidents that require medical treatment do not differentiate between adults and minors. It speaks volumes that when 'non-native' children were to be 'removed', the government did not even think it necessary to give them or their guardians any prior warning.[9]

From xeno-racism to anti-Muslim racism

Once structures of exclusion are erected for one group in society, they can easily be adapted for others. Thus, following the September 2001 attacks on the World Trade Center and the Pentagon, Europe's Muslim communities began to be caught up in the ever-expanding loop of xeno-racism. In mainland Europe, the notion that Islam was un-European and dangerous led to the introduction of laws prohibiting Muslim teachers, civil servants and students from wearing the veil at school or at work, a total ban on the wearing of full-face veil coverings in public spaces (in France and Belgium) and in Switzerland, amendment of the Constitution to expressly forbid the construction of minarets.

In the UK, where the harmonisation of discrimination law brought about by the Equality Act 2010 gives protection from discrimination on grounds of religion and belief, there are far fewer cases where Muslim women and girls are forced to mount legal challenges to laws that discriminate than on the Continent (though see Penketh, Chapter Eight, this volume). On the other hand, the structural racism emanating from the British intelligence services' approach to 'Islamism' has embedded itself within the criminal justice system in a way that is more advanced than in most other European countries (and here, see Lavalette, Chapter Nine, this volume, for discussion of the 'Prevent' agenda). Laws, procedures and mechanisms have been created that remove Muslims from the ordinary rule of law, deny them access to justice, legitimise special courts and secret evidence, detention, house arrest and deportation under cover of dubious diplomatic agreements to countries that practise torture – all part of a process whereby Muslims have been subjected to a parallel criminal justice system characterised by harsher penalties and fewer rights. In this, the crucial impetus driving structural anti-Muslim racism was not so much the populist anti-Muslim rhetoric of the nativists, as the fears and preoccupations of the intelligence services. For in the immediate aftermath of September 11, when the focus on al Qaida might have been expected to be at its sharpest, the British government introduced the first of seven emergency laws, with new laws and measures to prevent the radicalisation of young Muslims proliferating after the trauma of the 7 July 2005 bombings in which 52 people, as well as the four British-born suicide-bombers, died.

Some of the approaches that were adopted during the prolonged conflict in the north of Ireland, and gave rise to numerous miscarriages of justice (underscored by a general anti-Irish racism) have come to characterise the post-September 11 counter-terror policy in Britain. The Diplock courts in the north of Ireland suspended trial by jury for those on charges relating to terrorism and gave police extraordinary powers of arrest and interrogation. Similarly, emergency powers that involved the suspension of civil liberties and legitimised the use of secret evidence and special courts are central to the anti-terrorist laws and measures introduced in Britain over the last decade (for the best account of the history of this processes see Peirce 2010). In the first instance, in line with xeno-racism, it was refugees and foreigners (particularly from the Middle East, but also Algeria, Chechnya, and so on) who were targeted when the UK government further extended its emergency powers in the Anti-Terrorism Crime and Security Act (2001). This allowed for indefinite detention without trial – internment by any other name – of non-Britons. But when in December 2004 the House of Lords ruled that such internment was discriminatory (as it applied only to non-nationals), the government introduced control orders for terrorism suspects, both foreigners and citizens – although in reality, it has been mostly foreigners who have been subjected to this form of house arrest (on this, and the mental and health implications of control orders see Brittain [2009, 2010]). (The coalition government has renamed control orders, Terrorism Prevention and Investigation Measures [TPIMS].)

Even though, since the 2004 House of Lords ruling, foreign nationals cannot be interned, in reality, a number of foreign nationals continue to be detained without charge, but this time as immigration detainees. The government continues with the fiction that these foreigners have a choice, and that they are free to leave the country at any time, while aware that someone detained for deportation as a terrorist suspect in the UK would, in all likelihood, be detained and subjected to cruel and degrading treatment and probably tortured, if sent back to their country of origin. Foreign immigration detainees have no right to hear sensitive evidence against them, and a special court, the Special Immigration Appeals Commission (SIAC), is the sole appeal court for foreign nationals whom the home secretary wishes to deport on national security grounds. SIAC operates within an Orwellian system of special advocates, senior lawyers with security clearance, who can see the evidence against those whose interests they represent, but who cannot then have contact either with them or their lawyers.

The general popular discourse against Islam ensures that the British Muslim community as a whole is stigmatised for the actions of a few. This process is further reinforced by the institutionalising of religious profiling, which now takes many forms. It includes the increased use of stop and search, the mining of databases for information on Muslims whose personal profiles correspond to specific criteria on the police's search grid for potential terrorist sleepers, dragnet operations aimed at mosques and Muslim meeting places, increased questioning of Muslim airline passengers (ironically described as 'travelling while Asian'), pressure on young Muslims targeted by police to inform on the Muslim community and the instruction to universities to monitor the activities of Muslim students for signs of radicalisation and violent extremism.

Islamophobia and the parallel world of Muslim youth

The civil liberties lawyer Gareth Peirce, who has represented many young Muslims arrested under anti-terrorist laws, believes that our emergency laws are counter-productive; they create anger, resentment and despair, particularly when 'courts cannot, or will not provide a remedy', she says, adding that there now lies ahead the 'bleak prospect of imprisonment for thousands of young people, all Muslim, who have accessed the internet prompted by an interest – shared with millions of their contemporaries around the world, Muslim and non-Muslim – in the workings of political or radical Islam' (Peirce 2007).

What Peirce had in mind, when she made these comments, was a whole range of new criminal offences brought into the law under successive terrorism acts, based on very vague definitions of speech, behaviour or even thought that in and of themselves have never before come under the scope of the criminal law. The Terrorism Act 2000 gave police wider powers to stop and search at random. However, while the stop and search provisions were subsequently deemed unlawful by the European Court of Human Rights, the creation of new offences based on the possession or circulation of information useful for terrorism, was not. Section 57 of the Terrorism Act 2000, for instance, made it an offence to be in possession of books or items for the purpose of terrorism, while section 58, which carries a sentence of up to 10 years, made it an offence to collect information useful for terrorism. The Terrorism Act 2006 created specific offences of acts preparatory to terrorism and indirect encouragement by the 'glorification of terrorism' (distribution or circulation of a 'terrorist' publication was also criminalised). The 2008 Counter-Terrorism Act further widened the net of innocent people who can be incriminated, at the same time as affording greater penalties for those convicted of the vague offences outlined above, including confiscation of property, bans on foreign travel and requirements to report to the police whenever staying away from home.

The wording of such laws is deliberately vague, making it easy for the authorities to secure convictions on the basis of suspicion about a person's intentions and speculation about whether possession of certain texts is a prelude to future criminal acts. All this leads to a sense of injustice among young Muslims. While Islamophobia in society and the stigma attached to their faith erode the young Muslim's sense of belonging, the police's failure to clamp down on the crimes committed by members of groups like the English Defence League as they stage their drunken and provocative marches through Muslim neighbourhoods confirms them in the belief that they are a second-class community with second-class rights (see Copsey 2011; Erfani-Ghettani 2011). And controversies over the government's counter-radicalisation programme Prevent (Preventing Violent Extremism), add a further sense of victimisation (see Kundnani 2009; Lavalette, Chapter Nine, this volume). There have been a number of cases where youth workers and students have stated publicly that the police have pressurised them to act as informers on their community.[10] A number of other cases, involving heavy-handed police tactics, have further eroded trust. One case in particular, that of Nottingham University master's student Rizwaan Sabir and Nottingham university staff member Hicham Yezza, heightened discontent. After Rizwaan Sabir, as part of his PhD research on radical Islamic groups, downloaded an edited version of the al Qaida handbook (from a US government website) and Hicham Yezza printed it out, both men were detained following police raids. At the same time, the anti-terrorist police maintained a high profile at the university, questioning students and lecturers who, furious at the intimidatory atmosphere on campus, mounted a highly effective political campaign for academic freedom (at one point a demonstration was held in which prominent academics gave public readings from the al Qaida manual).[11] And there was anger, once again, in 2009 following the disproportionate sentencing of 22 young Muslims, convicted of public order offences as a result of taking part in demonstrations in London, in December 2008 and January 2009, following the Israeli invasion of Gaza (Athwal 2010). The young Muslims were targeted for arrest months after the demonstrations in dawn raids. The list of grievances included the fact that many of those arrested were students in full-time education and with no criminal record; that they were required to surrender their passports, despite the fact that the vast majority of those charged were British citizens; that British Muslim citizens were served with immigration notices, which stated that they could be deported, depending on the outcome of criminal proceedings; and that Muslim demonstrators were sent to prison for lengthy terms, often against recommendations in pre-sentence reports from the probation service.

Popular racism and violence against Muslims across Europe has increased massively in the years since 2001, and firebombing of mosques, death threats against prominent Muslims, physical attacks on Muslim women who wear the hijab, are now an everyday feature of European life. (For a documentation of anti-Muslim violence and other related provocations, Autumn 2010–Summer 2011, see IRR 2011.) Such cases are naturally picked up and discussed by Muslims, who increasingly view Islamophobia as a European-wide and global phenomenon. One of the most horrific incidents occurred in Germany, where the Egyptian-born pharmacist Marwa el Sherbini was stabbed to death by a known neo-Nazi sympathiser in a Dresden courtroom in 2009. (In yet another example of the dangers of religious profiling, the court guard went on to shoot and seriously wound el Sherbini's husband, believing him to be the perpetrator.) As Islam is viewed as foreign (despite being part of European culture for centuries) and has been (mischievously) conflated with political Islam, and then with terrorism, any sign of visible Islam can now be deemed threatening.

Since September 2001, there has been a proliferation of stereotypical generalisations about Muslim culture and the Islamic mind-set, reducing Europe's diverse Muslim communities into a monolithic mass, with Muslims represented as having characteristics that are immutable and innate. A religious identity has effectively become racialised. Hence what has emerged should justly be described as anti-Muslim racism, rather than mere Islamophobia, which implies personal prejudice – just as racism against Jews is not just Judaeophobia, or prejudice against Judaism, but antisemitism.

From cultural paradigms to the culture of poverty

It was, of course, September 11 and the 'war on terror', that led, at the level of ideas and discourse, to the creation of 'new' frameworks that essentialise Islam and demonise Muslims. One of the most influential of these frameworks was the 'clash of civilisations' thesis, which is associated with a group of American academics (including Bernard Lewis and Samuel Huntington) who, from the 1990s onwards, wrote a series of essays in support of American and Israeli foreign policy goals in the Middle East. Lewis suggested that the backwardness of Arab culture and economy was leading to feelings of enmity and rage directed at American, Israeli and European targets, while Samuel Huntington argued that with the cold war over, world politics had entered a new phase in which the fundamental source of conflict was not primarily ideological or economic, but cultural, with 'the principal conflicts of global politics occurring between nations and groups from different civilisations' (Huntington 1993: 22).

The popularisation of the clash of civilisations thesis is only one example of the ways in which cultural and religious paradigms are now widely used in popular debate to explain societal and political issues. The fact that culture is now treated as the key analytical tool for understanding developments in society has given a massive boost to those who seek to promote hate and popularise the reactionary idea that the clash of civilisations is an inevitable feature of the modern world. Formerly, racial supremacists used to talk about protecting one's race, and warned of the inevitability of 'race wars'. Nowadays, they talk about protecting one's culture, and the inevitability of 'culture wars'. Refugees, foreigners, Muslims, all pose a threat to 'our culture', because they harbour feelings of enmity to 'our way of life'. Asylum seekers who uproot their families, flee their homelands and risk their lives in perilous journeys over several international borders are seen as making an unnatural lifestyle choice – their weakness, pathology even, cannot be condoned by granting them access to refugee rights. (An exploration of the way those who cross borders to seek asylum are demonised is provided by Khosravi [2010].) Similarly, treating Islam as a pathologically insane and violent religion allows one to ignore political frameworks in which anger over Western foreign and economic policies in many parts of the world can be analysed and understood. Instead, one is taught to categorise and pre-judge Muslims, even in everyday encounters.

However, the same holds true when it comes to the debate on integration, where failures in integration are equated with 'self-segregation' or the desire of the Asian community in particular to live 'parallel lives'. Sociological explanations are discounted in favour of an overblown conspiracy thesis that blames, in the words of David Cameron, 'the state doctrine of multiculturalism' and decades of 'passive tolerance' for encouraging 'different cultures' to live 'separate lives' (Cameron 2011a; see Jenkins, Chapter Seven, this volume, for a critique). Previously, in February 2007, David Cameron had attacked Muslims for 'living apart' and the head of the former Commission for Racial Equality, Trevor Phillips, had attacked multiculturalism and warned that Britain may be 'sleepwalking to segregation' (Phillips 2005).

Sociologists Nissa Finney and Ludi Simpson (2009) have provided all the facts to rebut the 'sleepwalking to segregation' myth, while Arun Kundnani (2007) has located the rise of the 'self-segregation' and 'an excess of cultural diversity' framework to the Oldham, Burnley and Bradford riots in the summer of 2001. He showed that there was, indeed, a growing geographical segregation of communities in these northern towns, but the explanation for this did not lie within Muslim culture but in the 'interaction of industrial decline with institutionalised racism in housing and employment' (Kundnani 2007: 47). This industrial decline in the Lancashire and Yorkshire textile towns left towns on the scrap heap, there was discrimination in favour of whites in public-services employment and council-housing provision, and it was as a reaction to discrimination and racist violence that the Asian community were driven to settle in certain neighbourhoods and retreat into a self-provided safety. However, this history was completely forgotten, as was successive governments' responsibility for social and economic problems. Structural barriers to integration have not emerged overnight, but have solidified over time.

Another summer, another set of 'riots', and the same cultural lens is in operation, this time to explain the riots of August 2011, which occurred in neighbourhoods where BME communities are over-represented. These BME communities are now more diverse than in that earlier period of struggle that preceded the death of Stephen Lawrence and the Macpherson inquiry and include the new refugee and migrant communities from the Middle East, North Africa and Eastern Europe. And there have been other important changes too, particularly for Gypsies and Travellers, who are being forcibly assimilated into the general population owing to the criminalisation of the nomadic way of life, lack of official sites, and constant evictions (such as that at Dale Farm), so that they now live in a similar structural and spatial location to other deprived and marginalised groups (Smith and Greenfields 2012).

Today, we are being encouraged by politicians and certain sections of the media to judge people from poor neighbourhoods through a cultural lens and to blame their lifestyle choices for their poverty. Those who seek to draw attention to the way our economy and our society is structured – to issues like poverty, inequality, policing, institutionalised racism – are sidelined by a coalition government that emphasises 'violent gang culture' (May 2011) or an 'educational underclass' linked to a subversive culture in which young people feel able to ignore 'civilised boundaries' (Gove 2011). As a *Guardian* leader commented (in the context of a February 2012 Commons debate on welfare), a 'belief in couch-bound idleness as an inherited underclass trait is spreading', as media stories about 'shameless estates' proliferate.

The culture of poverty thesis popular in government circles and amongst elements of New Labour (Tony Blair was a zealous proponent) holds that the chaotic lives of poor people are the cause, not symptom, of the collapse of their communities. It is a way of thinking that holds that those who are culturally hostile to work and social order must not only feel the full force of the law (and in public order situations that means curfews, water cannon and plastic bullets), but that their access to the welfare state should be restricted and rigorously policed.

As we sift through the governmental and societal response to the summer of 2011 'riots' and begin to evaluate the policies that have emerged in their aftermath, we would do well to ask ourselves what exactly Michael Gove had in mind when he referred to subversive culture and civilised boundaries? We could try substituting black for subversive and add white, or Christian, to civilised boundaries. Or we could ask ourselves whether his words represent another example of dog-whistle politics. The historian and broadcaster David Starkey, when addressing the causes of the 'riots' during a *Newsnight* interview said 'the problem is that the whites had become blacks'.[12] It certainly does not seem that Starkey has been schooled in dog-whistle politics. Nor have the leader writers and sub-editors at *The Daily Mail* and *The Daily Express*. Neither Michael Gove nor David Starkey seems to have much sympathy for those black communities whose experiences have been shaped by a long history of violent encounters with the police. Among the mourners at the funeral of Mark Duggan, the 29-year-old father of four whose fatal shooting by the police sparked the August 'riots', were the relatives of Cynthia Jarrett, whose death sparked the Broadwater Farm disturbances in 1985; of Colin Roach, who died in Stoke Newington police station, north London; and of Sean Rigg, who died while in the custody of police in Brixton, south London. *The Daily Mail*, covering the funeral procession from the New Testament Church of Wood Green to Broadwater Farm, captioned a picture of young people touching the funeral cortege of Mark Duggan with the words 'Gangsta salute for a fallen soldier'. *The Daily Express* commented that 'In chilling scenes, youths dressed in black and baseball caps lined Tottenham with their arms outstretched in a "gangsta" salute to a "fallen soldier"' (Pilditch 2011). Both newspapers were guilty of a shocking disrespect to young mourners at a funeral. These dignified young people were merely responding to a request by Pentecostal bishop Kwaku Frimpong-Manson to stretch their arms towards the carriage as he prayed: 'We come to stretch our hands towards the casket and thank God for Mark's life as he begins his heavenly journey' (Muir 2011).

Conclusion

While race has been scientifically discredited as a way of classifying people, racism based on culture, religion and even poverty informs relentless attacks by politicians and the media, on groups such as asylum seekers, Roma, BME youth and Muslims, and institutionally racist laws, policies and practices targeting these groups. Vulnerable asylum seekers are criminalised, segregated, excluded from welfare, health and housing provision, detained and brutally removed, while the wholesale privatisation of detention and asylum support services has reduced accountability while providing further sites for racist practices.[13] Children are not exempted, and the damage wrought by their and their parents' treatment is one of the most tragic unseen effects of the institutionally inhumane asylum system.

In the UK, Muslims are targeted by policies driven by security services' fears and prejudices that see young Muslims as potential terrorists and subjects them to stop and search, questioning at airports, pressure to inform on their communities, and the risk of arrest for harbouring 'Islamist' reading material or ideas. As cultural and religious practices are reified, racialised and used to explain issues as diverse as global terrorism, riots and residential segregation, the real causes are disguised, and inequality and discriminatory policies go unaddressed. At the same time, the double standards revealed in the policing of BME and Muslims on the one hand, and of the far right and perpetrators of racial violence on the other, exacerbate alienation and distrust.

Social workers, whose work is likely to bring them in contact with vulnerable people of all religious and ethnic groups, need to understand the dynamics of the different racisms, against asylum seekers, BME and Muslim youth, the cultural stereotypes and the institutional racism embedded in policies and practice, if they are not to be part of the problem, but part of the solution.

Suggested further reading

Fekete, L. (2011) 'Understanding the European-wide assault on multiculturalism', in Hassan Mahamdallie (ed) *Defending multiculturalism: a guide for the movement*, London: Bookmarks, 38–52.

Hayes, D. and Humphries, B. (2004) (eds), *Social work, immigration and asylum: Debates, dilemmas and ethical issues for social work and social care practice*, London/Philadelphia: Jessica Kingsley Publishers.

Hayter, T. (2000) *Open borders: The case against immigration controls*, London/Sterling, Va.: Pluto Press.

Notes

[1] Macpherson defined institutional racism as 'the collective failure of an organisation to provide an appropriate and professional service to people because of their colour, culture or ethnic origin'. (1999 para 6.34)

[2] The Race Relations (Amendment) Act 2000 extended the provisions of the previous act on direct and indirect discrimination to public authorities and placed a statutory duty on such bodies to promote race equality.

[3] The phrases are those used to describe those migrating to the UK, including refugees, by the UK Home Office (1998) White Paper *Fairer, faster and firmer.*

[4] A reference to the anti-immigration campaign led by Prime Minister John Howard in the run-up to the Australian federal elections in 2001, in which Howard's government portrayed itself as strong on border protection measures while the opposition was weak. In the lead up to the election Howard's government had alleged that a boatload of asylum seekers had thrown their children overboard in a presumed ploy to secure rescue and passage to Australia. An Australian Senate Select Committee 'inquiry into a certain maritime incident' later found that no children had been thrown overboard and that the government had known this prior to the election (see Fear 2007).

[5] Australian indigenous critic, Tony Birch, speaks of the 'unpeopled', the 'non-people' whose human suffering may not be seen or recognised. See Suvendrini Perera, 'What is a camp....?', *Borderlands* ejournal, vol 1, no 1 (2002).

[6] For more information on the case of Jimmy Mubenga and other cases of concern, see the IRR Race and Refugee News Service (www.irr.org.uk) and the website of the National Coalition of Anti-Deportation Campaigns (www.ncadc.org.uk).

[7] Unaccompanied children are defined by the UNHCR as children under 18 who have been separated from both parents and are not being cared for by an adult who, by law or custom, is responsible to do so. Separated children are children under 18 who are separated from both parents or from their previous legal or customary primary caregiver, but may be cared for by extended family members. Child experts have also pointed out that some children arrive in Europe with adults (hence they are not strictly unaccompanied) who are not their parents or legal or customary primary caregivers as the result of being trafficked or smuggled. See Jacqueline Bhabha and Nadine Finch, *Seeking asylum alone: Unaccompanied and separated children and refugee protection in the UK,* Human Rights at Harvard, 2006.

[8] Although the Conservative–Liberal Democrat coalition, which came to power in 2010, claimed to abolish the immigration detention of children, over 220 children were detained during 2012, according to official statistics.

[9] In December 2011, the policy of no-notice removals was outlawed by the Court of Appeal on the grounds that it deprives deportees of access to justice.

[10] One case that was publicised involved six youth workers from Kentish Town who say they were harassed and interrogated after holidays abroad in 2008. See CagePrisoners, *The Horn of Africa and the new community profile*, 2010.

[11] For the full story see Nottingham University Students and Staff, press release, 21 May 2008, www.indymedia.org.uk/en/2008/05/399290.html; *The Times Higher Education Supplement*, 22 May 2008; *The Education Guardian*, 31 May 2008, www.theguardian.com/education/2008/may/31/highereducation.uk; Hicham Yezza, 'Britain's terror laws have left me and my family shattered', *The Guardian*, 18 August 2008, www.theguardian.com/commentisfree/2008/aug/18/terrorism.civilliberties.

[12] Interview available at www.guardian.co.uk/uk/2011/aug/13/david-starkey-claims-whites-black.

[13] The escorts who killed Jimmy Mubenga (see note above) were employed by G4S, the company which, with fellow multinational security giants Serco, Reliance and Mitie, run most of Britain's immigration detention estate and, now, most asylum housing. For damning critiques of privatised housing provision see John Grayson's blogs for Open Democracy, for example, 'Their secret is out, but for G4S and friends 'abject disregard' for human dignity persists', 18 March 2013, www.opendemocracy.net/ourkingdom/john-grayson/their-secret-is-out-but-for-g4s-and-friends-'abject-disregard-for-human-dign.

THREE

The catalysers: 'black' professionals and the anti-racist movement

Charlotte Williams

In this chapter Williams looks at the strategies for implementing anti-racist practice. In the 1980s the anti-racist social work movement argued that effective anti-racist practice would also require the significant recruitment of black and Asian workers who could challenge practice on the frontline and change the culture of social work organisations. Williams revisits some of the early debates of the 1980s and traces the history of the anti-racist social work movement, and the role of the early leaders. However, rather than an overt focus on policy regimes and bureaucracies, which many in the 1980s became concerned to focus on, she argues that we need to look at the practices and the networks of anti-racist practitioners, 'the catalysers' who can bring about significant organisational changes to services.

Introduction

At various points in post-war history, the recruitment of black and minority ethnic individuals into the social services workforce has received government sponsorship for a number of reasons: to address labour shortages, for symbolic and tokenistic imaging of public service agencies or for its transformatory potential. The bedrock assumption of this latter line of argument is that altering the racial composition of the social service workforce ensures that services would become more attuned and, therefore, more accessible to the 'special needs' of black service users and act as a counter to institutional racism. This strategy has steadily gained in momentum in public services in the post-Stephen Lawrence era, with a range of public bodies and agencies seeking to attract representation from minority ethnic individuals within their ranks. In many ways social work, like education, was at the forefront of this trend from the 1970s onwards, signalling the key role minority workers could play in the production of so called 'ethnically sensitive' service delivery (ADSS 1978).

The decade from the early 1980s can be identified as a significant period of 'black recruitment' in social work, when largely left-wing Labour-controlled local authorities sought to incorporate the welfare demands arising from grassroots minority ethnic communities and political activists and translate them into local government equal-opportunities policies. This was overtly the liberal settlement of a central state seeking to deflect a tense and unsettled period of race relations. Gail Lewis's seminal argument (2000: 206) proposed that the employment of black/Asian (largely female) social workers articulated with this very specific 'moment of racial time' in the UK, in which racial discourses of black and Asian family lifestyles suggested the need for a political response of control and appeasement. Social work accordingly came to occupy a very specific place in the repertoire of government strategies of the time in assuaging dissent, moralising and normalising black and Asian families, and mediating contestation over welfare resources. This *moment* led directly to the recruitment of black/Asian social workers who had hitherto principally occupied ancillary roles in such departments, largely as unqualified social work assistants or residential and home care-workers (see Bryan et al 1985). However, this settlement was fundamentally flawed in a number of ways, not least because of the competing ways in which the multiplicity of local authorities interpreted their equal opportunities brief and, indeed, the ways in which these equality ambitions became entangled with professional discourses.

If this racial moment has passed and other statist multiculturalist ventures overlaid it, it represents an interesting point for us to ask 'What happened to anti-racist social work? There remains a substantial number of black and minority ethnic (BME) workers in the social services system whose positioning vis-à-vis the racial-justice project forms a complex dynamic. Contemporary policy and practice and, indeed, professional discourses have successfully changed the terminology, the rules of engagement, the priorities and the perspectives of the race debate such that this constituency of workers has apparently lost its political significance and visibility.

This chapter returns to the debates about the role of 'black' professionals within the anti-racist movement, as practitioners, academics and students, looking specifically at their potential as catalysers in terms of political-agenda setting, framing and claims making, and critically debates their ambivalent positioning within 'White' public-sector institutions today. The term 'black' itself has been subject to considerable debate and transformation in this racial discourse, but I use it in this chapter in the way in which it was first inscribed in the debates in social work to encompass those of us of black, mixed and Asian descent. This chapter tracks the incorporation of black professionals into mainstream social work practice and education and training, and it critically debates aspects of their positioning within the anti-racist struggle and raises questions about shifts in the locus of effort for change in improving the lives and circumstances of BME peoples.

Black professionals and social work: infiltration

Local government can be said to be the pivotal site of anti-racist professional activism, and social work as a profession has provided a key arena where such activities have been played out. In a post-Scarman (1981) Britain in which the demands for appropriate welfare services were being more and more forcefully articulated by BME individuals, grassroots groups and activists, and in which government sought to muster a response to the 'problem' of immigrant minorities, the recruitment of BME professionals potentially held the promise of a more responsive service-delivery and a medium for countering institutional discrimination.

The core of this idea emerged most forcefully in local government of the 1980s under a variant of what Paul Gilroy (1987: 136) has called 'municipal anti-racism'. This particular brand of anti-racism engaged local authorities as an instrument of change in terms of actively campaigning against racism, targeting funding and initiatives towards marginalised groups, and recruiting from the ranks of underrepresented groups. This 1980s equal opportunities politics inevitably resulted in an increased recruitment of black and minority ethnic people into the professions, and especially into occupations such as social work, where the remit was to respond to locally based unmet needs using short-term section 11 funding made available under the Local Government Act 1966. This special funding of up to three-quarters of the cost of a post aimed at meeting the 'special needs' of minority ethnic communities led to the popularly called 'section 11' jobs. Singh (1992) argues that Black people were 'climbing over each other' for section 11 jobs, and black organisations were fighting among each other for a slice of local authority grant monies such that an 'ethnic parochialism replaced black activism' (1992: 23). Thus a twin tactic of cooption and divide and rule effectively operated to tame the street-based racial fury.

This recruitment was also an exploitation of a cheap pool of available labour. The position of the section 11 workers was very quickly noted. Their status and remuneration was notably lower than their counterparts with similar workloads and responsibilities and they 'often felt hopelessly isolated, misunderstood, at times snubbed and overwhelmed by totally impossible responsibilities and an unsupportive administrative structure' (Cheetham et al 1981: 93). The anomaly was that far from commanding a positive value for their work, these workers were placed in marginal positions within organisations, found themselves overburdened, subject to conflicting and additional demands by comparison with their white counterparts, and experienced high levels of workplace discriminations. Their relative powerlessness, however, was not considered an obstacle to their potential to operate as change agents.

The question of black professionals' ability to achieve change formed the basis of a study by Paul Stubbs undertaken as a PhD research project in 1983/84. Stubbs (1985) addressed the question '*what difference do Black social workers make?*' based on evidence from interviews undertaken in two London boroughs. He sought to explore the position of black social workers along three main lines of enquiry: the extent to which social work functions as part of the state apparatus or whether it can achieve relative autonomy (as a site of resistance) within the statutory context; the hierarchical nature of social service bureaucracies that determine particular types of manager/worker relationship in which few managers are black; and the claims regarding social worker–client relationships producing heightened responsiveness. Stubbs' work exposed the anomalies and contradictions that lie at the heart of the 'ethnic sensitivity' model deployed within local authorities of the 1980s, which he argued produced particular types of pressure for black workers forcing them into roles as 'good black social worker' that at best posed no threat to the reproduction of racist structures and at worst actively aided their reproduction (1985: 17). The misconception of the role of BME staff compounded the often untenable position of such staff within largely white organisations: assimilate or face marginalisation and exclusion. Stubbs concluded that the actions of black workers, when they form strong collective political groups within workplaces, may make some inroads into social work practices but that fundamentally they could only but fail to permeate the institutional reproduction of racism within state social work agencies. The working practices, ideologies and organisational modes lay largely beyond the scope of their influence. He pointed forward to a form of 'black professionalism' based on 'strong, effective black managers and senior social workers' that might penetrate social services departments in the longer term along the lines of models apparent in the US (1985: 26). In this sense

Stubbs did not let go of the idea of a constituent group of racialised actors that could transform service delivery.

By contrast Lewis's (2000) work, which tracked this 'new cadre of social workers' (2000: 8), is scathingly critical of what she calls 'the black staff model' (2000: 129), which she argues pivots on the assumption of essentialised cultural knowledges. Lewis problematised the privileging of 'black experience' or 'black perspectives' when she provocatively asked 'What, if any, are the particular skills or attributes which black women can bring to social work; and why are these important?' (1996: 29), and went on to critically explore what is meant by this experience and how it may be deployed authoritatively but only as part of what she calls 'occupational situatedness' (1996: 53). While she is not rejecting the added value that such subjective foundational experience can have in client/worker relationships, for Lewis it works in complex ways within and across racial category and is linked or mapped onto professional discourses producing a 'simultaneity of discourse'. As black women, she argued, these social workers' experience speaks across both race and gender and enables them 'to move within an across discourses as they communicate in modes of identification and differentiation with those who constitute an element of themselves' (1996: 53). It is accordingly both a (non-)hegemonic message and a situational one that must reflect their position of relative powerlessness within organisational hierarchies, where they seldom hold managerial positions because of their race and gender.

Lewis work calls for a reconceptualisation of how race/ethnicity is utilised to position these subjects in relations of power (2000: 131), taking into consideration the contest over the meanings given to ethnic difference and to the ways in which ethnicity can intersect with other social status such as age, class, gender or sexuality to structure experience. Her postmodern approach argued for complexity in the intersections of relations of power that structure both the lives of client's and those of the worker, in which ethnicity is just one of a number of factors at play and may not be the primary factor at any particular time. Ultimately, therefore, she refuted concepts such as ethnic matching in client/worker relationships or indeed the axiom that these women could influence agency ideologies and agenda.

For Lewis, black and Asian (largely women) social workers were effectively constituted as racial/ethnic subject by the state and were paradoxically provided with employment opportunities but, at the same time, this racialised status was the very factor that ultimately constrained their professional autonomy through determining for them a marginal positioning within the workforce. They became, in effect, problematic for the organisation (Lewis 2000: 14). They were not team leaders, managers, top civil servants or chief executives but caught in the Catch 22 of being both valorised for their racialised experience and being undervalued for it (Prevatt-Goldstein 2002). Far from being in lead roles in relation to a new model of service delivery, in Prevatt-Goldstein's terms the dominant 'race based ethos' of the organisation (2002: 777) essentialised, homogenised and exploited black workers on the one hand and negated their experience and skills on the other.

If the practice arena were to undergo change, so too this implied change to social work education and training, to its literature base and to its professional discourse. Alongside developments within SSDs (Social Services Departments) came the development of an academic literature reframing a professional discourse that had previously focused on responding to the particularised needs of minority ethnic groups to one resplendent with political, material and racial causality in individual and community distress (Ely and Denny 1987; Dominelli 1988). Individual treatment models were being rapidly decentred by an overtly radical anti-racist analysis and stance. The anti-racist project had been launched. Social work was interrogating itself and black professionals were crucially identified in their potential role as catalysers of this change: in the development of alternative perspectives, in advancing progressive initiatives as part of the broader black struggles against racism and for their 'experience' as part of minority communities themselves (Hutchinson-Reis 1989). Key grassroots groups and activists effectively formed a fundamental social movement that pushed this agenda from the bottom up and infiltrated professional discourses. Black workers both in the statutory and the voluntary sector were deployed as key agents and legitimators of this transformation (Alleyne 2002; Dabydeen et al 2008).

The partnership of local state social service departments and higher educational institutions under the oversight of the then regulating body the Central Council for Education and Training in Social Work (CCETSW) was the key medium for delivery on the new agenda within social work. CCETSW as an organisation was also cognizant of its need to get its own house in order and to recruit from the ranks of the BME population. Key movers and shakers were appointed to executive positions within the organisation with a specific brief to lead developments on race equality. The Black Perspectives Committee (1987–94) brought together academics, intellectuals, practitioners and activists to influence policy, practice, education and training issues. There was representation on this Committee from all four nations of the UK, which at the time secured the author's recruitment to this influential body. I took the messages 'home' and translated them into my own context in Wales pushing out the frontiers in remote and rural places (Williams and Short 1997). We, as black workers, had achieved presence – on the front line, in the teaching and training rooms, within the regulating body and were formulated as a black collective irrespective of the huge diversity of backgrounds, place, identity and experiences. The success of this cross UK forum was undoubtedly its high level of institutional support.

The movement: presence

There can be little doubting that the contributions made by BME professionals and students both within and beyond state institutions to the anti-racist effort within social work. Their physical labour, emotional investment and intellectual capital have been considerable. These day-to-day labours of love are important to recognise. They are the informal contributions and challenges to the unequal structures and practices within social work levied by these minority actors – work that is less quantifiable, visible or valued and that has for too long remained hidden from view. Their presence had both a caretaking and a 'watchdog' effect on practices within the bureaucracy. Recognition of these quiet narratives is important because these stories indicate the ways in which BME staff can and do muster strategies of resistance, mobilise counter cultures and act as active agents of change in their day-to-day work.

The momentum for change may have come from grassroots black activism but it was swiftly adopted and incorporated into the academy and the professional body and embodied in these catalysers. Alliances were formed across the service user/provider divide, across the lecturer/student divide, the practitioner/academic, and the statutory/voluntary sector divide pushed forward an agenda for change. Professional ideologies, which defined the nature of professional interventions, were questioned and reinterpreted. Types of skill and competency, the commitment to detachment of professional involvement with clients, the nature of leadership were all being reworked. The black managers that existed were cautioned that they had been inculcated with 'essentially white conceptions of knowledge and practice that have been promoted within a white system' (Husband 1991: 55) and invited to consider the ideology of professionalism as an important facet of institutional racism. Thus the proposition of a black professionalism was being advanced and black perspectives in social work was expounded in a growing literature (Singh 1992).

One such set of tangible products that were developed from these networks were the CCETSW Curriculum Development (CD) materials, which in themselves were transformative both as a resource and perhaps even more importantly as a process. Stubbs (1995 quoted in Patel 2002: 37) speaks to the collective effort that were the CD materials:

> Looking back the CD project represented some kind of new social movement in which in Audre Lorde's terms differences were acknowledged and even celebrated and used as a force for change. We were united by recognition of the need for anti-racist change at all levels, including, crucially, the curriculum, and we developed some kind of collective action, which transcended hierarchies of white/black, teacher/student, and academic/practitioner. The CD texts are both a process and a product containing for all their faults, innovative curriculum material.

A number of such formal and informal networks emerged to take the anti-racist work forward that are significant in themselves to the notion of a cross national 'collective action'. Some examples are the Association of Black Assessors, Black Probation Officers, Black Social Workers and Allied Professions – all of which offered advice, consultative work, training and crucially mentor support to black professionals. Strong links were formed with key non-governmental organisations (NGOs) working with black communities. It was indeed a movement in the classic sense, a movement whose hegemonic grip held the seeds of its own downfall.

Lewis's argument is that this was a very specific and time-limited period, which came to be very successfully eroded by the Thatcher government and the right-wing media as new discourses of service delivery emerged (Lewis 2000: 204). Sivanandan (1991), however, foresaw the fragmentation of the black struggle and its disengagement from the street anti racism that spawned it: 'firstly on the basis of the bourgeoisification of black people. Secondly on the emptying of "black" of its political content' (1991: 43). Others in this volume have documented the demise of the movement, what is perhaps of relevance here is the notion of fragmentation and bourgeoisification. One thread in theorising the question – *what happened to anti-racism?* – must be a consideration of the assertion that somehow these critical actors themselves were implicated both in terms of the increasing assertion that the term black no longer encompassed the various identity claims that differentiated them and indeed their own comfort and instrumentalism within state institutions, which arguably deradicalised them.

Paul Stubbs' anticipation of the rise of the middle-class black professional – conscious of itself as a substantive grouping and able to use its power to effect change has not emerged within social work despite continued and consistent recruitment into the profession. Currently just under 15% of the social work workforce are identified as being from BME backgrounds. Of the workforce as a whole 70% are known to be white, around 10% are known to be from the census black categories and 4.3% are Asian (GSCC Annual Report 2010). The Council with Social Services Responsibilities in England estimated around 6% of the workforce are recorded as of unknown ethnic origin. Interestingly, the not-knowns are largely recorded in the shires where it may be that ethnic monitoring is not robust or where people are more reluctant to mark out their ethnic origin. The BME staff whose ethnic origin was known mainly work in Inner London where 46% of social work staff are from BME backgrounds. Percentages of BME representation above the England average minority ethnic population of 9% were recorded by all London boroughs. Eight have a high percentage known to be from BME groups: Brent (63%), Ealing (49%), Hackney (59%), Haringey (53%), Lambeth (61%), Newham (55%), Tower Hamlets (54%) and Waltham Forest (54%). The highest outside London was in Birmingham (40%) (National Statistics 2011).

Despite these concentrations – the 'voice' of black professionals in social work is not a collective one. Their voice is strangely muted and their potential political clout diminished: but are they the self contented bourgeoisie that Sivanandan suggested?

Being black professionals or professionally black?: 'outsiders within'

The experiential narrative of this '*cadre of black workers*' within social work is surprisingly under-researched and under-theorised (Butt and Davey 1997; Lewis 2000; Prevatt-Goldstein 2002). In the main, it is the stuff of blogs and anecdote that form the body of evidence and in the last 10 years there is a deafening silence. This is not the case in relation to those of us in Higher Education institutions (HEIs).

Accounts from the ranks of what I call *Blacademics* of the dilemmas of managing their positioning in HEIs have come from the broader feminist literature or from disciplines such as education (Ahmed and Swan 2006; Mirza 2006). Concerns about BME staff in the HEI sector have long been documented with extensive evidence amassed to show

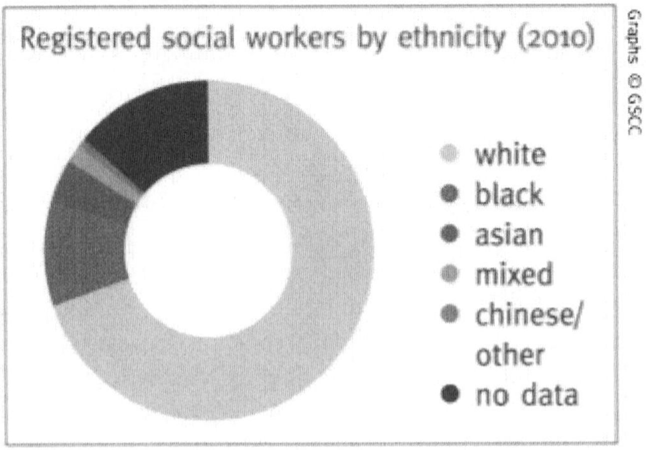

that BME staff are underrepresented at senior levels in HEIs and subject to a significant 'race penalty' in terms of promotion and progress in the sector (Equality Challenge Unit [ECU] 2011). The recent ECU research finds a disconnect between policy and implementation by reference to management practices of recruitment, workload allocation and promotion – all of which impact negatively on BME staff, with the worst instances of discriminatory treatment related to casual racism in the behaviour of managers.

> The majority of BME staff who participated in the research had experienced the damaging effects of being treated in a subordinating or excluding way because of their race. This highlights that the daily experience of working relationships and institutional support matter a great deal. The corrosion of confidence created by lack of respect, support and recognition affected some BME staff so severely that they simply gave up. (ECU 2011: 22)

The ECU research indicates that BME staff are less likely than non-BME staff to be in leadership and management positions in institutions. The number from minority backgrounds who have found their way from qualifying training to the front line, and on to become professors of social work, can be counted on one hand despite the relative healthy recruitment into the profession from the 1980s onwards. Social work is a very white profession in its higher echelons and its occupational culture. Like our counterparts in the field we spend years and years trying within this most benign and liberal of professions to break through the 'ivory ceiling' with little or no sponsorship from our white colleagues. When we do we may be subject to allegations of being 'uppity', assimilated, losing sight of our responsibilities to those we should represent, over-promoted or as has been too often said to me '*you've done well because you're black*'.

Punwar (2004) refers to us as 'space invaders', somehow 'out of place' occupying spaces not previously attained by black people or not seen as being rightfully in these positions. In her conference presentation Cathy Aymer (2010) depicted us as *aliens* in the host institution and Mirza uses the term 'disorientation' to describe '*the double-take as you enter the room, as you are not supposed to be there*' (Mirza 2006: 105). As external examiner (not the student), as chair of the recruitment panel (not the cleaner), as senior team leader or director of children's services (not the service user), as just being myself (not the race equality adviser) in these ways we face and then challenge the assumptive world of social work. Mirza (2006) poignantly highlights many of the processes of exclusion that Blacademics encounter. Beyond the immediate disorientation there is infantalisation, whereby you are assumed to be less capable of being in authority. There is the burden of invisibility, not being able to be yourself, or hyper-surveillance, whereby any mistakes are magnified as confirming incompetence or misplaced authority. In all of these ways the black worker has to work harder on credentialism, legitimacy and managing the confines of stereotypical expectations (Back 2004). There are costs to being in the HEI, says Mirza (2006), costs both emotional and psychic to BME students, costs to academics, costs to practitioners negotiating what Back has referred to as 'the sheer weight of whiteness' (2004: 1). Prevatt-Goldstein's (2002) evidence from a very small-scale study in social work largely confirms this type of experience. She finds workers experiencing major stress in managing additional tasks and the conflicting expectations of colleagues and black service users, having to over-justify themselves and being subject to isolation, over-scrutiny and interpersonal racism, and yet deeply concerned about their contribution to the wellbeing of BME service users.

Managing this positioning is not without a hefty price. In very few cases is it without pain. In his classic statement Du Bois (1903) identified the special responsibility of 'facing both ways' and the additional duties the black professional carries in respect of their wider constituency. Like Gramsci's (1971) organic intellectuals who retain their affiliation with the sections of civil society that they represent and who must play a key role in advocacy and change – we have work we must do. In addition, we must navigate a terrain riven with casual, inadvertent, banal racisms and confront the 'ethnic' dilemma – to *pass* or to claim.

For ethnicity is fluid, contextual, contingent, variously visible or not, it involves both the 'voluntary' assumption of self, claiming as well as the ascription of that identity by others, as McLaughlin (2007: 72) powerfully acknowledge when she asks:

> *Should one seek to maximise one's own power, influence and possibilities of success in a given set of circumstances by disclosure or nondisclosure of some traits?*

This decision making is, as she points out, strategic, instrumental and moral in nature:

> The behaviours involved in manipulating social identity may be argued to be a form of work, and a burden of work largely unknown to those from majority groups. The work is that of securing legitimacy and credibility of presence; presence being inherently questionable in relation to people identified in terms of minority group traits' (McLaughlin 2007: 73)

This extra work is complex and significant in a number of ways. It strikes to the heart of the hidden costs of the anti-racist project: the emotional investment of these actors that lies unrecognised. Patel's account (1995; 2002) of her time as a civil servant at the helm of '*The Firm*' – CCETSW's Race Equality Officer – is one such valuable contribution to social work history for which there is little such documentation. Using the third person she describes the mission to implement CCETSW's pioneering anti-racism policy:

> *She* was fired by a strong ideological commitment to fight racism, but was aware of the limitations of individual workers and their ability to challenge institutional racism.... *She* also recognised the context in which *She* and others in the area were required to operate: many regarded the goals of anti-racist policies as a search for something unachievable. This attitude, *She* felt, by and large reflected a generalised (but fortunately not *en masse*) resistance to change, as well as, in varying quantities inertia, narrow mindedness, short term thinking and racism. As for her own position, marginalisation, work overload and colleagues attitudes that anti-racism is not proper work were all to be expected – a

> situation no different to the experience of many other black people. (Patel 1995: 17–18)

The ambivalent positioning and fortunes of black students on social work programmes has perhaps received more attention not least because of their startling failure rates in qualifying training (de Gale 1991; de Souza 1991; Pink 1991; Channer and Doel 2009). Interestingly the HEI statistics indicate social work is a discipline of choice for many BME students given their preference for vocational training degrees and yet overall they fare badly.

The work experiences and well being of these individuals is clearly a factor that circumscribes their ability to 'speak out' against personal injustices and to influence and transform services. Patel provides insights into this story:

> And what of the human, personal, economic (job wise) costs to those ... who take a stand against such behaviour?
>
> This takes us to the heart of how black professionals conduct themselves and organisations' response to black professionals who are in the system. Black professionals with an anti-racism remit are a nuanced sub set of this group. After many months, *She* reflects on the context in which *She* arrived in the Firm. '*She*'ll set the place ablaze'. 'Do we need such posts when there are more pressing things to be done, such as child care work?' '*She*'s only been employed because *She*'s black'. ... *She* also knew that in the organisation the majority of black workers, as elsewhere, were to be found at lower levels in the organisational hierarchy; whereas black professionals such as herself were expected to be Jacks of all trades. (Patel 1995: 28)

The dilemmas are complex and manifold. The anti-racist project as it emerged within social work did provide the context in which individuals could exercise their agency toward change as a collective but the price was to essentialise them and to essentialise their claims such that they were always vulnerable to marginalisation when the bandwagon moved on. Perhaps the important distinction here is between types of political struggle: those that reflect a community of interest and collective action, and those that reflect the myriad forms of control and resistance played out as a result of our differential experiences in the workplace. If at various moments the opportunity structure has enabled the emergence of black people as a community of interest, there is nothing to suggest that they have been any the less active in both managing and addressing racisms in the micro-politics of their day-to-day existence within social service organisations and the academy.

As a result of such ruminating over the fixing of essentialised identities, more recent theorising has engaged with the ways in which race and ethnicity are 'performed' in particular contexts as opposed to being determining factors to action. In this sense people are neither black professionals nor professionally black but part of a complex apparatus in which anti-racism is situated and performed.

Loose cannons: white liberal institutions and the diversity mandate

If the *ethnic-sensitivity* professional discourse and the equal opportunities era of the 1980s provided a specific moment in racial time, then the emergence of the late 1990s *diversity paradigm* and the associated institutional responsibilities post-RRA 2000 provides another. The responsibility question is an interesting one: *Whose business is anti-racism?* In the 2000s the answer to the question came with the shift to institutional culpability for the reproduction of racisms.

For many black professionals the 'diversity' era as a formalised policy movement raises a number of issues in relation to their positioning. It brings into view the extent to which they take responsibility for this remit and undertake (or get burdened with) equalities '*work*' on behalf of agencies; the extent to which their presence is usurped for the purpose of showcasing/imaging diversity within the organisation; the extent to which they tangibly benefit (or not) from improved working conditions and prospects as a result of equalities policies; and crucially what potential remains for the aspiration of equality activism?

Mirza (2006: 109) has argued that the diversity movement within the academy has had little to do with transforming the experiences of black female staff and students (2006). The most recent evidence from the ECU (2011) supports this assertion. Patel's (1995) early account implies a similar situation within social work but there is a noticeable lack of evidence in relation to current experiences. While there exists some research evidence and monitoring data relating to BME NHS professionals and health-care staff, there is a serious evidence gap in relation to the social care-worker and social work (Williams and Johnson 2010). It is not that there have not been workforce surveys and workforce research particularly documenting the impact of neoliberal methodologies on social work practice and social workers' wellbeing, but the impacts of the modernisation agenda on minoritised groups has not been pursued. In the contemporary context of recession the precariousness of their position is exacerbated. BME workers may indeed be among some of the most vulnerable in the current economic climate and subject to the downward pressures of managerialist technologies and discriminatory practices in terms of recruitment, training and promotion. It is known that black workers are highly represented in the public sector and that they are less likely to be members of a union. In September 2010 as the recession in Britain began to take a grip, Diane Abbott put forward the claim that the planned government cuts to public services would hit BME workers harder than their white British counterparts because a higher proportion of their jobs were in the public sector (FullFact.org). There is little evidence to suggest equality policies will mitigate this ill wind.

Diversity action plans, equality statements, widening participation strategies, ethnic monitoring, audit and impact assessments all represent the ascendancy of the technocratic approach over the moral case for inclusion but, for Ahmed and Swan (2006: 97), these become 'technologies of concealment' whereby inequalities and distributions of power are hidden by measures of 'good' performance. For Ahmed diversity policy has been more about 'speech acts', more about saying than doing, and she suggests that these function to block rather than enable action. This type of critique could imply a narrowing of the scope for equalities politics, a de-radicalising and constraining of its effects and focus. Such equalities policies can effectively aid the politics of containment of black activism through subtle process of incorporation, assimilation, divide and rule.

Yet between the end points of marginalisation or assimilation there are huge sites of contestation in professional arenas where black professionals and their allies exert their agency. Hunter and Swan (2007: 377b) in editing a fascinating collection of essays that 'trouble' the traditional dichotomies in equalities studies, such as professional/activist, equality good/corporate diversity bad – put forward this space as an arena where a complex micro-politics in played out in fluid and contingent relationships between the state, activists and professionals. In this space those who will negotiate a path through the ambiguities and contradictions (the see-saw of hope/failure as they call it) that characterises much of this work manage to open up the potential for race equality work. This work is a complex of daily *oscillations* and contradictions that those involved in the messiness of equalities work must live with but one in which alliances and networks can be mobilised. In the bringing together of human and non-human resources such as agendas, policies and protocols, equality work is translated, interpreted and acted upon. These actors are involved in 'framing' claims, in generating debates, in translating or 'diversity interpretation' and in deploying the 'tools' of a range of types of intervention to effect change (Hunter and Swan 2007b).

This type of theorising enables the emotional and intellectual complexities of being involved in such interventions, the partnerships that are forged in these processes, the points of resistance that are opened up and the ways in which contexts shape the work and in which infrastructures are profoundly relational to be noted. It is not simply a case of top-down policy or indeed concerted collective bottom up pressures but a dynamic constellation of activity:

> rather than view professionals as complicit in the narrow bureaucratisation and quantification of inequalities and activists as 'impotent' in the face of managerialism, the very diversity of the infrastructure itself is constituted through a complex network of relations where activists, professionals, organisations and states are interdependent. (Hunter and Swan 2007: 413a)

We, therefore, need to revisit the anti-racist project in social work and consider the ways in which the locus of change has been re-sited from notions of a black caucus or a critical partnership of black and white activists. Patel writing over 10 years ago (2002: 36) spoke of '*those in charge of it...*' as if to identify a top-down model of action. Alternatively, questions have been asked about the dissipation of collective action and pointed to the demise of anti-racism as a social movement within social work. Social workers find themselves in the paradoxical position of acknowledging the persistence and pervasiveness of racism yet puzzling how to remobilise the effort, questioning where to look for the locus of change now that social work (as an institution) appears to have 'moved on'.

Whose business is anti-racism?

Lots of arguments and debates have emerged recently that focus on a retheorising and reorientation of the anti-racist effort in the light of socio-demographic changes, the rise of Islamophobia, the shift from single strand to generic equalities legislation and measurement and the incorporation of race equality duties into organisational behaviour. The anti racist project is rapidly being seen as 'so eighties', and somehow out of step with contemporary realities or at best embedded or mainstreamed. The literature and the anecdote cite the effect of neoliberalist methodologies as the culprit for this state of affairs. The logic of neoliberalism has, it is argued, served not only to strip the 'race' effort of its moral content through bureaucratic incorporation but also to fragment, demoralise and depoliticise social work itself such that the luxury of an anti-racist stance cannot be afforded. Much as this argument forms the dominant discourse within contemporary social work it does not explain why the profession has so easily coalesced around this position. Is it more the case that the profession has never found deep anti-racism comfortable because of what it implies for its liberal value base, its predominant methodological orientation, the normative whiteness of its elite profile? The lesson of the 1980s is one that suggests the profession focused far too heavily on the energy, passion and emotional commitment of a caucus of black people themselves; that the profession's ownership of the mantle was tentative and provisional – nay ambivalent, the alliances thin, permissive and voluntaristic. It is such disavowal that keeps these issues beyond examination and permits racism to be sustained within the profession itself. For our own part we as black workers are easily dispersed and fragmented, vulnerable to the demands of the day job, relatively powerless and subject to being cut off from the fuel supply that is our social care workforce – our minority students and service users – those who are best placed to keep the flame burning. As any type of collective Black workers are too diverse, too conspicuous, too visible, too easily disabled or dismantled.

Institutional support means an environment conducive to debate, trial and error experimentation and risk taking in the allocation of leadership roles – all critical to nurturing of anti-racist effort. It means a blurring of boundaries between public institutions and the organs of civil society and a mutuality that has not yet been seen. Where the bureaucracy has failed so indeed has the profession. The reorientation of the professional discourse on race and ethnicity is everywhere present. We find ourselves in a moment when our models of analysis have proved wanting, when policy has failed those we seek to serve but when there is considerable uncertainty about the way forward and considerable disagreement about what are the appropriate models of analysis and action. The profession is subject to and acquiescent in the popularist and knee-jerk directives of government and it is unlikely that bodies such as the Health Professions Council or even the College of Social Work will significantly resist, reframe or reorientate these debates. Yet anti racism is not a luxury, an 'if we've got time' set of tasks, or a special effort necessary for the special needs of a particular public. It is core to our primary business of rectifying injustices, of combating disadvantage and of speaking truth to power. It is in fact everyone's business.

Conclusion

Black workers have made and continue to make a significant and important contribution to the transformation of services and to the anti-racist effort within social work. This chapter has illustrated the highly political terrain in which they negotiate these efforts within their day-to-day work and the ways in which this effort affects them individually and as a collective.

The argument I put forward here is that it is more useful to look at the ways in which anti-racism is being 'performed' by a range of actors with an investment in social justice: via strategies that are protective, resistant and proactive. This will take us beyond the bureaucracy to networks of alliance, productive relationships from which practices and projects are built and take hold, toward an analysis of contexts conducive to change, toward micro politics which emerge, form and mobilise in particular context at particular times and become critical to claims making, agenda setting and change. It will take us toward an analysis of how and why certain professional discourses emerge and take hold. This will necessarily be an uneven project, one that is dispersed and patchy, recognisable by its outcomes. The emphasis becomes one of capturing and capitalising on this potential, nurturing and evaluating it and collating it to form a sustainable bedrock of knowledge for analysis, action and intervention.

Suggested further reading

Hunter, S. and Swan, E. (2007) 'Oscillating politics and shifting agencies: Equalities and diversity work and actor network theory', *Equal Opportunities International*, Vol. 26(5): 402–19.

Williams, C. (1999) 'Connecting anti-racist and anti-oppressive theory and practice: Retrenchment or reappraisal?', *British Journal of Social Work*, 29: 211–30.

FOUR

"Same, same, but different"

Philomena Harrison and Beverley Burke

In this chapter Harrison and Burke look at shifting anti-racist discourses from anti-racism, to anti-oppressive practice and on to notions of 'cultural competencies'. They trace this shifting debate through a range of perspectives, including the work of black feminists, the assertion of black perspectives, a focus on human rights and engagement with the service-user movements. The chapter includes discussion of the challenges facing social work educators (academics), who have tried to include this discourse in education and training in a way that makes it meaningful for professional practice.

> What is crucial to such a vision of the future is the belief that we must not merely change the *narratives* of our histories, but transform our sense of what it means to live, to be, in other times and different spaces, both human and historical. (bhabha 1994: 256)

Introduction

In Hanoi, as in many cities where tourists are plentiful, hawkers have developed ingenious ways of trying to persuade you to buy something, often exactly the same object that you are holding prominently in your hand! When one such vendor approached one of the authors (Philomena)on a trip to the city,[1] Philomena held up a previous purchase and said, with confidence, "See, I already have one!" The reply came, "Yes, yes, this one same, same, but different!" So began a dialogue about the nature of 'sameness' and 'difference'.

Using this theme of similarity and difference, the authors will critically evaluate the three areas of anti-racist practice, cultural competence and anti-oppressive theorising, and engage in an informed discussion of how these different ways of conceptualising and addressing racial discrimination have influenced social work practice.

Responses to oppression and inequality are not only informed by our similar and different lived experiences but also by our belief that responses to social issues are inherently political and require an analysis that recognises the specificity of particular forms of oppression as well as how intersections and interconnections between the various oppressions are played out in the lives of individuals, families, groups and communities.

The experiences of, and gains made by, a range of social movements led by disadvantaged social groups (Mullaly 1997, 2006), ideas developed by radical structural theorists (Bailey and Brake 1975; Ferguson and Woodward; 2009; Lavalette 2011) and, the authors' own exploration of Black feminist literature and theorising (Lorde 1984; hooks 1989, 1991, 1994; Morrison 1999; Hill Collins 2009; Ahmed 2012) contribute to the understanding and responses to social issues. The notion of intersectionality (Crenshaw 1989, 1991), individual agency and collective action inform our own understanding of power, powerless and oppression. Alongside this, it is crucial to recognise that the struggle for social justice and equality has to be more than a single response to any one particular individual, group or social movement. The problems of living are inextricably linked to particular structural arrangements and require social action that challenges the systems that contribute to, and sustain, patterns of inequality and oppression.

In this chapter the authors take into account concepts of fairness, human rights, equality and diversity, social inclusion, social justice and how they have informed a range of practices that have attempted to deliver equitable and just services to black and minority ethnic (BME) groups. The authors will explore and comment on the development and role of anti-racist, cultural competence and anti-oppressive discourses and their impact on social work practices, service delivery, education and training. In doing this national events and attendant debates, which have influenced the development of these perspectives within social work, will be considered.

In addressing the challenges for the future the authors explore how the shift from the clarion call of anti-racism (which attempted to look at structures that produced and sustained racist practices), to the idea of cultural competence and notions of fairness, diluted the challenge to discrimination and oppression on the grounds of race. This work intends to reassert the political and ethical potentiality of practice that is anti-oppressive. The ways in which anti-oppressive practice addresses the multilayered nature of oppression and discrimination and shifts the dialogue from dichotomous ways of thinking (which we believe to be one of the weaknesses of anti-racist and cultural competence approaches) to providing ways of addressing the complex interconnections and intersections of the lives of individuals; reaching beyond the all-encompassing definitions of any one social division is discussed. We believe that the social work and care professions, and social workers, in particular, are in a strong and unique position to bring voice to the complex lives and locations of vulnerable and socially excluded individuals and provide effective responses and resolutions to issues of inequality and oppression.

To be able to move away from a strategy of change that focuses merely on one aspect of difference (whether or not it deals with structural issues) an anti-oppressive approach that actively makes links between individual differences and structural issues brings a political potency to the discussion. Within such an approach issues of power, particularly in relation to understanding the processes of oppression and resistance (Ferguson and Lavalette 2004; Smith 2008), a commitment to social justice and human rights is actively acknowledged and addressed (Clifford and Burke 2009; Hugman 2013).

The personal and the political

The tragedy of the racially motivated murder of Stephen Lawrence exemplified the relationship between structural oppression and the impact on the individual, family and community. The impact of Stephen's death, 20 years on, can be seen today in changes in policing, the criminal justice system and other public services.

The life of Doreen Lawrence, mother of Stephen, was irrevocably changed not only by the racist act which killed her son but also by the deeply entrenched racism of the justice system. Institutional discrimination and racially motivated individual actions made their particular mark on her and her son – both psychologically and physically (Jordan 1989; hooks 1992; Byrd et al 2009; Ahmed 2012. Oppression is not simply understood in the mind – it is felt in the body in myriad ways' (Hill Collins 2009: 293; Ahmed 2009). Doreen, in response, resisted and reclaimed her humanity, as well as that of her son, and in turn the daughters and sons of communities where such injustices have been perpetrated. The police failed to provide a service that was 'fair' and just. Their reaction to the case was characterised by personal prejudice, stereotyping and institutionalised racism (Macpherson 1999). Doreen the woman, proud mother, denied the basic rights of a citizen in this country and justice for her son was catapulted into the role of political activist. Her identity as a black woman living in a society that is divided on many levels, including race and gender, was shaped not just by the brutal killing of her son but the responses to it by major public institutions. She has had to, through her extraordinary courage and determination, engage in battle from which others may have shrunk. Along with her family, and the support of legal advocates, action was taken against the police, the criminal justice system and the government and in that process brought to public attention the invidious and destructive realities of racism.

However, it still remains a singularly shocking and upsetting fact that racially motivated crimes continue to exist in British society (for example, Anthony Walker murdered in a racist attack in 2005 in Liverpool). Differences, based on skin colour distort and deny people's basic rights to be accepted, to be treated with dignity and respect, and to have fair access to services. The use of 'racialised' differences to discriminate and oppress in a society, which wears its democratic credentials on its sleeve, as it makes pronouncements regarding inequality and oppression on the globalised world stage, is morally unacceptable, dubious and suspect. However. is not entirely surprising given Britain's imperial and colonial past (Paxman 2011). A society that focuses on culture (and then only certain cultures) as the main determinant of difference and neglects the structural nature of racism and ethnocentrism fails to acknowledge the role that power plays in relation to dominant and subordinate group interactions. This depoliticised, conservative analysis of difference has led to the development of a plethora of liberal policies that maintain the status quo rather than address the causes of inequality. The increase in observable forms of racism within various cultural, social and political arenas - from the football field, the academe (Ahmed 2012) to Westminster – is suggestive of the need to once again, in a very real and direct way, discuss issues of 'race' and racism and what these concepts mean in a multicultural society.

The authors understand and appreciate that within sociological discourse and theorising, 'race' and racism are problematised and disputed terms as they are generated by social, cultural, political and economic factors which are subject to change. It is also important to acknowledge that 'whiteness' should also be problematised as the term is also informed by a particular set of racialised beliefs. This in turn will bring particular and complex meaning to 'racist' experiences of the 'white' majority in Britain. In this the authors support Lentin's (2000) position that it is necessary both to understand the historic specificity of the structural nature of the ways in which racism is endemic in Western societies and has had impact on the inclusion and exclusion of particular groups, and also to have an analysis that acknowledges that it is difference per se, and not difference based on particular biological and cultural traits, that enables us to explain the 'persistence of racism over time' (Lentin 2000: 104).

Anti-racist social work practice

Anti-racist social work practice was one direct response to acknowledging the impact of race and racism on the lives of those affected by racism. It went beyond assimilationist and integrationist ideas and practices that were directed at managing black and minority ethnic (BME) communities and questioned the Eurocentric base of social work training and practice, where 'race' problems were seen as a result of cultural differences and not endemic racism within institutional policies and practices (Keating 2000). Anti-racism highlighted the presence of black workers (including the establishment of black workers' groups) and saw the development of black perspectives (Burke and Harrison 2000) that critiqued the 'received wisdom' of a then mainly 'white' profession of social work. Anti-racism, by focusing on a structural analysis of racial oppression, radically shifted the emphasis from individual pathology and addressed the structural patterns of racial inequalities (Burke and Harrison 2000).

Anti-racist practice gained particular prominence in the 1980s (Grahame 2009) and can be defined as 'forms of thought and/or practice that seek to confront, eradicate and/or ameliorate racism' and as 'ideologies and practices that affirm and seek to enable the equality of races and ethnic groups' (Bonnet 2000, cited in Berman and Paradies 2010: 218). It provided a theoretical and practice framework in which issues of 'race' and racism could be discussed and practice developed that actively responded to racial oppression. Anti-racist practice not only brought attention to the unequal power relations that shaped the relationship between white and black people (Dominelli 1988) but it also attempted to address the disparity in power between professionals and service users. There was a clear acknowledgement of the racialised relationship between those who used deterministic belief systems and structures in society to dominate those who are seen as different by virtue of their 'race' (Bonnet 2000).

Although a very necessary step in the journey to equality, anti-racist practice has particular limitations. However, it is important to acknowledge the fact that commitment to anti-racism has led to necessary changes and challenges within social work (for example, work with black children and families Barn 1993). A focus on 'race' and racism drew attention to the presence of black workers and the failure of the profession to address and meet the diverse needs of black people. However, the failure to encompass the concept of intersectionality (Hill Collins 2009) and the 'simultaenity' of oppression (James and Busea 1993)has meant that anti-racism as both discourse and practice has failed to fully demonstrate how the experience of racism is mediated through other social divisions such as gender, class, disability, sexuality, religion. Racism needs to be understood as a multidimensional and complex concept, where the racial identity of the individual is but one aspect of the experience of racism (Burke and Harrison 2000). It is important to note that being critical of anti-racist practice does not mean that racism is a thing of the past as this is definitely not the case.

Cultural competence

It is relatively recent that welfare-service-delivery organisations have begun to seriously address ways in which service delivery needs to change. In some cases this had been in response to major enquiries where race and ethnicity were identified as major factors in oppressive practices. Two major reports that have had an effect on practice design and delivery are the Macpherson Report in 1999 (on the death of Stephen Lawrence and racist practices on the part of the police) and the independent inquiry into the death of David Bennett in 2003 (on the death in a medium-secure psychiatric unit of this young Afro-Caribbean man). These reports, alongside The Race Relations (Amendment) Act 2000) now oblige public organisations to respond to racial discrimination within a culturally plural society.

It became evident that health and social care services need to respond to the rapidly changing demographics in populations that accessed the services. Changes in Britain's population were brought about by distinct patterns of immigration and migration, not just by colonialism and imperialism, but by new connections between nations states (for example, the European Union) and devastating wars that have led people to seek refuge and asylum. Further, it was assumed that the development of culturally sound practices would also respond to, and appreciate, the distinctions and connections between notions of 'race', culture, and ethnicity. Specifically, the legislation required public organisations to develop race equality schemes and carry out race equality impact assessments.

Following these changes in the law policy guidance began to emerge that demanded service developers to address issues of 'culture' as a source of discriminatory practices. Notions of 'race' merged with concepts of ethnicity and culture. Professionals were required to become culturally competent in their practice. Many models of cultural competence have been developed since (Laird 2008; Tedam 2013). One such example is the work of Papadopoulos et al (2004), who produced a training tool for assessing cultural competence that was to be used with health-care professionals. This model provided a framework for professionals to develop culturally competent ways of working using a self-assessment tool and engaging in specific training. The training itself was based on a conceptual map that included the areas of cultural awareness, cultural knowledge and cultural sensitivity through which the worker could achieve cultural competence. They would then be able to self assess post-training and measure their levels of cultural competence. So the focus had shifted to addressing aspects of culture as contributing to discrimination in the delivery of services. It could be argued here that this shift seemed a more concrete way for practitioners to address racism. It assumed that racist practices were based on a misunderstanding of the service user's culture and cultural practices by the professional, rather than the deep-rooted prejudicial practises based on structural and historical racism.

Cultural competence training, though used widely in Britain in health and social care is subject to criticism. The following are critical issues and questions that the authors feel arise for practitioners using 'Cultural competence' as the main focus for achieving change where there is 'racial', discrimination in practice;

- By ignoring the intersectionality and interrelationships between race, ethnicity and culture, other identities or social differences on the grounds of class and caste could be ignored. So workers could privilege one aspect of social difference over another leaving a service user vulnerable, for example, on the grounds of gender (forced marriages).
- Given that knowledge and meaning around culture can be controlled by dominant ideologies it must be questioned who owns and controls the 'cultural knowledge' that is provided to students and practitioners.
- How far is it practically possible for practitioners to hold the range of cultural knowledge required to work in a complex multicultural society, where different ethnic groups may share a common religion but have developed, over time, different ethnic and or cultural affiliations (for example, being a British Muslim within a Bangladeshi community in the north of England)?
- How far can cultural groups demand the right to self determination where discriminatory cultural practices may perpetuate – such as

domestic violence, gender-based discrimination or religious/cultural practices such as female genital mutilation? Where does that leave the culturally competent worker?
- How far can organisations support practitioners when dealing with the complexities of a range of cultures – in terms of cultural knowledge and cultural sensitivity? A good example (coming out of engaging with practitioners experiencing cultural competence training) is the case where nurses working with a mother with a diagnosis of puerperal psychosis, whose cultural practice was not to take part in any care of the infant for a specific period of time after the birth. In order to respond to this specific cultural practice the nurses took on all the practical care of the baby. This produced complaints of unfair treatment from other mothers (of white British origin) in the unit and left the nurses in question at a loss as to how to respond appropriately in the interests of fairness for the other mothers. Would they be considered 'culturally incompetent', in this case, if they ignored the needs of women from the majority culture?

It is the authors' contention that the concept of cultural competence shifted the gaze away from discrimination on the grounds of race, and encouraged workers to develop new ways of working predicated on trying to respond to specific cultural practices; they ignored the complexities brought about by the intersections of other differences, such as class and poverty. This has led to workers being expected to appreciate and have knowledge of a whole range of cultures and religions rather than appreciate the specific historical and structural reasons why BME groups and individuals would suffer from a lack of appropriate services. Practitioners and educationalist in social work and social care have to question as to whether it is easier to challenge discrimination based on cultural differences rather than deep-rooted personal and institutional racism.

We agree that the work on addressing the notion of cultural competence in health and social care has enabled some practitioners to explore their own and others' cultures, enabling them to produce fairer practice and develop their cultural knowledge, cultural awareness and sensitivity. However, cultural competence cannot be achieved without an acknowledgement of the complexities of the development of culture for people in the diaspora.

Anti-oppressive practice

In the early 1990s the authors' experience as social work educationalists found them in a team, headed by Beth Humphries,[2] that was addressing new ways of facilitating students to explore the nature of oppression and discrimination for people receiving social work services. This was informed by debates taking place about the inadequacy of the anti-racist paradigm. It began to acknowledge that there could not be a meaningful analysis of race and racism without addressing other social divisions (major and minor) and the 'simultaneity' (James and Busia 1993) of oppression. Black feminist thought as articulated by writers such as Patricia Hill Collins brought about a

> fundamental shift in how we think about unjust power relations. By embracing a paradigm of intersecting oppressions of race, class, gender, sexuality and nation, as well as Black women's individual and collective agency within them, Black feminist thought reconceptualizes the social relations of domination and resistance. (Hill Collins 2009: 291-2)

This discourse enabled a move forward, and away, from some of the limitations inherent in a purely anti-racist perspective.

Since its development anti-oppressive practice has been defined in a number of ways. The following definition encompasses Clifford's (1998) key anti-oppressive principles (informed by black feminism and other non-dominant perspectives) of social systems, power, social difference, historical and geographical location and reflexivity. These principles are used to reflect on the similarities and differences in anti-racist practice, cultural competence and anti-oppressive practice. As previously discussed anti-racist practice and cultural competence are approaches that enable practitioners to address inherent discrimination in service delivery for minority groups in Britain. However, the authors argue that anti-oppressive theorising informs practice that is inclusive and deals with power and multi-oppressions in systematic and complex ways. Further, that the anti-oppressive principles provide a clear framework for assessment and intervention in social work:

> Anti-oppressive practice is a radical social work approach which is informed by humanistic and social justice values and takes account of the experiences and views of oppressed people. It is based on an understanding of how the concepts

> of power, oppression and inequality determine personal and structural relations.
>
> Anti-oppressive practice is based on a belief that social work should make a difference, so that those who have been oppressed may regain control of their lives and re-establish their right to be full and active members of society. To achieve this aim practitioners have to be political, reflective, reflexive and committed to promoting change. (Dalrymple and Burke 2000: 14)

Differences between people can be used to separate and divide. The use of power and the experience of powerlessness are the processes through which discrimination based on social differences occurs. The social divisions most familiar to us are those of race, gender, class, sexuality, disability and age. An anti-oppressive analysis of social difference enables the social care practitioner to address other social differences that may impact on the life chances of the individual. This shifts the focus from the given 'protected characteristics' (Equality Act 2010) to addressing other areas of differences in that individual's life; and how these differences contribute to their particular experiences of oppression.

For example, a woman coming to a social care resource, which focuses on mental health, requires the practitioner to explore other aspects of her social identity that go beyond her social difference as a woman. This means the worker has to address other differences such as class, sexuality, religion and status as a carer that will be important in any holistic assessment, not least her experience as a mental-health-system service user. These other identified forms of oppression will interact to produce a particular picture of her need and experiences. It is this complex form of knowledge that the worker should use to inform any planning and intervention. This form of analysis is anti-oppressive because it shifts the focus from one major social division to the interactions and interconnections between the various social differences that shape the nature and impact of oppression on any individual. This view of intersectionality captures both the structural and dynamic aspects of multiple oppressions.

Power is an essential concept to address when looking at issues of oppression. It operates at different levels and is influenced by a range of factors including the social, cultural, economic and psychological. Power is very influential in relation to how service users and practitioners are able to access services and resources given the structural inequalities in the distribution of power within both the public and private spheres of life. In any practice relationship power dynamics will direct and influence both the nature of the relationship and the outcomes. Power is socially constructed and, thus, not solely possessed by either the practitioner or the service user.

The worker needs to be aware of their own professional and personal power in this situation and how that has a bearing on understanding and interpreting the narrative brought by the service user to that situation. This process must also include an appreciation of the power and powerlessness of the service user.

Power, as an anti-oppressive principle of analysis, requires the practitioner to engage in the narrative of the service user in a way that places it in the wider social context and in relation to a range of social systems. These systems will include the family, the community, large organisational structures and other formal and informal social networks. All of these interacting social systems must be explored with reference to their historical and geographical dimensions. So for a woman seeking asylum in Britain we would need to take into account the historical and current relationship between her country of origin and the place of refuge. The social, political and economic systems relating to migration, immigration and asylum will have an impact on any service or intervention provided. Her life chances will be shaped by the interconnections and intersections between these macro and micro social systems. An anti-oppressive analysis will include an appreciation of the agency of the individual and the practitioner to bring about changes in those very systems; including the racialisation of the immigration system.

The concept of reflexivity as a principle in anti-oppressive practice requires the practitioner and the service user to engage in critical reflection that deconstructs meaning and reality brought to the situation. Each participant will bring to the situation their socially constructed lived experiences, values, power and powerlessness, which in turn will construct and reconstruct that mutual engagement. Each will begin with a partial view of the other's power, social difference, world view, personal biographies, values and belief systems. The act of critical reflexivity will bring them nearer to a more complex appreciation of the other person's social and cultural identities. It will challenge and reconstruct, bringing new meaning and perspective to the mutual involvement of practitioner and service user. This goes beyond a mere focus on one aspect of the individual or social situation; the mutual engagement then becomes a dynamic interplay between the participants' social constructions, values, beliefs and assumptions thus creating new shared realities.

The authors argue that anti-oppressive practice includes the principles of anti-racist practice. An anti-oppressive perspective highlights issues of race and racism as one aspect of social difference. Race does matter, but within a context. It is only then do we fully appreciate the complexity of racism and its interconnectedness to other forms of oppression.

Anti-oppressive practice provides a detailed analysis that responds to structural issues at every level in the mutual engagement of practitioners, service users and the organisation. It includes the complexity of differing levels of meaning and enables the worker to make sense of practice in a systematic way. It deals with the processes and the goals, such as they might be – produced by the mutual engagement of service user and professional; allowing for analysis of institutional and organisational values in current and historical contexts.

The principles of working in an anti-oppressive way require the practitioner to respond to the social context as well as the personal biography of the service user. This means a response to the detail of the person's life, including the meaning placed on the aspects of difference as defined by the service user. It will also point to where the challenges need to be made either by the practitioner, the organisation or the service user.

Conclusions

Working with the principles of anti-oppressive practice provides a means through which all workers can come together to combat racism and other oppressions. They will value and work with the differences and strengths of individuals and communities. Practitioners will develop a professional response that is sensitive to and takes into account the diverse family patterns, religious and cultural traditions and values of BME people. This form of practice enables practitioners to challenge Western eurocentric interpretations of human experiences, allowing them to see the historical and current interconnections between race and culture and other aspects of difference. Racialised state policies (for example, current immigration policies that require social workers to carry out age assessments of young people) are being delivered, at times uncritically, by social work practitioners (Humphries 2004). Social work continues to engage in practices of cultural management that contribute to the depoliticisation of race relations. Yet an exclusive focus on race leads to a partial understanding of the complexity of living in a society that is divided on a number of lines – race being just one of them. With a narrow focus on race and culture other pertinent factors are left to fade away in the background and yet it is these very factors that shape and define the very complex picture of inequality.

We may as practitioners and academics ponder at what is 'Same, same, but different' as we continue to work to fight a range of discrimination in social work practice. Anti-racist practice is part of practice that is anti-oppressive. What is different is the way in which the principles of anti-oppressive practice explore and critique any understanding of the complex nature of oppression for the individual or community. Cultural sensitivity and awareness alone cannot challenge the received ideas about 'race', culture, ethnicity, citizenship, multiculturalism and belonging. Anti-oppressive practice principles require the practitioner to ask continuous questions that develop accounts of the experience of 'race' as difference in conjunction with other aspects of the human experience and critical understandings of privilege. The production of such critical practice (Fook 2012) will require a workforce with the capacity to engage in and develop knowledge about a range of social divisions and their dynamic interconnections and intersections.

Meaningful change will come only when driven by political activism, not just by the individual practitioner, but by the profession being committed to challenge the oppressive processes of social systems (especially professional social work), motivated by principles of equality, human rights and social justice. Practitioners will need to use their relative power and influence beyond the direct engagement with the service user. They must intervene in organisational and political structures that can define and limit ways in which they as participants of wider social movements (at local, regional, national and international levels) may bring about changes in systems of inequality, power and privilege. We must continue to question what has changed in relation to the relationship between social work as a profession and the delivery of services to all communities who are disadvantaged and oppressed.

Stephen Lawrence and Anthony Walker were both cut down in the prime of their lives for being black and in the wrong place. For Stephen, his parents had to fight for 18 years to get justice.[3] They have as individuals and as a family paid an emotional price that we will never truly understand or appreciate. Their lives were dramatically transformed.

As practitioners we cannot divorce ourselves from the powerful social and political contexts that generate damaging experiences of racism and other oppressions. We must as practitioners and educationalists draw on and learn from the legacies of these powerful personal experiences to better understand the complex and structural nature of oppression, its historical and geographical specificity, and develop new challenging and complex ways of learning and practising. The death of Stephen Lawrence opened up the space for ordinary people's narratives to be heard and connected the impact of racism to other aspects of people's lives – housing, poverty, health and education.

As bhabha reflects, 'What is crucial to such a vision of the future is the belief that we must not merely change the narratives of histories, but transform our sense of what it means to live, to be, in other times and different spaces, both human and historical'(bhabha 1994: 256). Now, more than at any other time, we need to seek out the contested spaces, spaces of division, and work collectively to challenge racism and all other forms of oppression.

Suggested further reading

Burke, B. and Harrison, P. (2009) 'Anti-oppressive approaches', in Adams, R., Dominelli, L. and Payne, M., eds *Critical practice in social work*, 2nd edn, Basingstoke: Palgrave Macmillan.

Dalrymple, J. and Burke, B. (2006) *Anti-oppressive practice: social care and the law*, 2nd edn, Maidenhead and New York: Oxford University Press.

Fook, J. (2012) *Social work: A critical approach to practice*, 2nd edn, London: Sage.

Notes

[1] Between 2001 and 2002 Philomena Harrison travelled around the world.

[2] Head of social work at Liverpool Polytechnic (Liverpool John Moores University).

[3] In 2012 Gary Dobson and David Norris were eventually convicted of the murder of Stephen Lawrence, which took place in 1993.

FIVE

Antisemitism and anti-racist social work

Barrie Levine

When the history of anti-racism in social work is examined, there is a notable gap: a developed analysis of one of the oldest 'racisms' – antisemitism. In this chapter Levine explores why this omission has occurred and locates opposition to antisemitism within the wider social work anti-racist discourse. In doing so the chapter examines the nature of antisemitism today in the UK and internationally. In addressing these issues, the chapter will further explore the fundamental debate surrounding the distinction between anti-Zionist and antisemitic discourses that have been conflated in recent years. Levine argues that this conflation leads to confusion and serves to undermine a full understanding of the true nature of racism and antisemitism.

Introduction

It is axiomatic that a core component of social work is its value base and related commitment to anti-racist and anti-oppressive practice. This is borne out by the weight of social work literature that is committed to challenging racism, discrimination and oppression in their widest forms through a clear focus on achieving social justice for marginalised and oppressed groups in society. This focus on anti-racist values is enshrined in the International Federation of Social Work (IFSW) Statement of Ethical Principles (2012), which guides social work practice and education from a perspective firmly rooted in principles of human rights and social justice. Social work practitioners and students need to grapple regularly with the ethical contradictions thrown up in practice situations to ensure they are acting from anti-discriminatory and anti-oppressive perspectives. Such contradictions and ethical dilemmas are unfortunately all the more apparent in a period of economic crisis and associated 'austerity' measures as are now being imposed by central banks and national governments across Europe and worldwide (Ferguson and Lavalette 2013a).

Within this broad context, there are deepening and continuing attacks on previously accepted ideas of welfarism and multiculturalism, which pose significant challenges for social work practice. As McKibbin (2013) and others argue, in the UK it is the poor, the disabled and the vulnerable who are increasingly bearing the brunt of the coalition government's ideologically driven attacks on welfare, leading to increasing impoverishment and misery for tens of thousands of people; many of whom will be in contact with social work. Related to attacks on welfare, discourse from political parties such as the UK Independence Party (UKIP) in Britain or the Golden Dawn in Greece, seeks to further push the blame for the economic crisis onto foreigners and foreign migrants rather than the economic and banking system where true blame lies. Across Europe there is a perceived growing concern about immigration and a developing demonisation of immigrants, which can often be read as code for thinly veiled racial attacks that particularly target Muslims, alongside growing persecution of Roma people in numerous European states. In this context it is further notable that there has been a recent resurgence of openly espoused antisemitism in countries such as Hungary and Greece. This is a worrying development and adds urgency to the need for a greater level of understanding of racism, including antisemitism, and the social forces that give rise to the issue. The growth of racism across Europe is discussed further in this chapter and elsewhere in this volume. However, racism, like other forms of discrimination, is not a static entity, but shifts and changes according to material circumstances that are reflected in dominant ideas and discourse. Given the role that social work plays in responding to the needs of the poor and the marginalised, it is therefore essential that social workers have a comprehensive and nuanced understanding of racism in all its forms to enable the aims of anti-racist and anti-oppressive practice to be met. At the same time, as this chapter will argue, there is evidence that current theory and practice in understanding and challenging racism is at best uneven; and in this context, it is further argued here that there is a relative absence from social work literature of a meaningful focus on one of racism's oldest and most pernicious forms: that of antisemitism.

It is perhaps surprising that social work anti-racist literature makes little reference to antisemitism despite its history and the plethora of writing in the field of antisemitism itself. Overall, this chapter aims to redress this balance somewhat through examining where the neglected subject of antisemitism should be located within anti-racist theory and practice. In doing so the chapter seeks to develop a greater understanding of the experience and phenomenon of antisemitism and develop discussion over how this should be responded to, particularly in a UK context. Links will be made to social work practice, although the main focus of the chapter will concentrate on developing an understanding of the complexities associated with antisemitism and the development of key arguments that underpin discussion of the issue. This is felt necessary given the relative lack of emphasis on the subject in current social work teaching (Soifer 1991) and will further facilitate the ability of practitioners to respond appropriately to the needs of Jewish service users and instances of antisemitism where this may arise. In this respect the discussion has direct relevance to the components of knowledge and understanding of social issues contained within the Professional Capabilities Framework (PCF) which is being applied to social work in England as well as the respective occupational standards applicable in Wales, Northern Ireland and Scotland.

In approaching the issue, it is important to acknowledge that antisemitism is a complex and contested issue where current-day manifestations can only be understood from a historical and political perspective. At the same time, a full and detailed analysis of all aspects of antisemitism is outside of the scope of this chapter. The purpose, therefore, is to provide a broad overview of the subject drawing practitioners and students towards a greater level of understanding while pointing towards further sources of study and investigation.

Understanding antisemitism

In order to address expressions of antisemitism today it is necessary to understand what antisemitism is, its historic origins and current debates over its manifestations. Surprisingly perhaps, antisemitism is a fiercely debated and contested issue, which is subject to differing forms of interpretation (Beller 2007; Cohn-Sherbok 2002; Hellig 2003; Julius 2010; Rose 2004). Debate even exists as to how the term should be written and for the purposes of this chapter, I have used the convention or other variants. A further initial thought is that when in social work reference is made to anti-racism this is deemed a 'positive' concept, yet antisemitism is a 'negative' concept implying hatred or dislike of the semitic subject of the term. This may seem a matter of semantics, but the use of language is important and a more positive construct such as 'anti-racism towards Jews', which underlies our understanding of tackling antisemitism, is perhaps overly complex to be used consistently. However, we need to maintain this awareness of tackling racism towards Jews as the object of the discussion while referring to the broad experience of antisemitism.

In terms of a starting point, and at its most basic, antisemitism can be defined as a dislike or hatred of Jews (Hellig 2003) and has also been described as the 'longest hatred' by Robert Wistrich (1991). The Anti-Defamation League based in America offers the following definition:

> The belief or behavior hostile toward Jews just because they are Jewish. It may take the form of religious teachings that proclaim the inferiority of Jews, for instance, or political efforts to isolate, oppress, or otherwise injure them. It may also include prejudiced or stereotyped views about Jews. (Anti-Defamation League 2001)

There are competing definitions that will be discussed later, however, discussing antisemitism is a complex task, not least due to the powerful emotions raised through considering an issue that has been shaped by arguably one of the most defining points of the 20th century: the Holocaust. While this is neither the start or end point of antisemitism, reference to the Holocaust is an essential component of the discussion due to its impact on Jewish experience in the 20th century. It is difficult to underestimate the impact of the Holocaust, but it is important to recognise that the attempt by the Nazis in Germany during the Second World War to systematically murder all European Jews touches every Jewish family worldwide and continues to resonate to the present day. The reasons why the Nazis developed their policy of *Judenpolitik* (Longerich 2010) and pursued such a murderous strategy has spawned a huge amount of literature and debate on the subject. At its most basic, the question is raised as to how hatred of the Jews developed to the extent that their racist characterisation as *untermenschen* ('sub-humans') resulted in the extermination of six million Jews; equating to 80% of European Jewry. In this context, the memory of the Holocaust is a sombre reminder of the depths of barbarism that racism can lead to and should act as a warning to the dangers of fascism as a political ideology (Longerich 2010).

Yet despite the horrors of the Holocaust, antisemitism continues to exist as a pernicious force in society, accompanied by continuing attempts to deny the Holocaust took place or to minimise its extent. One example is that of Jean-Marie Le Pen, the former leader of the French Front National, who stated that 'The gas chambers are only a mere detail in the history of the Second World War' (France 24 News online 2009). Despite the fact that Le Pen was convicted as a Holocaust denier, it is particularly worrying that in recent national elections, almost 20% of French voters were prepared to vote for Le Pen's Front National.

The continuing hold of xenophobic and racist ideas in political parties such as the Front National is of immediate concern to anti-racists and an issue that will be returned to later in the chapter.

Holocaust denial is a recognised crime in a number of European countries and those prosecuted include the British Historian David Irving (Julius 2010). Beyond Europe, numerous allegations of Holocaust denial have, for example, been levelled at the Iranian President Mahmoud Ahmadinejad (BBC News 2005). However, despite such instances, the vast majority of people are aware of the scale and the horror of the mass murder carried out by the Nazis in the 1940s. The need to commemorate the Holocaust is now institutionalised in the International Holocaust Remembrance Day as designated by the United Nations in 2005, marking the liberation of Auschwitz-Birkenau on 27 January 1945. The US President Barack Obama was uncompromising on International Holocaust Remembrance Day in January 2011, when he stated '"Never Again" is not just a phrase but a principled cause. And we resolve to stand up against prejudice, stereotyping, and violence – including the scourge of antisemitism – around the globe' (Mozgovaya 2011). However, despite this level of international awareness of antisemitism and its tragic culmination in the Holocaust, antisemitism remains a persistent and potent force. The reasons why this might be so are complex and contested, but will be examined as the chapter progresses.

Although antisemitism has a long history stretching back over two thousand years, the term itself is a comparatively recent formulation, which was first used in or around 1879 by Wilhelm Marr, a radical antisemitic German Nationalist, who coined the term to replace the German word *Judenhass*, or Jew hatred (Hellig 2003: p 70). Marr was a conscious antisemite who founded an organisation known as the Anti-Semites League and published a treatise called '*The victory of Jewry over Germandom*' .This document posed the threat of Jews to Germany and Aryan Germans in racial terms, and was an important presage to the development of Nazi ideology. However, in understanding the development of antisemitism it is also important to consider the social factors that contibuted to 'Jew hatred' at this time. While some may argue there is something uniquely inherent in the German psyche that lends itself to hating Jews, this would be akin to arguing that all whites hate blacks, which is patently untrue, and in any event explains nothing, while reducing explanations of racism to vague and problematic notions of racial superiority and inferiority. Instead, a closer examination of the social circumstances that existed in Germany at this time provides a different, and more important, level of understanding of how racial hatred can grow. As Longerich (2010) explains anti-Jewish agitation around this period emanated from the German stock market crash of 1873, known as the 'Grunderkrach'. Prior to this, from 1871, Jews had enjoyed full citizenship rights in Germany, although in common with many other European countries, Jews had historically been confined to certain areas of economic activity including finance. In the context of the financial crisis that erupted during this period, the search for scapegoats developed and the Jews were blamed for the economic crisis. This is not to minimise or excuse the virulent levels of anti-Jewish racism that developed in Germany and other European countries in the late nineteenth and early twentieth century, characterised by the formation of numerous antisemitic leagues, but it is an important reminder that the root causes of racism are often underpinned by material circumstances or economic problems. Currently, this level of scapegoating is particularly evident in Greece where the country is wracked by austerity measures and mass unemployment (Ferguson and Lavalette 2013a). In response to the problems of the Greek economy, the neo-Nazi Golden Dawn seeks to target immigrants and foreigners for the economic crisis and has tried to organise 'Greek only' blood drives and food hand-outs alongside direct violence against immigrant communities (*The Guardian* 2013). So, in order to understand and explain the rise of racism, there is a need to consider the ways in which economic and social circumstances provide an ideological rationale for discriminating against certain groups. Historically, a strong example of this is reflected in the so-called 'theories,' which the British ruling class developed for justifying the slavery of black African people. Such 'theories' were based on spurious pseudo-scientific notions of racial characteristics including ideas of intelligence and supposed inherent levels of immorality. Eugenic theories had their roots in these historical developments and later helped to justify the Nazi programmes of forced sterilisation and euthanasia of the so-called 'unfit'. Gypsies, psychiatric patients, people with learning disabilities, Jews, homosexuals and people of mixed race came into this category and were all subject to such treatment during the Nazi regime. However, while antisemitism reached a murderous peak in Europe during the Nazi era, its history is much deeper and as Bale (2010: 431) points out, is a history that is fractured, often irrational and ambivalent. It is necessary to develop an understanding of the history of antisemitism to make sense of present-day ideas and attitudes.

Historical antisemitism

Authors such as Cohn-Sherbok (2002) would argue that antisemitism can be traced back to the period of classical history, well before the birth of Christianity. However, as others have argued (Rose 2004; Sand 2009), this is a contentious view of history that may be more related to a Judeo-centric perspective on history and too literal a reading of Old Testament texts. However, there is no doubt that antisemitism has deep historical roots following the birth of Christianity and linked to ideas of the Jews' rejection and 'killing' of Jesus Christ (Cohn-Sherbok 2002). Such attitudes become especially evident from the period of the crusades onwards and is further reflected in the later medieval period when Jews were at points tolerated and allowed certain prescribed occupations by Kings and Rulers across Europe, while at other times were actively persecuted. In England, for example, the Jews were forcibly expelled in 1290 and only allowed to return in 1657.

During this medieval period, dangerous myths developed regarding the Jews, which were based on superstitious religious beliefs, and resulted in the development of pervasive ideas such as the 'blood libel' or ritual murder of children in the run-up to the festival Pesach (Passover); 'desecration of the host' and the 'poisoning of wells'. These ideas and others continued to resurface across Europe on a regular and sporadic basis up until the beginning of the 20th century, and provided the basis for episodic, violent oppression and persecution of Jews. Such persecution included anti-Jewish riots and murderous pogroms, which were a regular feature in the Pale of Settlement.[1] The Pale was where the majority of European Jewry were confined legally and in terms of occupation. The Pale progressively came under the rule of the Russian Empire, and in the late 19th and early 20th centuries anti-Jewish persecution and agitation reached new heights on the back of a combination of religious superstition, modern ideas of antisemitism linked to developing ideologies of 'race' and racism, and economic and social circumstances. As Hellig (2003) notes, Tsarist Russia developed increasingly anti-Jewish policies during the 19th century that had severe impacts on the social and religious freedom of Jews, and as a consequence, triggered waves of Jewish emigration from Eastern Europe. European antisemitism was also fuelled by events such as the notorious Dreyfus affair in France in 1894, which involved false accusations of treason against a Jewish army officer, Alfred Dreyfus, and the publication in Russia of the equally notorious *Protocols of the Elders of Zion* in the early 20th century around 1905. The 'Protocols' were a fabrication of the Tsarist secret police that accused Jews of a conspiracy to take over the world primarily through economic control of the banking system and the media. Despite being a forgery, the 'Protocols' gained huge popular purchase and were even distributed in the US in the 1920s by Henry Ford of automobile fame, who had 500,000 copies printed. The impact was to significantly link Jews to ideas of financial control, which in the context of economic turmoil and financial crashes in the early 20th century, provided a convenient basis for the scapegoating of Jews for the ills and problems of capitalism. The 'Protocols' still circulate to this day, particularly in some Middle Eastern countries, indicating the deep-rooted nature of the antisemitic tropes the document has given rise to. In Germany in the 1930s, Nazi anti-Jewish propaganda developed these themes, with Jews being slandered as capitalist exploiters, while at the same time being characterised as revolutionary agents of Russian Bolshevism and in line with Christian antisemitism, even as a demonic force (Hellig 2003). To underline the centrality of Nazi antisemitism and its perceived connections between Jews and communists, it is worth considering the Nazi party's guidelines published in 1925 which stated that 'The energy of the whole movement is to be directed against the worst enemy of the German people: Judaism and Marxism' (cited in Longerich 2010: 15).

Responses to Jewish persecution

During the late 19th and early 20th centuries, as a result of continuing persecution, there was a massive emigration of Jews from Russia and Eastern Europe mainly to Western countries such as the US and the UK. Estimates suggest that at least three and a half million Jews fled Eastern Europe at this time from an overall Jewish population of approximately eight million (Weinstock 1979). However, it is important to note that the history of Jews in Europe does not solely reflect persecution or 'suffering', which tends to dominate historical accounts. As Rose (2004) points out, what is overlooked is that many tens or hundreds of thousands of Jews threw their lot in with the workers' and peasants' revolutionary movements of the day and joined the Bolsheviks, or the Bund Jewish revolutionary movement. A much smaller number were influenced by the ideas of Zionism, which advocated that Jews should build their own state in the historic land of Palestine and emigrate there to found settlements. To illustrate the limited extent of the hold of Zionist ideas at this time, Fieldhouse (2006: 123) indicates that the Jewish population in Palestine in 1914 was approximately 85,000, of whom 35,000 had migrated since 1881 when anti-Jewish pogroms had developed in Eastern Europe. This is in stark contrast to the millions who migrated to Western counties including Britain during this period.

Thus, in the battle of ideas regarding how to respond to antisemitism in the early 20th century, three distinct currents emerged which continue to reverberate today. The first current was one of emigration and assimilation into liberal, democratic Western societies that were perceived as being less antisemitic. The second current was linked to socialist and revolutionary movements that argued that Jewish emancipation was intrinsically bound up with the emancipation of the working class and the overthrow of capitalism. The third, and at the time, minority current, was that of Zionism that argued, in what can be construed as a deeply fatalistic and pessimistic way, that antisemitism was endemic to non-Jews, and the only solution was for Jews to separate themselves from the rest of society and create an exclusively Jewish state. In analysing Zionism in the context of responses to racism, there are some parallels with the black nationalist movement with its 'Back to Africa' call proposed by the Afro-American leader Marcus Garvey in the late 19th and early 20th century. Garvey's black nationalism promoted the idea of racial separation in addressing the historical racism experienced by the black population in the Americas. Zionism advocated a not dissimilar position with its call for an exclusively Jewish State, although as Weinstock (1979) makes clear, Zionism was at heart a colonial enterprise, albeit one partially shaped by the experiences of European antisemitism. Furthermore, the idea of Zionism reflected the growth of ideas of nationalism and imperialism during this period among Western powers, particularly Great Britain (Rose 2004). However, while Zionism was not the majority current at the time of the mass migration of Jews from Russia prior to the First World War, it is now the dominant ideological force which permeates debate about the nature of antisemitism and the state of Israel today. A detailed discussion of Zionism is beyond the scope of this current chapter, but an essential component of any discussion of contemporary antisemitism requires some understanding of the growth of Zionist ideas.

Anti-Semitism in the 20th century and the growth of Zionism

As has been discussed, the growth of fascism and extreme antisemitism in Europe in the 20th century led to the annihilation of 80% of European Jewry on the basis of racial ideology. Mass murder on such a scale had never before been experienced. The Nazi programme of the 'Final Solution', to what they termed the 'Jewish Question,' was not confined to Germany, but was also viciously pursued in Poland, Hungary, Lithuania, Latvia, France and other countries under Nazi domination in Europe. Following the end of the war there was as Hellig (2003: 15) ably puts it '…a stunned silence'. The scale of the catastrophe was such that it was not until the 1960s that scholarly activity in relation to Nazi atrocities developed, and the term 'Holocaust' entered common language.

As the war ended, there was a massive humanitarian crisis in Europe with hundreds of thousands of displaced Jewish refugees among approximately seven million displaced people. Neither America nor the UK was willing to provide a safe haven for Jewish survivors of the Holocaust, as both countries had developed anti-immigration legislation prior to the war itself. In Britain, this dated back to the 1905 Aliens Act, which was specifically developed to restrict Jewish immigration. In this respect it is important to note there had been a strong current of antisemitism in Britain in the early part of the 20th century, with a visible example being the racist British Brothers League (the forerunner of Sir Walter Moseley's British Union of Fascists, which was formed in 1932), agitating for an end to Jewish immigration (Julius 2010; Rose 2004).

The position of Jewish displaced persons at the end of World War II was particularly problematic. For the vast majority, the prospect of return to their countries of origin in Eastern Europe was simply impossible due to the level of antisemitism they had experienced. Post-war, the problem was intensified in July 1946 following the pogrom against Jews in the Polish town of Kielece which claimed 42 lives (www.ushmm.org/wlc/en/article.php?ModuleId=10007941). Following this event approximately 150,000 displaced Jews in Eastern Europe fled to Western Europe, further compounding the refugee problem. In the context of the harsh conditions of the displaced peoples' refugee camps Zionist ideas gained a greater hold, although for the majority, emigration to the US remained their preferred, if unattainable, choice. Therefore, at the end of the war, the only seemingly practical solution for many Jewish refugees was emigration to Palestine, which at the time was under British Mandate control although ostensibly closed to Jewish immigration. As indicated, prior to the war, the idea of emigration to Palestine was not viewed as a positive life choice by many Jews. Thus, it was only from the 1930s onwards, and specifically in the context of the end of World War II, that Zionist ideas in the form of an escape from murderous antisemitism through a Jewish homeland in Palestine gained weight among Jews themselves; notwithstanding that the concept had been supported by Britain in colonialist terms since the Balfour Declaration of 1917. The role of Britain in exercising the Mandate in Palestine and its abrupt evacuation of troops in 1948, were major contributory factors leading to the subsequent conflict between Jews and Arabs in Palestine. In 1948 the state of Israel was declared and the subsequent war led to the displacement of approximately 750,000 Palestinians (Pappe 2006; Piterberg 2008; Weinstock 1979). Following the end of the Mandate in 1948, mass migration to Palestine was opened up and, by 1951, 300,000 Jews had fled the displaced persons camps in Europe to arrive in the newly formed state of Israel.

Waled Khalidi, a Palestinian historian (cited in Fieldhouse 2006: 217), described the British record in Palestine as 'perhaps the shabbiest regime in British colonial history', and following the ending of the British Mandate in May 1948, Fieldhouse goes on to state in tragically accurate terms, 'Palestine was left to find its destiny in blood' (Fieldhouse 2006: 217). The shameful role of British imperialism in Palestine, and the subsequent role of American imperialism as the main sponsor of Israel through financial and military support, is intrinsic to understanding the present-day conflict in the Middle East and for that matter, contemporary antisemitism. In this context, it would not be inaccurate to say that the twin narratives of the formation of the state of Israel on the back of the Holocaust and the forced displacement of the Palestinians known as the Nakba (catastrophe) in 1948, arose out of a combination of European antisemitism. Zionist colonialism, Western imperialism and a collective failure of the victorious Western powers after World War II to respond to the crisis of Jewish survivors of the Holocaust in Central Europe.

The 'new' antisemitism

Anti-Semitism, as we have briefly discussed, has taken different shapes and forms throughout history, and as Beller (2007) discusses, the complexity regarding antisemitism is deepened when focusing on what is known as the 'new' antisemitism. In approaching the issue it is important to note that historically, antisemitism had mainly been a Central European phenomenon with early roots in Christian theology, which was further shaped by the development of modern capitalism (Weinstock 1979). As Rose (2004) and others discuss, in historical terms, Islam had not been a consistent protagonist of antisemitism due largely to the Jews being viewed as 'People of the Book' in Muslim scripture. 'People of the Book' in the Quran refers to the followers of the monotheistic faiths, including Jews and Christians; and as such, subject to tolerance or protection under Islamic law. However, in historic terms, Jews did not experience full civil, religious or social rights in Arab or Islamic countries and experienced periodic instances of oppression and persecution (Green 2010; Sebag Montefiore 2011). Despite its mainly European roots, much discussion of contemporary antisemitism is referred to in terms of Arab or Islamic antisemitism. In this context, the specific hostility to Jews in the Middle East, cannot be discussed without reference to the State of Israel itself. This in itself raises a fundamental question. If there is hostility towards the state of Israel by Arabs across the Middle East due to the continuing oppression of Palestinians and the illegal occupation of Palestinian lands as defined by the international law; can such hostility be deemed antisemitic.

Certainly, the state of Israel is constituted as a 'Jewish' state with a Law of Return that allows Jews anywhere in the world to move to Israel and become full citizens. At the same time Palestinians who originate from what is now Israel have no right to return and become citizens of the state. While the concept of Israel as a homeland and refuge for Jews may have had a moral imperative following the Holocaust, authors such as Pappe (2006) now point to the fact that the exclusivist nature of the Israeli state can be construed as racist through its design and intent. Plus, there is considerable and growing criticism of Israel for its human rights abuses such as the jailing of Palestinian children (Horton 2013) and administrative detention without charge of Palestinians adults. Alongside this, there is huge and evident discontent among Palestinians and their supporters across the Middle East due to the injustice of Israeli policies such as the continuing settlement expansion in the West Bank and the blockade of Gaza. To describe such legitimate criticism as antisemitic in itself is highly problematic and raises further complex arguments. Of course, it *is* possible for criticism of Israel to be couched in antisemitic terms and it is critical that this is avoided. However, when a state defines itself in racial terms, as the Israeli state does, there should be little surprise that some victims of Israeli state oppression may couch their criticism in 'racial' terms that reflect many of the claims of the state itself.

This issue of conflating criticism of Israel with being antisemitic is the subject of what can be described as a highly vitriolic and controversial debate both inside and outside of Israel. An example of the tone of debate can be found in an article in *The Guardian* in 2003 by an Oxford University academic, Emanuele Ottolenghi, entitled 'Anti-Zionism is antisemitism – behind much criticism of Israel is a thinly veiled hatred of Jews' (Ottolenghi 2003). The blogosphere is consumed with such debates on a daily basis, and the views held by commentators are strongly held. However, the debate is also fuelled by a level of policy development at an international level. The following quote taken from the front page of the Inter-Parliamentary Coalition for Combating Anti-Semitism's (ICCA) website exemplifies this when it states:

> The world is witnessing today an escalating, sophisticated, global, virulent and even lethal anti-Semitism, that is arguably without parallel or precedent since the end of the Second World War. (ICCA 2011)

If accurate, this statement would be deeply concerning for anti-racists everywhere, but the claim needs to be examined in more detail.

The ICCA is an international grouping of parliamentarians, which was founded in London in 2009, and held its second conference in Ottowa in 2011. The ICCA formulation of antisemitism is itself based on the European Union Monitoring Centre on Racism and Xenophobia's (EUMC) working definition of antisemitism, which was published in 2005. The EUMC was the forerunner of the European Union Agency for Fundamental Rights (FRA), an advisory body of the European Union established in 2007 with a remit to ensure fundamental rights are protected across Europe. The FRA's published Working Definition of AntiSemitism (EUMC 2005) begins with:

> Antisemitism is a certain perception of Jews, which may be expressed as hatred toward Jews. Rhetorical and physical manifestations of antisemitism are directed toward Jewish or non-Jewish individuals and/or their property, toward Jewish community institutions and religious facilities.

This formulation helps to clarify the nature of antisemitism. However, the FRA's definition goes on to add less helpfully that 'In addition, such manifestations could also target the state of Israel, conceived as a Jewish collectivity'; and further, 'Denying the Jewish people their right to self-determination, e.g., by claiming that the existence of a State of Israel is a racist endeavour' (EUMC 2005). The key implication of the latter quotes is highly problematic, as it repeats the state of Israel's often cited case that any criticism of Israel is antisemitic.

There is considerable debate both within the Jewish community itself and among academics as to the nature of this 'new' antisemitism The debate is such that Jewish critics of Israel have been tarred as antisemitic or 'self-hating Jews' by other Jews who support a more uncompromising Zionist perspective. Rosenfeld's influential essay

'"Progressive" Jewish thought and the new anti-Semitism' (Rosenfeld 2007), written in response to anti-Zionist Jewish critics such as the late Tony Judt (2003), came up with the term 'proud to be ashamed to be Jews' in describing Jewish critics of Israeli policy. There have been numerous responses to Rosenfeld by Jewish authors such as Braverman (2012), and the debate is too extensive to explore fully here, but at its core is an attempt to understand, and distinguish between, antisemitism and anti-Zionism.

The highly contentious nature of this debate places great constraints on a full and open discussion regarding the reality of antisemitism *and* on any justified criticism of Israel. As such, activists and anti-racists can be disarmed in responding to what are key issues in the global fight for social justice, if they are described as being antisemitic. In this context, the 'new' antisemitism can have the effect of closing down debate rather than opening it up by tarring critics of Israeli policy as antisemitic. Given this, it is possible to postulate that fear of being labelled antisemitic is a possible reason for the relative absence of a discussion regarding antisemitism in social work anti-racist literature, despite evidence that it is essential for anti-racists to be able to navigate their way through the debate. Without this level of understanding, the alternative is to leave the field open for potentially ill-informed discussion and to miss the very real dangers posed by the growth of 'old' antisemitism far-right and neo-Nazi political ideas that are gaining ground across Europe.

The return of 'old' antisemitism?

In contemporary society there is a worrying tendency for mainstream politicians to pander to anti-immigration views, and, in the process, demonise whole groups in society, particularly Muslims. When leaders of European political parties such as David Cameron make speeches on the 'end of multiculturalism', they give real succour to racists and reinforce negative stereotypes of immigrants and refugees (see Jenkins, Chapter Seven, this volume).In the context of a growing economic crisis, openly racist parties have grown across Europe, and their growth can be seen to be reinforced when politicians such as Cameron, Merkel and Sarkozy feed into anti-immigrant discourse.

It could be argued we are witnessing in some respects a slow-paced rerun of events from the 1930s, with all the dangers this poses in terms of racism and antisemitism. To provide an example, one of the most dangerous manifestations of the 'old' racism exists in Hungary with the openly fascist and xenophobic Jobbik party. In 2010 Jobbik gained 17% of the vote, and are now the third largest party in the Hungarian parliament, with a reputed 25% level of support among young people in the country. Jobbik espouse an openly racist and antisemitic stance and are further bolstered by their uniformed fascist wing, the Hungarian Guard, who have carried out regular attacks on Roma people (*Tablet* 2012). The Hungarian Guard are the direct descendants of the Hungarian Nazi Arrow Cross Party, which were in power in Hungary in the 1940s and oversaw the extermination of over 550,000 of Hungary's Jews. One of Jobbik's three MEPs even turned up to the opening of the EU Parliament in 2009 in full Hungarian Guard uniform, in defiance of his country's laws. In a nod to one of the oldest antisemitic slurs, Jobbik resurrected the Blood Libel in April 2012 with a speech in parliament by one of their MPs about the supposed murder of a Hungarian girl by Jews before the Passover festival in 1882 (Tablet on-line 2012). This resurrection of fascism is a very real danger and takes place in a country that is suffering hugely as part of a wider global economic crisis, and is massively indebted to the world banks. The shift to the right in Hungary is deep-rooted and has even seen homelessness criminalised and a social worker, Norbert Ferencz, threatened with three years in prison for speaking out against anti-homelessness legislation.[2] A similarly disturbing development is the emergence of the openly fascist and antisemitic Golden Dawn Party in Greece, which entered the political arena in 2012, and captured 7% of the popular vote in national elections. More recent opinion polls have shown a growth in its support to approximately 22% (*The Financial Times* 2012). As discussed, Greece is wracked by austerity as it struggles to pay off massive debts imposed by the European Union and IMF bailout conditions. The Greek people have witnessed a serious deterioration in their living conditions, with the youth unemployment rate at 50%, public service workers going unpaid, the growth of soup kitchens in Athens and a 40% rise in suicide rates. In this economic environment, Golden Dawn campaigns on a viciously anti-immigrant programme under the slogan 'So we can rid the land of filth' and holds frequent rallies, chanting 'Foreigners out of Greece'. The party parades in black shirts, with insignia that is very similar to the Nazi Swastika, and its members have been involved in violent attacks on immigrants. In addition, its leader, Nikos Michaloliakos, has claimed that Nazi concentration camps did not use ovens and gas chambers to exterminate Jews during the Holocaust, stating in a television broadcast, 'There were no ovens – it's a lie. I believe it's a lie. There were no gas chambers either' (Israel National News 2012).

The dangers posed by Jobbik and Golden Dawn are extremely worrying and pose significant challenges for anti-fascist and ant-racist activists, not only in Hungary and Greece but in other parts of Europe. In Austria the Freedom Party has been achieving 25–30% of the vote in elections, and also campaigns on a right-wing programme of anti-immigration, Islamophobia and euro-scepticism. The leader of the party, Heinz-Christian Strache was recently criticised for posting an antisemitic cartoon online with distinct similarities to the type of crude propaganda used in *Der Stürmer*, a weekly paper published by the Nazis in Germany (BBC News 2012). Fascist movements have also grown in Germany with the National Socialist Underground (NSU) as well as in Russia, Estonia, Latvia and Lithuania. Meanwhile in France, the Front National, achieved 17% of the vote in 2012 on the back of an anti-immigrant, anti-Islamic campaign. Front National leader Marine Le Pen has argued against Muslim women wearing the headscarf, as well as opposing the sale of Halal and Kosher meat; an argument taken up by the then President Nicholas Sarkozy in the 2012 French elections. In a further development, Marine Le Pen has even argued against observant Jews wearing Kippas (ritual skullcaps) in public, basing this on ideas of 'equality' linked to the ban on Muslim headscarves (Jerusalem Post 2012).

The growth of racist, xenophobic, anti-immigrant and anti-Islamic political parties is replicated in other countries with the Dutch Freedom Party, the Sweden Democrats, the True Finns in Finland, who gained 19% of the vote in 2011, and the Norwegian Progress Party, which is the second largest grouping in the Norwegian parliament and counted among its members the notorious Anders Breivik, who killed 77 people in his 'war' on 'multiculturalism' in 2011. There are numerous other examples of so-called 'respectable' mainstream anti-immigrant parties across Europe and smaller explicitly avowed neo-Nazi parties. In the UK there are the British National Party and the English Defence League, as well as smaller, offshoot Leagues in Scotland and Wales. While antisemitism is not an explicit theme among these groups, their growth and overt anti-immigrant and anti-Islamic rhetoric reflect a significant and worrying growth in racism. Although such far-right and Nazi groups remain relatively small in the UK, the 2013 English Council elections have indicated a 25% share of the vote for the intensely nationalistic and xenophobic UKIP. This demonstrates a dramatic surge in support for what was previously a fringe party and suggests a hardening of attitudes towards immigration among other issues, with a worrying potential for this to feed into further levels of racism (BBC News 2013).

Anti-Semitism in the UK today

While there is a discernible growth in antisemitism of the 'old' order in mainland Europe, it is also necessary to examine in more detail, the situation in the UK today to draw out lessons for social work. There is a long history of antisemitic attitudes in Britain, dating as far back as the medieval period (Julius 2010). In the late 19th century, Britain witnessed a significant growth in antisemitism, which coincided with the large-scale immigration of Jews to the UK. Approximately 250,000 Jews arrived in the UK between 1880 and 1906 (Boyd 2011), mostly penniless and having escaped severe repression in Eastern Europe. In the 19th century Jews were subject to various forms of social and civil restriction resulting a in a long struggle for Jewish emancipation, with full equality finally being achieved in 1890 (Green 2010). During the 1930s the British Union of Fascists grew significantly and was involved in promoting antisemitic propaganda. However, they were challenged by Jews, trade unionists and communist activists, which culminated in the famous Battle of Cable Street, when these groups stopped the fascists marching, under the slogan of 'They shall not pass!' There is in fact, a forgotten history of Jewish radicalism in the lead-up to this period, with many Jews becoming active in Trade Unions, the Communist Party and the Bund (Fishman 2004). Anti-Semitism in more recent historical periods has at points become institutionalised to a degree, with antisemitic attitudes common in the media and in literature. As Julius (2010: 242) argues, antisemitism takes various forms, from the murderous obsession of the Nazis to quotidian or 'every-day' forms of antisemitism. This was reflected in significant sections of the British ruling class who perceived Jews as both potential Bolshevik or anarchist agitators and as financial speculators; as well as being racially inferior. For example, Julius (2010: 61) points to John Buchan's *The thirty-nine steps,* published in 1915, with its characterisation of Jews as 'Jew-anarchists' and 'capitalists who rake in the shekels'. Post-1917, and in the context of the Russian revolution, *The Times* reported the events as '…engineered by "adventurers of German-Jewish blood and in German pay"' (Julius 2010: 287). As Julius (2010) discusses, there was systematic evidence of antisemitic attitudes in the British political establishment throughout the early part of the 20th century demonstrating hostility, dislike or antipathy towards Jews.

Such antisemitic attitudes did not disappear following the end of World War II with the dominant experience of British Jews being that of insecurity and fear of further persecution. Institutionalised forms of antisemitism still existed well into the 1970s and later, such as Jews not being able to join golf or tennis clubs. From my own experience of growing up in Scotland in the 1960s, anecdotal as it is, antisemitic attitudes persisted and were in many ways deeply ingrained. As a child, I remember being segregated at primary school where we were sent to the 'Jews' room during religious assemblies. Casual antisemitic remarks were regularly encountered at secondary school, and on occasion, antisemitic violence occurred. This would be a not uncommon experience among British Jews at this time, however, evidence would suggest this degree of open discrimination no longer exists and the bulk of equalities legislation has changed the political landscape. However, the experience of antisemitism helps to explain why Jewish communities in the UK have remained relatively insular and have created their own cultural and social institutions, including embryonic social services targeted at the Jewish community.

It would be wrong to characterise Britain as an antisemitic country today institutionally, or in terms of attitudes. The experience of the majority of British Jews in the 21st century is that of social and economic integration with full participation in terms of employment and involvement in political and cultural institutions. It is important to recognise that, over the past forty years, many other groups have borne the brunt of racism. For example, the Irish, Gypsies, Afro-Caribbeans and immigrants from the Indian sub-continent have all been affected by direct and indirect racism. Today, with the rise of Islamophobia, Muslims are the focus of much racist rhetoric and are particularly demonised.

However, there are commentators who would argue that antisemitism is in fact on the rise, particularly when analysed in the context of attitudes towards Israel. Anthony Julius's *Trials of the diaspora: A history of anti-Semitism in England* is an essential source in tracing the development of antisemitism in the British context. However, Julius, along with others, is a firm proponent of the view that quotidian antisemitism is alive and well and growing in Britain; and that anti-Zionism is a cover for antisemitism or Jew hatred. However, this is a problematic position that tends not to be borne out by evidence, but may also be a contributory factor in the failure to integrate antisemitism into anti-racist theory and practice. To reiterate the argument being made here, fear of being tarred as antisemitic for raising criticisms of Israel, alongside confusion over the nature of antisemitism itself, can have the unintended effect of antisemitism being excluded from anti-racist theory more generally. Even more dangerously, it can be argued that the stated position that perceives an increasing, quotidian, 'new' antisemitism obscures and diminishes the very real dangers of the 'old' antisemitism where it exists and grows today.

A brief review of the available evidence regarding Jewish attitudes to antisemitism in Britain today is helpful in analysing the extent of the problem. The initial findings from the 2010 survey conducted for the Institute of Jewish Policy Research (Graham and Boyd 2010) on the attitudes of Jews in Britain towards Israel are illuminating. The survey focuses on the relationship of British diaspora Jews towards Israel rather than antisemitism per se, but many of the findings are directly related. Out of 4081 responses, 82% of respondents felt Israel plays a 'central' or 'important but not central' role in their Jewish identities; at the same time, 67% favour giving up territory for peace with the Palestinians, and 74% are opposed to the expansion of existing settlements in the West Bank. In relation to antisemitism itself, 23% of the sample had witnessed some form of antisemitic incident over the previous year. Of these, over half (56%) believed that the incident was 'probably' or 'definitely' related to the abuser/assailant's views on Israel; and 11% said they had been subjected to a verbal antisemitic insult or attack in the 12 months leading up to the survey. The results paint a complex picture and as with any survey, there are different ways to interpret the results. However, in terms of antisemitic incidents, the figures indicate that the percentage of Jewish people who had experienced antisemitism *not* as a result of views on Israel was approximately 5%. While any degree of antisemitic incident is clearly concerning and needs to be tackled with appropriate vigour, overall 71% of those involved said they felt comfortable as a Jewish person living in Britain. However, the perceived lack of security among over a quarter of respondents is concerning.

A further perspective is provided by the Community Security Trust (CST), a UK charity that advises and represents the Jewish community on matters of antisemitism terrorism, policing and security. In its latest Antisemitic Incidents Report (CST 2010), 586 antisemitic incidents were reported to the organisation The majority involved incidents of abusive behaviour and damage or desecration of Jewish property, with 92 of the total incidents being violent in nature, but most were characterised by random verbal abuse. There is also evidence that the total number of reported incidents was down by 9% from 2010, which was the second year in which reported incidents had decreased from a record high of 929 incidents in 2009 (incidentally, 2009 was the year when Israel launched Operation Cast Lead against Gaza resulting in the deaths of over 1,100 Palestinians). A large number of the reported incidents occurred in Greater London and Greater Manchester where the largest Jewish communities are located, and were directed against members of the Jewish ultra-orthodox community suggesting that 'public visibility' was a contributory factor. Helpfully, the CST report makes some distinction between anti-Israel and antisemitic incidents generally, suggesting a reasonable level of accuracy in its figures, although as the organisation itself acknowledges, 'Drawing out these distinctions, and deciding on where the dividing lines lie, is one of the most difficult areas of CST's work in recording and analysing hate crime' (CST 2011: 32).

An on-going study commissioned by the Scottish Government in 2011 provides a further glimpse into the lives and views of Jews in the UK today. The 'Being Jewish in Scotland' study, being carried out by the Scottish Council of Jewish Communities (Scojec), produced interim results in June 2012. The report provides valuable information regarding the experiences of a small minority community. The Jewish community in Scotland now only numbers some 6,500, whereas in the mid-20th century that number was about 20,000, with the majority centred round suburban Glasgow, and to a lesser degree, Edinburgh. In the 2011 study, the majority of the 300 respondents surveyed displayed a largely positive view of living as Jews in Scotland, although many felt isolated; particularly those living in remote areas where there was little understanding of Judaism and associated religious requirements in health and educational establishments. This lack of awareness is further reflected in the way social work services to Jewish people in Scotland have historically been provided by organisations established by the Jewish community itself, rather than through generic services. In relation to antisemitism respondents to the survey indicate limited actual experience of antisemitic incidents although '... four fifths of people who completed surveys or participated in one-to-one interviews mentioned the increasingly acrimonious attacks on Israel as an area of concern' (Scojec 2012). Overall though, despite these areas of concern, it would be difficult to argue that Jews in Britain are experiencing the virulent growth in antisemitism referred to by the ICCA earlier. This does not mean however, that anti-racists should be complacent and there are strong indications that continued attention should be paid to areas of social, health and education provision as part of a wider approach towards community cohesion.

There is a probable 'common sense' attitude that exists in the UK today that British Jews are a relatively materially prosperous community; and in this respect an example of a 'successful' immigrant community. However, there are risks here of stereotyping all Jews and even of recycling less favourable antisemitic tropes concerning Jews and wealth. It is, therefore, important to recognise that the Jewish community in the UK is not a homogeneous body and that in common with other minority communities has particular needs that require to be addressed by social work and other services. In this respect, a further study by the Institute of Jewish Policy Research into child poverty and deprivation in the British Jewish community carried out in 2011 is illuminating. The study indicates high levels of poverty and other social issues among the Jewish Haredi (strictly orthodox) community especially in London and Manchester (Boyd,2011). High poverty levels are not commonly associated with Jewish communities, but there is little in social work literature that focuses on the needs of Jewish communities, so the problem remains relatively 'hidden' and gains little discussion, which in itself is problematic. In reality there are numerous Jewish 'communities' in the UK that correspond to the cultural–religious backgrounds of Jews themselves, for example, Haredi, Orthodox, Reform, Liberal and secular. Although certain customs pertain to all Jews, there are considerable variations that apply depending on religious practice and background to this, from a social work perspective, we need to avoid potentially institutionally racist responses corresponding to the notion that 'the Jewish community looks after its own'. This kind of formulation has been applied to other BME communities, which in a similar context can make false assumptions about the nature of minority communities, the social relations that exist in such communities and the service needs which flow from this. It is unfortunately highly likely that there is a relatively low level of understanding of Jewish cultural and religious practices among the majority of social workers in the UK; and hence, limited awareness of how to work effectively with service users from a Jewish background. Although specific services have grown up such as Jewish Care in areas such as London, Manchester and Scotland, this does not obviate the need for social work to develop a greater awareness of culturally sensitive practice with Jewish people and by extension, grapple with antisemitism.

Social work, anti-racism and antisemitism

As discussed throughout, antisemitism is a complex phenomenon that has taken varying forms both historically and materially, and any real understanding regarding antisemitism cannot be divorced from an understanding of oppression more generally. As Ferguson, Lavalette and Mooney (2002: 101) argue, a Marxist analysis of oppression starts from an understanding that 'oppression has material roots and is historically specific'. Therefore, in contrast to essentialist analyses, '...oppression is seen to arise not from any biological imperative but rather from the material and social relations of class society'. This is important in recognising that racism is not a product of human nature, and also in revealing the ways in which racism can grow at periods in history in response to material conditions, and in times of economic crisis. The growth of racism in Europe today can be analysed effectively in these terms and reflects historical developments concerning antisemitism, for it was the material conditions of economic crisis in the 1930s that fuelled the growth of Nazi antisemitic ideology.

Taking the debate a step forward, how then, is the fight against antisemitism today reflected in terms of anti-racist practice, particularly in the field of social work. Anti-racist practice is, or should be, central to the value base of social work. Furthermore, given the historical importance of antisemitism and its continued centrality to racist thought and ideology, it would be expected that an analysis of antisemitism would be firmly rooted in anti-racist literature, especially within social work. Yet, this is not the case and antisemitism as an issue is largely absent from anti-racist literature in the UK social work field and beyond. A cursory review of the literature confirms this. For example, a publication by the UK Institute of Race Relations (IRR) in 1993, the *Resource directory on 'race' and racism in social work* has only one reference to antisemitism in the whole book. This is despite the book being designed as a comprehensive guide for UK social work students, educators and practitioners. It should be further noted that this guide was produced at what could be termed the highpoint of the development of anti-racist approaches in social work in the context of CCETSW's Paper 30 in the 1980s. The single reference identified in the *Resource directory* is to a chapter titled 'Racism and anti-Semitism' by Audrey Droisen in a 1989 publication, *Child sexual abuse: Feminist perspectives* (Driver and Droisen 1989). Without being overly critical of Droisen's chapter and its intent, there is unfortunately little that readers of the chapter would gain in terms of an understanding of antisemitism itself, never mind the social work response to Jewish families. Instead, the focus is mainly on child sexual-abuse and the development of a comparative discussion of the experiences of black and Jewish children's experiences of abuse. This is useful in itself, but not the basis for an informed social work analysis regarding antisemitism or important issues related to work with Jewish communities.

While a comprehensive review of the available literature is outside the scope of this chapter, currently limited research indicates that even in more recent, well-constructed and popular texts on social work and anti-racist practice such as Bhatti-Sinclair (2011), Dominelli (2008) and Thompson (2012), readers will struggle to find any reference to antisemitism or more than passing mention of issues impacting on the lives of Jewish people. This gap in the literature is not confined to social work and has also been identified in the field of education. Geoffrey Short (1991: 33), when reviewing contemporary texts on anti-racist teaching found '...there is not a single reference to the need to combat anti-Semitic prejudice' . There have, however, been some developments in the education field. For example, in England, teaching on the Holocaust is part of the national curriculum for secondary school pupils, although there are criticisms of the depth and nature of content. In Scotland, the situation is different and there is no similar commitment to explore the Holocaust, unless it reflects a particular teacher's interest in the subject.

This gap in addressing antisemitism is not solely confined to the UK. In North America, for example, antisemitism is better integrated into social work education, but again this appears to be variable. In the US, referring to social work education, Soifer (1991: 156) demonstrated clearly that 'The social work profession has overlooked the topic of Jews as a cultural-religious minority group and the problem of anti-Semitism.' This analysis was built upon through a subsequent study of diversity and oppressed groups within a context of multicultural social work education (Guitierrez et al (1999). Writing in 1994 for the *Canadian Woman Studies* journal, Reed identified 'The omission of Anti-Semitism in Anti-Racism' and developed Short's analysis in criticising the anti-racist movement for being too narrowly focused on race or colour to the exclusion of '...anti-Semitism in the overall anti-racist project' (Reed 1994: 70). Gold (1996: 77) goes further, and in the introduction to her article in the *Journal of Social Work Education* states: 'Yet, anti-Semitism has been almost completely excluded from discussions of racism and from anti-racism efforts (such as curriculum changes) within US and Canadian schools of social work'. In relation to anti-racist social work literature and education in the UK, the immediate impression is that the same would seem to be true, although the question has to be asked as to why this is the case.

There are a number of possible reasons why antisemitism is largely excluded from anti-racist social work's theoretical understanding. The first might be the reality of racism in the UK and the understandable focus on the racism experienced by black and Asian people both historically and today. In this context, antisemitism could be argued to be 'further down the list' of 'racisms' as it is not (thankfully) the dominant expression of racism in the UK. However, to come to this conclusion would arguably depend on a thoroughgoing analysis that encompassed all forms of racism, including antisemitism as part of a fully worked-through debate over priorities for anti-racist social work. There is however, limited evidence that this debate has taken place to date. If so, then the issue of Islamophobia, which is arguably the most virulent form of racism in the UK today, would be higher up the social work anti-racist agenda than it possibly is. Even if this rather reductionist argument were to be accepted, this would not in itself excuse or justify a lack of attention to antisemitism in its current manifestation. The deeper issue here is more likely related to the point that Charlotte Williams makes when she states that: '…the radical trajectory of anti-racism in social work has found itself in a *cul-de-sac* characterised by a politics of compromise' (Williams 2011: 61). In this context, it could be argued that anti-racism has become deeply formulaic and overly focused on issues of race and colour, thereby missing a more comprehensive analysis of racism and oppression in their widest forms, that is informed not just by the political issues that drive it, but also by seeing anti-racism as a dynamic process that needs constant re-evaluation and re-invigoration. Underpinning this, the perspective that social work has 'lost its way' and become compromised by the growth of managerialism and neoliberalism, thereby devaluing the radical potential for social work to be a genuine force for change has significant merit in helping to explain the issue further (Ferguson and Woodward 2009, Harris 2003, Lavalette 2011).

There is however, another factor that very possibly contributes to the omission of antisemitism from the canon of anti-racist literature – namely, 'that it is "too difficult", and therefore best avoided'. Again, this is very likely related to the contradictory and complex issue of the state of Israel discussed above, and accompanying issues relating to the disputed human rights of the Palestinian population within Israel itself and in the Occupied Territories. However, to raise criticisms of Israel risks the prospect of being accused of antisemitism under the terms of *The working definition of Antisemitism* (FRA 2012). The weight behind this argument of the working definition, or 'new' antisemitism is considerable. The following statement by the former Labour MP for Rotherham and former Europe Minister Denis McShane, writing in *The Washington Post* in 2007, and cited on the website of the Institute for the Study of Contemporary Anti-Semitism at Indiana University, reinforces this point. McShane states:

> Neo-antisemitism is a twenty-first century global ideology, with its own thinkers, organizers, spokespersons, state sponsors and millions of adherents. We are at the beginning of a long intellectual and ideological struggle.… It is about everything democrats have long fought for: the truth

without fear, no matter one's religion or political beliefs. The new antisemitism threatens all of humanity.

I would argue here, that what McShane is referring to is not the growth of fascism and racism in Europe, which poses real and dangerous threats if not checked, but the freedom for Israel to act in defence not only of its own stated interests but also in the interests of Western neoliberalism and imperialism in the Middle East.

The great tragedy here is that this ideological onslaught has arguably wrong-footed the anti-racist movement and in the process actually harmed the cause of fighting antisemitism. The task we have to address is how to find a way to resolve this conundrum and allow a full and proper analysis of antisemitism, which can be integrated into anti-racist theory and practice. Here I would make some interrelated proposals. The first is that anti-racist theory, education and practice needs to include a thorough understanding of antisemitism and a wholly uncompromising attitude to racism, antisemitism and fascism wherever it rises. The second is that social work in developing its understanding and awareness of antisemitism develops a greater level of cultural understanding of Jewish communities, and develops the potential to work with them in an effective manner, recognising their needs and issues. Third, and while it is necessary, culturally sensitive social work is not enough in responding to issues of racism and antisemitism. The concept of the 'social worker as agitator' described by the social work lecturer (and later, Labour Prime Minister) Clement Atlee, is one that perhaps needs resurrecting. (Ferguson and Woodward 2009: 15) In this context, it is arguable that social work needs to engage more actively with anti-racist and anti-fascist campaigns that go beyond individual advocacy and work collectively with such campaigns in championing human rights. Fourth is the need for an equally uncompromising approach in fighting for social justice and the human rights of oppressed groups both in the UK and elsewhere. In this context, there is no contradiction in supporting the rights of Palestinians to social justice, self-determination and freedom of movement alongside the struggle against racism, fascism and antisemitism.

Implications for social work education and practice

Soifer (1991) coins the term 'cultural-religious minority group' when discussing how Jewish people should be referred to within a broader context of racial, ethnic and cultural identity and social work education. There is a strong argument that social work education in the UK needs to consider the inclusion of a similar construct that can allow for Jewish experience to be incorporated within the wider framework of BME communities. As Soifer (1991) argues, although Jews can be identified as a minority ethnic community, this can cause confusion when considering the general interpretation of BME communities that is equally applicable in the US and the UK. Jews are a minority community within the UK although compose a heterogeneous body of differing communities. Social work education at the least needs to consider how diversity and identity is developed to include the experience of various minority groups including Jews. Without this, there is a risk of institutional racism to develop through lack of understanding on the part of social workers.

Tackling antisemitism as part of anti-racist practice entails a thorough understanding of oppression as it affects Jewish people and in being confident to identify and tackle antisemitic attitudes when they occur. While many practitioners will not come across Jewish people in the course of their practice; when they do, they need to be equipped to understand the basic aspects of Jewish culture and religious practice to enable them to respond appropriately to the needs of Jewish people. A detailed discussion of specific educational programmes is not possible here, although it is possible to discern how such approaches could be integrated within current teaching. For example, in considering life-course work, Jewish practice and customs in relation to birth, transitions to adulthood, marriage, ageing and death could be incorporated within existing teaching. Similarly, awareness of the range of Jewish communities in the UK and their differing practices would increase knowledge and avoid risks of stereotyping that can slip into forms of institutionalised racism. A key component would also involve awareness of dietary customs (*kashrut*) and the role of religious practice and festivals in shaping Jewish life. Underlying this is the issue of Jewish identity; an identity not only shaped by concepts of family and religion but also of historical persecution and oppression. For social workers and social care staff to successfully engage with Jewish people, there needs to be an awareness of these components of Jewish identity and how to ensure they are integrated into culturally sensitive practice. However, beyond this is also the ability to identify antisemitism and to challenge this effectively. As with other aspects of anti-racist practice, practitioners require knowledge and understanding of minority groups' experiences and an awareness and understanding of their own social identities and attitudes.

Conclusion

The rise of racism across Europe and the growing assault on anti-discriminatory initiatives in Britain such as multi-culturalism pushes at a door that is already ajar in relation to greater intolerance of the 'other'. As Liz Fekete, the Director of the IRR argues, 'We are witnessing the revival of arguments first used by Enoch Powell...in 1968 for his "Rivers of Blood" speech that warned of the dangers posed by mass immigration from the New Commonwealth' (Fekete 2011: 38). As Fekete goes on to explain, the growth of anti-immigrant rhetoric not just from far-right parties, but from centre-right and even social democratic parties has spread across Europe to the point where this has become 'a new popular "common sense" racism' (Fekete 2011: 38). A leading proponent of the attack on multiculturalism is Thilo Sarrazin, a former member of the Deutsche Bundesbank, whose 2010 book *Deutschland Schafft Sich Ab* (Germany Abolishes Itself), has become one of the most widely read books in Germany since Mein Kampf (Fekete 2011). Behind this ideological assault lies a context of deepening economic crisis and the failure of neoliberal policies to resolve the problems of modern-day capitalism beyond making the poorest and most vulnerable pay for the crisis. Sarrazin's central thesis that immigration is a threat to German society, culture and economic security has let a genie out of the bottle; and one which is not easily rebottled. Racism tends not to respect defined categories or boundaries and the threat to (Muslim) immigrants today is a threat to all minorities tomorrow. There are disturbing similarities between Sarrazin's book and Marr's antisemitic treatise from the 19th century in terms of attitudes to immigration and national identity. The evidence of the rise of antisemitism in Europe both historically and currently should act as a warning sign to the dangers of assuming that history does not repeat itself. The insidious growth of anti-Jewish measures and policy in Weimar Germany is instructive in how once fringe forms of racism can become mainstream policy. It may be easy to dismiss neo-Nazi parties such as the Golden Dawn and Jobbik as fringe extremists, however, this is to overlook that exactly the same attitude existed in relation to the Nazis in Germany before they assumed power in 1933 (Longerich 20101; Paxton 2005). While the xenophobia and 'little England' nationalism of Nigel Farrage and UKIP in warning of Britain being overrun by a (supposed) wave of Bulgarian and Romanian immigrants may seem a far cry from fascism in the 1930s, there is a real risk of such racist ideas developing and gaining hold to the detriment of all minority communities in the UK today.

Social work has a real and distinct role in challenging racism and standing up for the rights of oppressed minorities. However, this needs to move beyond the realm of what may often be rhetoric to more concrete application of theory to practice. In this respect there is an urgency to ensure anti-racist theory and practice integrates an understanding of the dynamics of antisemitism as without this we may be left with an incomplete understanding of the dynamics of racism. Anti-Semitism has shown itself to be a disturbingly pervasive and persistent form of racism, which requires a level of analysis to be able to distinguish between 'old' and so-called 'new' variants and in how to respond to them (Finkelstein 2003; Rose 2004). When in late 2012 Marton Gyongyosi, an MP for the Jobbik, who is also vice-chairman of the parliament's foreign-affairs committee, called for the authorities to compile a national list of Hungarian Jews, especially those in parliament and government, who represent what he described as a 'national-security risk'; we should collectively shudder over the antisemitic intent behind this move (*The Economist* 2012).

There are, however, forces of hope we can look to in this situation that build on collective fights against fascism and racism from the past, which brought together Jew, non-Jew, black and white. For example, Unite Against Fascism (UAF) in the UK has been exemplary in mounting protests in every situation where the EDL have tried to march or demonstrate. The lessons from history are that fascism takes on different forms and can adopt the 'clothes of the mainstream' through participation in parliamentary politics. However, fundamentally, fascism is about destroying freedom of speech and curbing civil liberties on the streets as well as in the debating chambers of parliaments (Paxton 2005). It is on the streets that fascists have to be confronted if they are to be stopped. The mass battle of Cable Street in the 1930s and the large demonstrations by the Anti-Nazi League in the 1970s and 1980s effectively put a halt to the growth of fascist movements in both periods. Similar protests have been organised in Spain and in Greece against the fascists and the far-right. This is a model that needs to be replicated across Europe through the building of united alliances with progressive social movements against fascism and racism. Even in Hungary where the fascists are on the march, there is opposition to their dangerous ideas. In response to Gyongyosi's dangerous speech a demonstration was called in early December 2012 which was attended by thousands and called for solidarity with Hungary's Jews (*The Economist* 2012). And in May 2012, in response to the electoral success of the fascist Golden Dawn in Greece, an open letter 'We are all Greek Jews!' was circulated across Europe to raise awareness and build opposition to Golden Dawn.[3]

Social workers in Hungary and Greece are daily involved in confronting racist and antisemitic ideas. There is an urgent need for social work in the UK and elsewhere to similarly confront the growth of racism and locate antisemitism as part of the mainstream body of anti-racist theory and practice. To avoid doing so diminishes not just the fight against antisemitism, but further weakens the anti-racist movement and anti-racist social work in the common fight against racism in all its pernicious forms.

Suggested further reading

There is a vast amount of literature in relation to antisemitism and an array of political perspectives in analysing the issue. There are currently no social work texts that focus on the issue, however, the following texts may provide some balance towards understanding of the issue and contrasting perspectives:

Beller, S. (2007) *Antisemitism: A very short introduction,* New York: Oxford University Press.

Julius, A. (2010) *Trials of the diaspora: A history of antisemitism in England*, New York: Oxford University Press.

Rose, J. (2004) *The myths of Zionism*, London: Pluto Press.

Notes

[1] 'The Pale' refers to the area where most European Jews lived. This is the geographical area that stretched from Poland through the Baltic States such as Lithuania and Latvia, to Western Russia.

[2] www.socialworkfuture.org/articles-and-analysis/international-articles/245-vote-for-norbert-ferencz

[3] http://weareallgreekjews.eu/

SIX

Anti-Roma racism in Europe: past and recent perspectives

Špela Urh

Following the chapter on anti-Semitism, Urh here looks at the history of anti-Roma, anti-Gypsy and anti-traveller racism. Across Europe Roma communities have, historically, suffered from racism and oppression – often a violent and bloody form of political action promoted by national states, by state employees and by far-right groups. Today the rise of far-right organisations (like the Jobbik Party in Hungary, which openly vilifies Hungary's Roma minority) has brought increasing levels of violence directed against the community. However, anti-Roma racism is not just a Hungarian, or East European, problem. Here Urh looks at the roots and origins of anti-Roma racism, its prevalence today and asks what social workers can and should do when working with the Roma community.

Introduction

Written sources bearing witness to the Roma population in Europe date back to the 14th and 15th centuries. On the basis of research and comparisons of the Romani language, linguists have identified the Roma migration route and agreed that the Roma came from India in the 14th century and began to settle in large numbers from the 17th century onwards (Hancock 1988). According to Okely (1996), the Roma as a European minority have one common feature, namely being perceived as 'others'. This 'otherness' has been evoked in traditional studies (for example, anthropology, sociology, social work, and so on) to orientalise them by emphasising their Indian origin (Said 1996). The orientalisation of the Roma produces the effect of a double exclusion in their representation as both biological and cultural foreigners. Taking this as a starting point, Okely (1996) rejected the thesis that all Gypsies are Indian by origin, in turn rejecting the notions of 'true' Roma and 'false' *Travellers.* According to primordialist conceptualisations, which see *ethnos* as a universal framework of the existence of human groups, the Romani *ethnos* along with its constantly emphasised nomadism originates in India.

Data shows that there are between 10 and 15 million Roma in Europe. Countries such as Bulgaria, Hungary and Romania have the highest numbers of Roma, with estimates that there are 700,000–800,000 in Bulgaria, 550,000–600,000 in Hungary, and 1,800,000–2,500,000 in Romani. In the European Union (EU), which includes cultural diversity among its officially declared values, 'the discussions regarding the identity of the Roma bring about the realisation that it is the Roma, the European nation without a state, who are the first heralds and protagonists of the idea about Europe without borders' (Klopčič 2007: 25–6). Yet, the notion of cultural diversity is not applied in relation to the Roma, who have become the European 'other', perceived as a threat to the dominant society in relation to their nomadism and their settlement.

The Roma community is recognised historically as one of the most oppressed and excluded ethnic groups in Europe (Okley 1994; Barany 2002; Fonseca 2007). Many agree that the history of the Roma is a history of persecution and racism, particularly under absolutist rulers, as witnessed in the genocide they experienced under Nazism (Zimmermann 1999; Barany 2002; Fonseca 2007). In Eastern European countries under communist regimes, hostility towards the Roma was, with a few exceptions, more covert. It is still the case today that Roma populations are victims of overt and covert racism, and are denied their formal and legal rights (see more on www.errc.org/). Research carried out in a number of European countries (OSI 2001, 2002) has shown that the Roma's social status is lower than the social status of other culturally diverse communities. For example, they experience much higher rates of unemployment, receive inferior rates of social assistance, and disproportionate numbers of Roma children are sent to special schools compared to non-Roma children.

Today, racism against the Roma continues to reflect notions of 'otherness'. This is often expressed in proverbs that portray everything Romani as deviant, undesired and contrary to mainstream values. There are also many cases of nimbyism, which represents one of the modern forms of cultural racism applied to people with psychiatric diagnoses, drug addicts, refugees, immigrants from the 'third world' and the Roma. Nimbyism – *Not In My Back Yard* – leads to the persecution of such populations and calls for segregation in, for example, centres for foreigners and Roma settlements (Sayce 2000).

In order to understand the levels of biological and cultural racism that the Roma have experienced over the centuries, and continue to experience today, it is necessary to explore levels of persecution from an historical perspective, and consider the ways in which this has resulted in separatism, exclusion and repression.

The history of the persecution of the Roma

The notion of 'Gypsy' began to gain ground in the 16th and 17th centuries during mass migration towards the European continent, although its meaning has changed since then. At the first World Roma Congress, which was held in 1971, the Roma considered it more respectful to adopt 'Roma' and 'Romani' in place of 'Gypsy' to counter negative connotations associated with the latter. Yet the Anglo-Saxon use of the name 'Gypsy' is still very common. Initially, in earlier centuries, the term 'Gypsy' referred to all travelling peoples or groups of people and individuals, regardless of their origin. However, the nomadic, travelling way of life was stigmatised, and accordingly people were divided into 'Gypsies' and 'Non-Gypsies' (Willems 1998). Thus in earlier periods of migration, numerous groups were described as 'Gypsies', who nevertheless differed from each other in terms of their ethnicity and other characteristics (for example, villains, beggars and pagans). In the 18th century, Grellmann wrote a comprehensive historical book on Gypsies and defined them as 'a mixed population of foreigners, oddballs and deviants who travel' (Willems 1998, p 18).

Lucassen (1998) carried out research investigating how the term 'Gypsy' was constructed in Germany, and found that in the 18th and 19th centuries, German police had the power to define who was a 'Gypsy'. It was believed that the travelling way of life was dangerous, and that with high probability these groups of people tended to be criminals. Names of potential criminals were kept by the police in special lists, which were then published in public newspapers. The lists included the names, and described the activities of, those suspected of burglaries and robberies, while also containing the names of vagabonds who were denoted as *Gauner*, *Vaganten* and *Zigeuner*. Lists were later expanded to include acrobats, refuse-metal collectors and travelling salesmen.

It was in the second half of the 19th century that *Zigeuner* started to focus on ethnic origin rather than a travelling lifestyle, reflecting the strong influence of newly emerging racist theories. The theoretical presuppositions of 19th century racism advocated the existence of diverse, biologically differentiated human races, and later became the basis for Hitler's idea of ethnic 'others', along with his belief in the superiority of the white German or 'pure Aryan race'. In the 19th and early 20th century, national–socialist politics against the Roma, called *Zigeunerkaempfung* (Zimmermann 1999), were based on the concepts of late absolutism. As early as 1783, a decree issued by Joseph II prohibited Gypsies from, for example, nomadism, changing names and surnames, living in forests, and breeding and trading horses. If someone was heard speaking Romani they were physically attacked. Gypsies were forbidden to marry each other or live in an extramarital partner relationship, and if they did, their children were taken away from them and placed in non-Gypsy foster homes to be re-educated to become decent Christians (Guy 1998).

Hostility towards Gypsies existed throughout Europe, and many other countries adopted similar measures to counter the dangerous 'Gypsy nature'. In Czechoslovakia as early as in the 15th century, Gypsies were considered to be Turkish spies, while in the 17th and 18th centuries they found themselves in an 'age of darkness' due to the devastation left behind by the Thirty Years' War (depopulation, plague, and famine). Romani girls and under-age children had their ears cut off, and adults were killed on a mass scale, with their bodies hung up in trees in order to intimidate the Roma and deter future Roma immigration (Guy 1998).

A Slovenian romologist, Pavla Štrukelj, gives examples of the strict and coercive attempts to prevent the Roma travelling in Slovenian territory during the early 18th century, which was then part of the Austro-Hungarian Monarchy (Štrukelj 2004: 83). Decrees prohibited travel, and later contained strategies for civilising Roma communities. For example, one law stated that Gypsies had to be recorded in parish and other registers under the designation 'new immigrants', they were not allowed to speak in their mother tongue or trade in horses, and they were prohibited from living in tents in the woods. There were also decrees specifying places where they were allowed to settle. Often children were taken away by the authorities from their Gypsy parents and given to families living in towns, or to farmers to learn craft and farm work. This was to re-educate and resocialise them.

Decrees in the 19th and 20th centuries were equally punitive and repressive. A report by Dinko Puc, the civil governor of the Drava province (Ljubljana, 8 June 1935) states that:

> The Gypsies are to have their movement outside the farmhouse embittered in every way, they should be troubled in every step. They should not be allowed to camp outdoors. They are to be forbidden to enter the fairground. They are not to be allowed to own dogs, as they do not need them and can also teach them to warn them by barking about

> the arrival of constables, or train them for game hunting. (Klopčič 1991: 4)

Gypsies were excommunicated from the Catholic Church, and roaming in towns was punishable with up to three months in prison or with forced labour in the workhouse. In October 1931 the royal provincial administration of the Drava province issued the following decree:

> The Gendarmerie has to search every Gypsy they meet while patrolling to find out whether they have a travelling permit and to establish their identity. The awareness of being controlled in itself averts Gypsies from vagabonding. During the controls, everything Gypsies carry or transport should be checked. (Klopčič 1991: 4)

Maček (2001) and Štrukelj (2004) discuss how proposals to solve the 'Gypsy problem' were put forward in 1918 in Slovenian territory. Ogrin, who was a lawyer, proposed that guardians be allocated for Gypsy children, whose up-bringing was neglected by their parents, and argued for the establishment of correction institutions for adolescents who lived immorally (as beggars and vagabonds). Adult criminal offenders were to undertake forced labour in workhouses and to be trained in handicrafts. Ogrin encouraged the employment of Gypsies when, after the World War I, there was a shortage of workers. He was also concerned to regulate their settlements.

Assimilationist approaches were based on the assumption that the integration of the Roma would only be successful through determining their place of settlement, their employment and education. The key to success was to socialise the Roma, so that in time, their culture (language, customs, clothing) would become obsolete and replaced by the culture of the majority wherever they lived. It was only then that they would be able to dispel negative connotations associated with the term 'Gypsy'. Similar proposals are reflected in contemporary social and political discourse, and there is continuing evidence regarding social exclusion in terms of employment, education and living conditions (OSI 2001, 2002).

Racism against the Roma during Nazism and World War II

Several authors (Lucassen1998; Willems 1998; Zimmermann 1999) portray the beginning of the 20th century as 'the golden years of racism', and the discourse about Gypsies reached its peak during the period of Nazi Germany. In the 1930s under the leadership of the German psychiatrist Robert Ritter, the Research Institute of Racial Hygiene (*Rassenhygienische Forschungsstelle*) had the legal power to determine who was a Gypsy. Rather than being grounded in ethnological and anthropological methods, Ritter's 'scientific approach' was based on the presupposition of biological racism – distinguishing Gypsies from non-Gypsies (a similar approach was taken against the Jews) according to phenotypical differences (such as colour of hair, eyes, skin, and shape of nose). Ritter's view of Gypsies was similar to Hitler's, and was imbued with stereotypical ideas proclaiming Gypsies as 'typical primitives without their own history'. Hitler designated Gypsies as antisocial, which was allegedly one of the primary reasons for the genocide against them. According to the Nurnberg law, Jews, dark-skinned people and Gypsies were an inferior 'race' and undesirable. The Roma were considered suspicious and culpable, for which they were punished or killed (Zimmermann 1999; Fonseca 2007).

In Nazi Germany, institutional racism towards Gypsies was most visible in legislation. In 1933, people labelled Gypsies by the racial institute were subject to mass sterilisation, prescribed by law. However, Ritter's institute was not the only implementer of racial hygiene policies that saw Gypsies being subjected to genocide. During that same period, racism was widespread across society, and racist ideas were evident in academic circles, with racially oriented research about Gypsies being carried out across universities in Germany (Zimmermann 1999).

Racially motivated genocide in Nazi Germany represented the essence of national-socialist politics towards the Roma. Zimmermann (1999) presents results based on his own research regarding the social–biological attempt to exterminate all that would make the Aryan race impure. For example, from a total of 22,600 individuals in Gypsy camps in Auschwitz, around 19,300 'Gypsies' were killed. Some 5,600 were gassed, while over 13,600 died of hunger, disease and epidemics.

Ritter was also the first to propose sterilising Gypsies as part of racial hygiene politics in an attempt to make them biologically harmless. After being sterilised, many Roma people described themselves as being 'like a tree without fruit' or 'the living dead' (Zimmermann 1999).

If, during this period, the Jews were deemed silent collaborators with the communists, the Gypsies were seen as racially subordinate spies and agents. Not only were they subject to racist attacks emanating from Hitler's Nazi politics but, as historical sources demonstrate, they were also viewed with suspicion by the partisans, who suspected the Roma of being collaborators with the Italian occupiers. The Slovenian historian Maček (2001) wrote about the mass killing of Gypsies in the

Kanižarica mining settlement in the Bela krajina region in the far south-east of Slovenia. In 1942 partisans burned down a Roma settlement, men, women, children and babies were killed. The exact number of those murdered is unknown, but an estimate is that there were 100 victims. The Roma who lived in Bela krajina during the war recall how the partisans also chased the Roma away from Slovenia across the Croatian border to the village of Zagradec, and pushed them into a Karst sinkhole. While some died immediately, many other were kept there for days and were tortured (Urh 2009, p 78). It was noted that:

> 52 Roma were killed then, only one pregnant woman and a small boy were saved. His name was Kido, and he knew how to sing beautifully. The soldiers promised him they would keep him alive if he sang. The boy was singing while his entire village, relatives and parents were being killed. (Urh 2009: 78)

An elderly Roma man who at the time was the youngest child in the family recalls how he lost his father and six brothers in the war:

> The Gypsies were deported to a camp or killed straight away. I was the youngest, my mother gave me to some farmers, where I helped with work and survived. My mother also went from farm to farm, helped with work and in this way she somehow managed to save herself. (Urh 2009: 78)

Although the Roma genocide was concealed from wider society, as evidenced in written sources, the elderly Roma still have vivid memories of acts of atrocity carried out.

The silent genocide by communist authorities

The post-war period was a time of mass migration among the Roma, who began to leave their isolated settlements in the countryside to move to industrial areas in bigger towns. As their numbers increased in towns and cities, partly due to migration and also due to population growth, they became increasingly visible and their presence generated high levels of political concern. The numbers documented need to be treated carefully, however, as censuses were not always reliable sources of data, as many Roma found ways to avoid exposing themselves to the authorities. Nevertheless, according to the first post-war national population census in Slovenia in 1953, 1,663 Roma were living in the country, but at the next census conducted in 1961, their numbers had declined sharply with just 158 people declaring themselves to be Roma. Such statistics point to the fact that as part of a strategy for survival the Roma concealed their identity thus avoiding assimilationist pressures from the communist political regime in Slovenia, which was then part of Yugoslavia.

This 'silent genocide' against the Roma continued after World War II. Stewart (1997) describes how the Roma in Czechoslovakia, Poland, the Soviet Union and in Hungary were the target of almost identical assimilationist policies. Guy (1998) notes how, in Czechoslovakia, every Roma had their own identity card including the designation of their Romani ethnicity, they could only seek employment in their place of residence and displacement was prohibited. Any violation of these policies could lead to imprisonment for up to three years.

In Slovenia, most state recommendations adopted to improve the Roma's position concerned employment and promoting the schooling of children (Urh 2009). Šiftar gives an example from a 1954 report written by the local authorities in the north-eastern Slovenian town of Murska Sobota, which reflects underlying values and assumptions regarding the Roma:

> Above all, it is urgent to displace the young ones and those capable of work to different places of our country, to separate families so they have no contact, and start their individual re-education, which will certainly bear fruit. Regarding the elderly, they should be enabled a decent life and should be forced with coercive measures to start living in a more hygienic and cultural way. (Šiftar 1970: 108)

In a session of the People's Committee in Murska Sobota, the president of the Health Council proposed that 'every person wanting to become employed of their own free will should provide a written statement that they will not return to their old settlement or, if they do, they will be expelled (Šiftar 1970: 108). A focus on assimilation into mainstream society was articulated in the requirements calling on the Roma to abandon all 'typical' Gypsy habits. The belief was, that only through employment and education would the Roma be able to integrate successfully into society. However, despite these political measures, the Roma experienced high levels of unemployment and as a result, came to the attention of social services.

Elsewhere in Europe employment was also seen as key to ensuring the assimilation of the Roma. When Varsa (2005) analysed the documents of the Central Committee of the Hungarian Socialist Labour Party between 1960 and 1980, she exposed how the communist authorities discriminated against the Roma. For example, they were not treated equally in the field of employment, and in the labour market Roma women were subject to racist treatment. During the 1950s, full employment was defined as the highest social value by the socialist authorities, and Hungarian women were systematically encouraged to find jobs. However, a decade later, when it was revealed that the birth rate was falling 'white Hungarian women' were encouraged to have children and stay at home. As a result, the socialist authorities began to employ Roma women instead, which, it was argued, would improve the position of the Roma in society. However, it has been argued that this was just ensuring integration by other means, and that the purpose was clearly racist, as it would limit the birth rate of the Roma, and act as a tool of cover social sterilisation, particularly as the Roma birth rate had always been higher than that of the indigenous population in the countries in which they lived (Barrany 2002).

There was also evidence of more overt measures being taken by the communist authorities to reduce the birth rate of the Roma in some countries (Stewart 1997; Varsa 2005). For example, in Romania the authorities were involved in sterilising Roma women, and in 1965, after coming to power, Nicolae Ceaucescu introduced the so-called 'The Children of the Decree' or 'the New Man' project, which prohibited abortion for women below 45 years of age and those with less than five children. However, this did not apply to Romani women who were instead, encouraged to have abortions. There was concern that the Gypsies would corrupt the pure Romanian 'race' and was an openly eugenicist policy implemented at a national level to exterminate the Roma and create a 'pure' Romania.

Modern anti-Roma racism

Since the end of the communist era, in parts of Central and Eastern Europe, there has been a resurgence of racism towards the Roma. After the political transition in Eastern Europe, the Roma began to migrate in large numbers from Romania, the former Yugoslav Republic of Macedonia and from Bosnia and Herzegovina. From 1991 and 1992 many migrated from Croatia and Bulgaria, and after 1995 migration increased from Poland, the Czech Republic and Slovakia. The Roma, in order to find a safe haven, free from political persecution and inferior economic conditions, began to migrate to Germany, Italy, France, and Great Britain. Yet they became victims of repressive asylum policies that were punitive towards asylum seekers from 'third countries' (Hayes and Humphries et al 2004), and also towards 'foreigners' such as the Roma. For example, Great Britain was one of the countries that rejected the asylum claims of the Roma, and by treating them as economic migrants, denied the discrimination and suffering they were experiencing in other countries, and the Belgium government violently expelled all Slovakian Roma asylum seekers from the country in October 1999, (Taylor 2001). With the accession of Eastern European countries (where the majority of Roma live) to the EU it is now the case that they can freely move across the 'united' territory and seek employment. However, this has given rise to high levels of fear and hostility regarding an increase in the Roma population, who are subject to negative stereotypes regarding their lack of education and their tendency to have large families. High levels of political concern regarding the rapid growth of Roma settlements have led European governments to introduce worrying measures. For example, in 2010, the French government, under Sarkozy, offered every Roma from Romania and Bulgaria living in France as EU members, 300 euros per adult and 150 euros per child to leave the country. As the enforced displacement or deportation of citizens of EU member states is not allowed, he paid the Roma to return to their country of origin at their own free will.

The Roma have also been subject to institutional racism in the field of education. In Central and Eastern Europe they tend to have fewer educational opportunities, partly due to poverty, but also as a result of marginalisation. In Germany and in the Czech Republic, a disproportionate number of Roma children are enrolled in special schools for intellectually impaired children, and Spanish schools attended by Roma children are becoming increasingly ghettoised. Moreover, many European countries in which the Roma are settled operate segregationist policies with special schools attended by Roma children called 'Gypsy schools'. One principal of a Slovenian special school made a public declaration that due to the increasing social integration of children with special needs, the school would have been closed long ago had it not also been attended by the Roma.

As well as policies linked to stigmatisation, segregation and widespread discrimination, there is also evidence of high levels of cultural racism against the Roma across Europe, reflected in public opinion. For example, a 1995 Slovenian public opinion poll published in the Human Development Report revealed that half of those interviewed would not wish to have the Roma as neighbours, while 36.6% expressed strong anti-Roma sentiments (OSI 2001: 74) In Slovenia, hostility to the Roma was exposed when in 2012, a family of 10 moved from an unregulated Roma settlement to a rented house in Vranoviči, a small village of about 15 to 20 houses in the south-east of Slovenia. The local residents collectively resisted their settlement and demanded that the mayoress force them to return to where they had come from. The mayoress expressed sympathy with the locals and encouraged the Roma to return to their original location, and the locals offered the house owner a higher purchase price to ensure they did not move in. Another case revealed how villagers in the region of Dolenjska burned down a house that the Roma had bought before they could move in, and there have been other cases where the Roma have been prevented from settling in an area as a result of protests and vigilantism

The Roma have also been subject to direct and violent racism. The European Roma Rights Centre (ERRC) has received numerous claims regarding violent attacks on the Roma in Poland, Bulgaria, the Czech Republic and Slovakia. In December 2000, neo-Nazi groups in Poland broke the windows of Roma houses and wrote racist graffiti on the walls. The local police immediately rejected the accusation that local youths carried out the damage, and accused the Roma themselves of carrying out the vandalism, so that they would be granted asylum in Western Europe. In March 2001, a Roma woman from Slovakia reported that she and her 10-year-old daughter had been attacked by a group of 15 skinheads who poured petrol over them and tried to set them on fire, while shouting 'Die, you Gypsy whore'. Although the woman was hospitalised for a range of wounds to her face and back, the head of the local police force expressed doubt about the nature of the attack, inferring that she had fabricated the story. He made a public comment, stating: 'I think the Roma woman made everything up ... I don't know why she did it, probably the Roma are trying to build up the background for them to be able to leave the country' (OSI 2001: 46). There is evidence that the police and other officials, not only fail to protect the Roma against violence, but that they are also, at times, perpetrators themselves.

The consequence is that the Roma are not accepted and find it difficult to participate in everyday social and professional life. Many representatives of Roma organisations, such as Roma writers, doctors, teachers, sports stars and singers, often hide their backgrounds to avoid being socially excluded and suffering negative repercussions in their personal and professional lives. Sadly, they can also be complicit in stigmatising Roma communities in order to distance themselves from being associated with 'common' Gypsies.

Reaching beyond racism against the Roma: social work responses

As a condition for their accession to the EU, candidate countries were required to respect the human rights of the Roma. This enabled the development of different programmes aimed at improving the Roma's position and reducing violations of human rights, discrimination and racial violence (Klopčič 2007: 36). However:

> despite all these measurements and programmes a large majority of the Roma in Eastern Europe live on the brink of survival experiencing poverty and hunger. In 2003 the international development fund the United Nations Development programme (UNDP) found that the living conditions of the Roma in Eastern Europe were at the level of those in sub-Saharan Africa. (Klopčič 2007: 37)

The European Roma Rights Centre (ERRC) in its quarterly publications often presents similar findings:

> Even today the Roma (Gypsies) remain the most de-privileged ethnic group in Europe. Their basic rights are endangered almost everywhere. In recent years alarming examples of racist violence against the Roma have been occurring. The Roma experience discrimination in employment, education, health care, administration and other services, which is common to many societies. Hate speech directed at the Roma has been deepening negative stereotypes which permeate European public opinion. (ERRC 2003)

It can be said that Gypsy/Romany communities of English, Scottish and Welsh origin and Irish travellers are in many ways similar to European Roma. For example, many members of these communities face persecution, are illiterate, and face discrimination from state institutions including welfare agencies. In relation to education, the UK emphasises the education of the children of traveller families (Cudworth 2008). Under section 13 of the 1996 Education Act 1996, local education authorities have a statutory duty to ensure that education is available for all school-age children in the area, corresponding to their age, ability and aptitude, and any special education needs they may have. This duty extends to all children residing in a particular area, whether permanently or temporarily, which is of particular relevance to travelling children. Yet, Cudworth (2008: 365) notes that 'despite this legal obligation to secure, allocate and retain a place for GypsyTraveller children, many children from these communities find themselves excluded from state schools, once enrolled, for reasons of non-attendance'. Derrington and Kendall (2007: 119) state that high numbers of traveller children are not registered at a school and if they do attend, they experience high levels of under achievement.

There are however, some recognised examples of good practice evident in parts of the country. In Haringey, community social workers play a positive role in promoting a positive educational experience for the children of Travellers, Gypsies and Roma families. Here, social workers have adopted a community social work model to ensure that these children can access education and achieve academically, and they promote positive cultural role models (Davis 2010).

The community model of social work has been recognised as being one of the most successful ways of working with marginalised Gypsy communities (Schuringa 2005; Rorke and Wilkens 2006). The main focus of this model of intervention is to move from 'the culture of poverty' towards 'the culture of development', and the approach has been described by Leida Schuringa, who has more than 10 years of experience researching, training, and working with Roma, as establishing mechanisms for mobilising community resources, in order to facilitate community problem solving from the bottom-up. Here, the Roma are seen as subjects who can fully participate in producing change, and not as passive objects of support from others, as reflected in top-down approaches. They key aim is to build on the strengths of the community and work in partnership in an emancipator way. One of the most influential organisations in Europe that, for almost 20 years, has helped to build better futures for European Roma is the Open Society Institute (OSI). Principles underpinning the work of the OSI are influenced by community models of practice that focus on working with Roma to help them mobilise their communities and help themselves. The aim was to move away from funding projects that neglect Romani involvement and partnership and that leave no worthwhile legacy or concrete lasting results. Instead there was emphasis on the inclusion of the Roma themselves in all aspects of project development, including monitoring and evaluating the success of developments.

Social work seems to be the 'ideal' profession to contribute to the abolition of inequality and discrimination against the Roma. First, because of its insights into people's everyday experiences, and second, because it has knowledge about working with marginalised social groups. However, despite this potential for working in a positive and anti-oppressive manner with Roma groups, intervention is not always constructive, positive or non-discriminatory. The Roma often describe their relationship with the personal social services as a 'paper relationship' that draws on bureaucratic measures to solve problems and seek change. There are also criticisms that intervention can be discriminatory reflected in much stricter controls regarding access to social benefits, a degree of indifference, and a tendency to 'victim blame' by seeing the Roma as perpetrators of their own misfortune (Urh 2009) In this respect social workers can be involved in reinforcing racist practices and procedures rather than challenging them.

Among the Roma there are also levels of fear and distrust regarding social work intervention, and the view that one of their key roles is to take away Gypsy children. In this respect social workers need to build up a level of trust when working with Roma families so that they do not fear contact with the social work profession. Social workers need to be culturally aware and act as advocates for Gypsies and travellers, defending and supporting them, and fighting to enhance their lives and their civil and social rights. The goal of cultural advocacy is to strengthen marginalised minority ethnic communities and to create the space to encourage and promote their emancipation. Cultural advocates understand and respect cultural differences and the varied experiences of minority communities, and can serve as mediators between groups with different cultures. They can speak out against repression and marginalisation and give voice to the often unheard views and experiences of minority ethnic groups.

Across Europe the failings of social work in responding effectively to the needs of the Roma is linked to the fact that anti-racist perspectives in social work have not been part of the curriculum in social work educational settings, which is particularly true of Eastern European countries. When, in 2002, at the first Slovenian Congress of Social Work, a Slovenian social worker showed photographs depicting measurements of the Roma for the size of their skull and other body parts that the Nazi's used to justify genocide, the audience did not react. A failure to recognise the racism inherent in these depictions, and to challenge them effectively, continues to promote the Roma as a problem for society rather than acknowledging the ways they have been persecuted and discriminated against. Instead, public discourse continues to reflect stereotypical and discriminatory views that portray the Roma as living off hard-earned tax payer's money, stealing from farmers, expecting the state to provide a living for them and ignoring planning restrictions.

When Slovenia was part of the Yugoslav republic and under communist rule, before gaining its independence, social work was strongly subordinated to social policy, and talking about discrimination and social inequality was prohibited as it was believed that, under political rule in these countries, social justice and equality had been achieved. In this respect discussions regarding the status of minority ethnic communities was seen as unnecessary. A further problem was that social work education did not involve critical reflection regarding elements of prejudice and discrimination, and social workers were also heavily influenced by a public discourse that discriminated against the Roma, and presented mythological images of 'typical' Gypsies. In the absence of any critical and theoretical discourse in the professional literature regarding social work with Roma families and communities, social workers looked for other existing ('romological') literature that offered a romanticised view of the Roma, presenting them as a homogeneous group with a common origin, culture and other set characteristics, while also portrayed them as inherently aggressive, dirty and lazy.

Conclusion

The absence of anti-racist social work theory in social work education settings, results in conscious and unconscious racist practises being implemented in social work practice. Much research has revealed that social work intervention with Roma groups is often culturally insensitive and fails to achieve outcomes that will respond to the needs of and improve the lives of the Roma minority. Instead, social work practice can reinforce the pathologisation and marginalisation of this population (Urh 2011).

A critical historical exploration reveals that the Roma have always experienced high levels of direct and indirect racism, and that this persists today, with widespread discriminatory practices and policies in place across Europe. Social work could play a key role in challenging discrimination and countering the effects of racist policies, practices and procedures, but in order to do so, a commitment to anti-racism is key. Social workers need an awareness of the historical experiences of the Roma to better understand their lives and experiences today and their distrust of state and welfare professionals who have often contributed to their persecution and exclusion. Understanding the dynamics of racism, as well as the lives and experiences of the Roma will enable social workers to work with them in a sensitive, informed and non-discriminatory manner, and in a way that does not collude with and reproduce oppression and persecution (Thompson 2001; Jones 2002; Dominelli 2007). Also, as European countries become more multicultural there is an increasing need for social workers to practice with cultural competence and to ensure that they can meet the needs of groups and families from diverse ethnic and cultural backgrounds. However, in order to ensure this is the case, there is a need for an increase in literature in the field, particularly in East European countries.

Suggested further reading

Barany, Z. D. (2002) *The East European Gypsies: regime change, marginality, and ethnopolitics,* Cambridge, New York: Cambridge University Press.

Hawes, D. and Perez, B. (1996) *The Gypsy and the state,* 2nd edn, Bristol: Policy Press.

Schuringa, L. (2005) *Community work and Roma inclusion,* Utrecht: Spolu International Foundation.

SEVEN

In defence of multiculturalism?

Gareth Jenkins

The Professional Capabilities Framework (PCF) domain 8 requires that social workers are aware of changing social contexts. Many social workers writing about anti-racist practice in the 1980s would have followed Sivanandan's (1982) critique of local authority 'multiculturalism'. Sivanandan's case was that too often policies of multiculturalism were reduced to a celebration of 'steel-bands, samosas and saris' while institutional and structural racism was ignored. However, from the perspective of 2013 the attack on multiculturalism has shifted the political terrain. Multiculturalism is being used as a code word by politicians to attack migration and the presence of minority communities in Britain itself – themes that Jenkins addresses in this chapter.

Introduction

The constantly repeated message is that multiculturalism has 'failed'. According to politicians and pundits, it has allowed 'tolerance of diversity to harden into the effective isolation of communities, in which some people think separate values ought to apply' (Phillips 2005); it has not succeeded in instilling belief in 'freedom of speech, freedom of worship, democracy, the rule of law, equal rights regardless of race, sex or sexuality' (Cameron 2011c); and the consequences are social fracturing in which Islamist terrorism can grow or, more recently, inner-city rioting can erupt.

The racism, implied or explicit, towards Muslims that anti-multiculturalism has given voice to has now been joined by a new enemy: young working class people (Jones 2011). This should alert us to a larger context: the attack on multiculturalism is not restricted to attacks on a particular ethnic and cultural minority. The venom aimed at a 'feral underclass', the new dispossessed on inner-city estates, is inseparable from the project that sees disciplining those on the receiving end of austerity (whatever their cultural background) into acceptance of neoliberalism as the only way in which society can be run. It is not just minorities that are affected (through discrimination or racism, including racist immigration controls). The mass of ordinary working people must be made to accept that there is no alternative and that their anger and resentment must be directed, where possible, at 'outsiders' for taking the limited resources that would (apparently) otherwise go to them. The defence of multiculturalism therefore has to involve more than defending cultural plurality. The broader struggle to resist racism has also to challenge the 'naturalness' of neoliberal economic policy.

As Peter Hain MP has put it, the attacks on multiculturalism allow far-right organizations to feed off:

> mounting popular grievances caused by the banking crisis, the economic recession and savage cuts in public services and jobs. … [S]lashing public spending is making our poorest communities even poorer, in turn providing easy targets for those who cannot get jobs or houses to scapegoat people of a different race or faith. This divide-and-rule politics has always been a trademark of the right. (Hain 201: 9)

The defence of multiculturalism, then, is inseparable from resisting the broader economic and social attacks on those at the bottom of society, whatever their cultural background, and from ensuring that anger is not diverted along race or cultural lines. It also involves understanding why it is in the interests of the vast majority to defend multiculturalism.

This chapter aims to set the debate about multiculturalism within the context of class divided societies. This is mainly because of the way in which the right has come to use culture as its preferred racist weapon. However, it is also to address the fault lines in multicultural theory, which also depends on a culturalist analysis of society (though naturally with better intentions). For if the right is desperate to use culture to obscure class (in the emphasis that irrespective of class 'we' all hold common values), multiculturalist theorists have largely underplayed (if not ignored) the importance of class. To see society as possessing a plurality of cultures is, of course, an advance on pretending that it is monocultural – it is a way of highlighting the necessity for a broader and more inclusive society. But what will be argued here is the *limitation* of seeing society as being defined primarily in cultural terms, as opposed to starting from the historical and material circumstances that shape it.

Culture – whose culture?

Defence of 'our way of life' is home territory for the right. It allows racism to be respectably clothed in cultural, rather than biological, terms – as demonstrated in Margaret Thatcher's notorious assertion in 1978 that British people were 'really rather afraid that this country might be swamped by people of a different culture' (Thatcher 1978). This allowed her to appeal to racist feeling without openly endorsing it. What this 'new racism', as Barker and Beezer [[not in Bibliog.]]noted a few years later, was to foreground the 'notion of culture and tradition'. Central to its way of thinking is the idea that a 'community is its culture, its way of life and its traditions. To break these is to shatter the community' (1983: 125).[1] This culturalisation of racism has remained central ever since – as has the notion that at risk is 'our way of life'.

The purpose of this abstraction of culture from the economic and social forces that have created and shaped it is to attempt to suggest a (national) collectivity that transcends divisions based on income, status and power. Such 'essentialisation' is false in a number of ways – for example, in its attempt to freeze-frame what is always a historically limited snapshot of 'all the characteristic activities and interests of a People' (Eliot 1948: 31).[2] In traditional society, culture may have been relatively unchanging. However, it is not in modern society, since the restless dynamism of capitalism constantly transforms production and social relations. Inward migration, trade, encounters with other societies have all altered, and continue to alter, what passes for 'English/British' culture. So essentialisation is false in another, more profound, way. For it is possible to accept this process as a constant updating of culture (chicken tikka masala replacing fish and chips as the national dish – all part of some New Labour 'cool Britannia') and still essentialise it. A culture is said to possess transhistorical values, even if they are manifested through history, because they characterise a 'people' (as if a people were some entity that entered history ready formed rather than being its product and as if its 'values' did not reflect an ongoing state of struggle, with one part of society constantly seeking to impose ideas about how life should be on another part of society and constantly finding these resisted or modified). So belief in 'freedom of speech, freedom of worship, democracy, the rule of law, equal rights regardless of race, sex or sexuality' (which David Cameron [2011c] offered as characteristic of 'our' culture when he attacked multiculturalism) is hardly something that has always existed. Historically, it was bitterly rejected by the ruling class in the past, which had to be forced into accepting it (or accepting aspects of it) consequent on a bitter fight from below by subordinate classes – a fight that goes all the way from the English revolution of the seventeenth century to votes for women in the 20th century. And it is not a settled question: what a neoliberal society means by the value of democracy is arguably, at least in terms of content, very different from that held in a social democratic welfarist society. Finally, of course, the fight to win this set of beliefs was not peculiarly British: it was part of a broader movement that transcended national boundaries – which rather makes the point that the best part of any culture is what is most international in origin and outlook.

'Our' culture, conceived in an essentialist way, requires its 'other' – an equally essentialised, but demonised culture against which to set it. If the antagonism is not between classes then it has to be between cultures, with a Muslim (and Islamic) identity acting to fulfil this opposing role. The power of this 'other' resides, of course, in the fact that it *must* be 'imaginary' – it *cannot* correspond to reality. Cultural critics, like Aijaz Ahmad, have drawn attention to how ungrounded this supposed unitary Muslim identity is at the global level:

> For most, being a Muslim mainly signifies the fact of birth in a Muslim family, at best a Muslim sub-culture within a wider national culture (Egyptian, Nigerian, Lebanese or whatever); while religion, even when observed, is lived as one of the many ingredients in one's complex social identity, which is always specific, and hence deeply tied to language, region, custom, class, and so on; religious observance, if any, remains largely local and personal. This subcultural Muslimness itself is contextual, deeply shaped by history, geography, politics, the larger multi-religious milieu, myriad rhythms of material life. (Ahmad 2007: 1)

And Cantle has made much the same point about Muslims in Britain. He argues that 'there is often as much "difference" within each identifiable group as between them':

> The present focus on the Muslim community ... generally assumes a high level of internal coherence and commonality, whilst in practice there is a huge variety in ethno-cultural characteristics, cultural heritage, theological traditions, kinship patterns and organization – and political views. (2008: 87)

To which we might add that more crucially there are splits along class lines – of greater importance than any commonality of culture. The modern Conservative Party may wish to show its inclusivity by having a Muslim chairperson, but the presence of a successful business woman is more likely to reassure the aspiring Muslim shopkeeper than appeal to Muslims who work in factories or on the buses, alongside non-Muslims.

The 'huge variety' referred to by Cantle is collapsed into particular details that are then constructed into a stereotyped image of Muslim culture. One striking example of this is the headscarf worn by some but by no means all Muslim women (see Penketh, Chapter Eight, this volume). It is made into the sign of a 'backward' culture and of a male oppression said to be inherent in Islam – to be constructed as the polar opposite of advanced Western culture and its liberated treatment of women, in the name of which intervention in Muslim countries (such as Afghanistan) or legal restriction on its public wearing (as in France) can then be justified. It goes without saying that this stereotyping ignores the real lives of Muslim women and their reasons for wearing, or not wearing, a headscarf (or other form of face covering). In particular, it manages to misrecognise the choice made by some young Muslim women to wear a head covering as one that cannot be free because of the oppressive culture surrounding them (a condescending argument never deployed in respect of young non-Muslim women's 'choice' of clothing and make-up). Interestingly, the stated reason for wearing a head or face covering seems frequently to do as much with a very 'Western' right of an individual woman to wear what she likes as to do with an assertion of religious identity – an interesting example of how cultures blend. A young Muslim woman who wears a head covering is also likely to be a facebook user, to talk in English that is identical with her non-Muslim peers, and to share many of their tastes in popular entertainment – as even casual observation of students leaving their local sixth form centre in a multicultural area can confirm.

The 'advantage' of essentialising cultures in this fashion is that discrimination and racism can be turned inside out. 'Their' culture becomes the reason why people who adhere to it, as opposed to 'our' culture, can be subjected to what would otherwise be clearly racist persecution. As Pitcher puts it, 'By reconstituting tolerance as the ethical property of a multicultural nation, it becomes possible to inoculate exclusionary practices against the charge of racism' (2009: 59). Racism in defence of a monoculture is made to seem 'non-racism' in defence of the toleration of diversity said to be the essence of the British 'way of life'.

Self-segregation: fact or fiction?

However, if skin (in biological racism) were destiny, so too is culture: those belonging to one culture 'naturally' tend to prefer their own over those belonging to others. As Goodhart put it in *Discomfort of Strangers*, discussing what he claims is 'the instinct to favour our own': 'we feel more comfortable with, and are readier to share with and sacrifice for, those with whom we have shared histories and similar values' (2004). So although we may (and indeed *should*) sympathise with outsiders and be tolerant of diversity, there are limits, necessarily and naturally, as to how far this can go: sharing welfare with 'stranger citizens' is 'more smoothly and generously negotiated if we can take for granted a limited set of common values and assumptions' (2004: 65). At the same time, if welfare is 'naturally' limited in relation to demand (which is the whole basis of neoliberal economics) then resentment towards 'outside' claimants is also 'natural' (if regrettable). This plays to the view that the host community (crucially, the white working-class) inevitably tends towards racism and downplays the idea of a multiracial and multicultural working-class that might be able to fight for better welfare all round.[3]

If multiculturalism represents an attempt to go against a natural tendency within 'our' culture to look after our own, it is also, and rather contradictorily, responsible for not stopping other cultures from doing the same. 'We' look after each other; 'they' do not integrate – indeed, such communities are increasingly prone, it is claimed, to self-separation. Trevor Phillips, then head of the now defunct Commission for Racial Equality under Labour, warned apocalyptically in 2005 that we were 'sleepwalking our way to segregation' by allowing 'tolerance of diversity to harden into the effective isolation of communities, in which some people think separate values ought to apply' (2005).[4]

Even Cantle, who, as we saw earlier, was not prepared to 'essentialise' Muslims, accepts the myth of self-segregation:

> The geographic concentration of the BME [Black and Minority Ethnic] community has … changed little over the last 40 years or so and has actually been reinforced by the recent trends. This clearly has an impact on many areas of daily life, particularly schooling, employment and leisure patterns. … In Britain it had been assumed that segregated areas were gradually being broken down' but the 2001 riots showed 'increasing evidence of 'parallel lives', in which physical separation of different communities

> was compounded by a complete separation in education, employment and in other spheres. (2008: 14, 76)

Yet, according to Finney and Simpson's scrupulous statistical and conceptual analysis, the trend is in the opposite direction – *away* from segregation and *towards* integration. Minority ethnic young people are more, not less, likely to have mixed-ethnicity friendships (and this is true at the most intimate level: 'Asian Muslims, Sikhs and Hindus all marry out of their own groups just as often as do White Christians' [Finney and Simpson 2009: 99]); that minorities wish to live in mixed neighbourhoods; that a town like Bradford is not ghettoised but is ethnically mixed, just like the rest of Britain; and that there is greater ethnic mixing in neighbourhoods across the country as a whole (Finney and Simpson 2009: 183–7). In addition, where there are 'concentrations' of minorities, this reflects not self-segregation, but lack of resources, poverty and racism. Thus, 'segregated schools' reflect not minority ethnic choice but the fact that the desire for mixed schools is not being met for other reasons (resources, educational policy) (Finney and Simpson 2009: 104–8). Finney and Simpson also destroy the 'reverse' myth to 'self-segregation' – that of 'white flight'. Far from its being the case that only white people are moving out of neighbourhoods with a high proportion of minority ethnic groups, the reality is that both 'white and minority groups are moving in the same direction and at the same rate' (Finney and Simpson 2009: 191).

The importance of Finney and Simpson's rebuttal of 'self-segregation' is that it pays proper attention to the way in which economic and social factors, rather than culture, determine patterns of integration or separation. To focus on a supposed self-segregation is to evade discussion on how resources might be increased for the benefit of all and to avoid racism dividing communities. It plays to the idea that the problem lies in the cultural *behaviour* of minorities. From this it is a short step to implying that they *invite* the very discrimination that is inflicted on them. What then becomes required of them is 'the impossible task of remedying the negative effects of their own racialisation' (Pitcher 2009: 90–1).

If minorities are in part to blame for their own fate, then racists are also partly let off the hook. Or, to put it another way, minorities can only be protected if the majority is seen as having legitimate concerns that need addressing to stop them becoming the exclusive property of the far-right. These revolve round 'conflicts that have arisen as a result of pressure on hard-pressed local services': 'Deriding the concerns about migration of the host community (both black and white citizens) is not sufficient. True, such concerns have often been used to underpin racist sentiment, but if change is to occur, difficult areas need to be tackled, rather than simply avoided' (Cantle 2008: 23).[5] The implication is the need to ration welfare in the context of a neoliberal Malthusian mismatch between population growth and resources. If overpopulation is the problem in the overconsuming Western world, then so too must immigration be, difficult though that is to 'de-couple' from 'race issues' (Cantle 2008: 23–4).

Multiculturalism and the perils of essentialism

Central to the multiculturalist critique is the inadequacy of the individual rights framework characteristic of liberal–democratic society. These rights may proclaim themselves as universal but are in fact culturally particularistic: they enshrine the value-system of the majority culture (in Western liberal–democratic societies) and fail to allow, if not actively discriminate against, the value-systems of other cultures (within these societies). True equality requires more than respect of a person's individual rights (the right of someone from a minority ethnic community to the same kind of job as anyone else); it requires social recognition of that person's right to live according to their culture even where this clashes with majority sanctioned rules (the classic example is the right of a Sikh man when driving a motor bike to wear the turban prescribed by his faith instead of the crash helmet prescribed by law). What this points to is the acceptance in a multicultural society of not just individual rights, applied universally, but group rights, reflecting the demands of culturally defined communities within society. Without this, minority cultures suffer from discrimination because they are not recognised as being of equal worth with the majority culture. Society, therefore, needs to be understood as no longer culturally homogeneous and therefore purely individual-rights based. As a leading theorist of multiculturalism has put it, modern society is both 'a community of citizens' and 'a community of communities' (Parekh 2006:ix; Modood 2007). So while the state has to be 'colour-blind' as far as the enforcement of individual rights are concerned, it also has to be 'culture-aware' in terms of the way it operates at the national and local level if it is to avoid prejudiciously favouring (if only unconsciously) the dominant ('white') culture.

However, this notion of group rights has been criticised as being radically in conflict with, rather than as complementing, individual legal, political and welfare rights (Barry 2001). A group might insist on its members conforming to a cultural norm from which one of its members might wish to break. The right of an individual to exercise self-determination comes up against the right of a cultural group to live according to practices that do not allow for individual rights. This poses an insoluble contradiction. Either universal values obtain (all human beings have the right to determine their actions) – in which case, cultures have no overriding 'rights' – or the values of a culture override the rights of an individual within it and no one from outside that culture has the right to intervene in the name of universal rights (to do so would be to act oppressively towards that culture). Multiculturalism thus stands accused of incoherence and relativism.[6]

However valid the accusation, the fact remains that multiculturalist theory has to fall back on an approach to culture that is not so different from that of the monoculturalist. The monoculturalist says that a society is its culture; the multiculturalist, that it is its cultures. The monoculturalist demands that 'our' culture is irreducible; the multiculturalist has to concede that minority cultures are also irreducible (unless there is some irreducible core the value of understanding society primarily in cultural terms makes little sense – one would have to concede the priority of non-cultural factors). The risk therefore is that multiculturalists fall into the same essentialising trap as monoculturalists. Multiculturalists are not unaware of this dilemma. Modood, for example, rejects the view that 'cultures are discrete, frozen in time, impervious to external influences, homogeneous and without internal dissent' and the view that 'group membership falsely implies the existence of some shared essential characteristics' (2007: 89). He is clearly unhappy with the prospect of dissolving society into a collection of discrete, non-communicating monocultures. However, he is also clearly worried about where this argument about heterogeneity within cultures takes him. If you make culture too internally differentiated, then can one talk of a culture at all? It would cease to operate at the 'deep' level (of overall shaping) and become no more than one perhaps very subordinate element of a person's individual identity. He is led, therefore, to reject the view that there is 'something false, fictitious and illegitimate about appeals to culture, ethnicity and so on …' (2007: 90). Groups do have, for him, a reality no less than that of individuals.

Modood tries to resolve the contradiction between seeing culture as essentialist and seeing it as no more than one element in a story we create about ourselves by resorting to the concept of 'family resemblances' (2007: 95–8). However much they differ in some respects, members of a cultural group share affinities that bind them together:

> The category 'Muslim' ... is as internally diverse as 'Christian' or 'Belgian' or 'middle-class', or any other category helpful in ordering our understanding of contemporary Europe; but just as diversity does not lead to an abandonment of social concepts in general, so with that of 'Muslim'. (Modood 2003: 100)

Whether this analogy with the (biological) family gives culture anymore of an objective basis is open to question. Compare this with arguments about the reality of class, where the objective factor (class as a relationship to the means of production) is not dependent on the subjective factor (the degree to which an individual sees him or herself as a member of a class).

Nevertheless, this attempt to see culture as both having a distinctive reality and being internally diverse does permit Modood to escape the idea of multiculturalist society being a collection of separate, incomprehending cultures. Fruitful interaction between cultures is also at the heart of Parekh's rejection of essentialism and of the notion that cultures are self-contained. The shared 'outside' to culture is 'human nature' – one born of the interaction between human beings and nature, of the transformation of nature to satisfy human needs and of human beings' own self-transformation in the process (Parekh 2006). However, this interaction that defines our common humanity has been given rise to different cultures and so different understandings of what 'the good life' is. There is no one right way of doing things ('human nature' is culturally shaped, not some false universal). Nevertheless, because all cultures stem from our shared species-given need to interact with the environment human beings 'are able to take a critical view of it and rise above it in varying degrees.' (Parekh 2006: 158). This depends on the degree to which any culture offers 'critical resources', either because internally the culture generates the capacity to self-reflection or because of familiarity with other cultures. So although the right to difference, the right to live one's life according to one's culture, should be respected, cultures do necessarily interact, making it possible for them to learn from each other.

A solid foundation?

Beyond the ability to learn from one another through cultural interaction, it is not clear how far this takes us. Mutual respect can involve a kind of diplomatic cover for what works pragmatically – as in Parekh's discussion of 'Asian values' (a peculiarly essentialist formula to cover very diverse societies and cultures). The societies that practise such values are said to 'wish to pursue such collective goals as social harmony and cohesion', with greater restrictions on 'individual freedoms than is common in liberal societies'. But that, Parekh, reassures us 'is not an argument against them' (2006: 139). One wonders whose perspective he is adopting here – certainly not those within Asian societies who might see such 'collective goals' as ideological cover for economic and social repression. Respect here seems to mean deferring to whatever works.

More broadly, cultural interaction seems designed to bring about 'just recognition and a just share of economic and political power' (Parekh 2006: 343) – but only within the existing social and political framework that constitutes the state as it is. So multiculturalism on this basis has no interest in transcending the national culture – only in creating a new synthesis in which different cultures are incorporated. As Modood puts it:

> A sense of belonging to one's country is necessary to make a success of a multicultural society. Not assimilation into an undifferentiated national identity; that is unrealistic and oppressive as a policy. An inclusive national identity is respectful of and builds upon the identities that people value and does not trample upon them. Simultaneously respecting difference and inculcating Britishness is not a naïve hope but something that is happening (2007: 150)

So a monocultural concept of citizenship is to be replaced by a multicultural one, one kind of Britishness by another. Modood argues that 'multiculturalists, and the left in general, have been hesitant about embracing our national identity and allying it with progressive politics' but that the 'reaffirming of this plural, changing, inclusive British identity [...] is critical to isolating and defeating extremism' (2007: 150).[7] This slightly embarrassed formulation seems very close to Cantle's demand about not 'deriding the concerns about migration of the host community' in that it is arguing that 'Britishness', customarily thought of as the property of the right (and far right), can be made progressive – that there is something in 'Britishness' (that 'imaginary container of belonging expressing an anxious demand for social conformity' [Pitcher 2009: 67]) that can be made 'ours'. Yet, as we saw earlier, 'Britishness' can now be made to look inclusive of tolerance and diversity by the very people who also demonise Muslims and push for ever tighter immigration restrictions. For multiculturalists to meet this half way (by embracing national identity) can only tie minorities to the very order that uses racism to marginalise and exclude them.

Harnessing multiculturalism to the flag can only weaken and destroy the anti-racist content of multiculturalism. A similar critique, about the absorption of multiculturalism into the existing structures of society, has been made by Sivanandan (1990) and his co-thinkers at the Institute of Race Relations. The right's attempt, under Thatcherism, to assert a homogeneous British or English culture was one half of the official response; the other half, Kundnani argues, 'was an attempt to soften the sharp edges of black politics through official multiculturalist policies that focused on managing the "ethnic identity" of different communities.' Though multiculturalism was essential 'for the survival of non-white communities', the policies implemented in the period 'were a mode of control rather than a line of defence'. These entailed taking African-Caribbean and Asian cultures off the streets, where they had been politicised and rebellious, and putting them 'in the council chamber, in the classroom and on television, where they could be institutionalized, managed and commodified' (2007: 44). Black culture ceased to be something to be acted on but to be 'celebrated':

> The method for achieving this was the separation of different ethnic groups into distinct cultural blocs, to be managed by a new cadre of ethnically defined 'community leaders', and the rethinking of race relations in terms of a view of cultural identity that was rigid, closed and almost biological; all of which aimed at adapting what were now called 'ethnic communities' to the British body politic in an unthreatening way and preventing any one group's militancy from infecting the others. (Kundanani 2007: 45)

Kundnani is dismissive of what this meant for the 'culture' taught in schools, 'based on hackneyed formulae of steel bands, samosas and saris' and argues that this meant a 'desiccated' view of ethnic identity:

> genuine education about other people, their histories and their struggles, was replaced with the grim essentialism of identity politics, as each group competed for 'ethnic recognition' in the classroom. ... [T]he error of multiculturalist policies was to confuse anti-racism with a superficial sort of cultural recognition. (2007: 46)

Or as Sivanandan put it much earlier:

> The ensuing scramble for government favours and government grants (channelled through local authorities) on the basis of specific ethnic needs and problems served, on the one hand, to deepen ethnic differences and foster ethnic rivalry and, on the other, to widen the definition of ethnicity to include a variety of national and religious groups – Chinese, Cypriots, Greeks, Turks, Irish, Italians, Jews, Moslems, Sikhs – till the term became meaningless (except as a means of getting funds). (1990: 94)

This critique of a competitive scramble for resources has also been made by radical egalitarians – though on a different basis. Barry (2001), for example, has sought to argue that the multiculturalist case for group rights is a step backwards. For him, the resurrection of what he sees as special rights for some is a regression to the pre-Enlightenment thinking that characterized the *ancien régime* in France. The great advance that the Enlightenment brought was a concept of citizenship:

> there should be only one status of citizen (no estates or castes), so that everybody enjoys the same legal and political rights. These rights should be assigned to individual citizens, with no special rights (or disabilities) accorded to some and not others on the basis of group membership. (Barry 2001: 9)

In the course of the 19th and 20th centuries legal and political were extended to cover economic and social rights. Thus enlightenment universalism was strengthened, even though practice often falls short of the ideal and inequality has massively increased under neoliberalism.

Multiculturalism, for Barry, is therefore either redundant – there is nothing it can deliver that egalitarian redistributionism cannot by way of eliminating discrimination – or it is harmful (because it is, ultimately, 'not uncongenial to the reactionary right' [Barry 2001: 11]). The harm it can cause follows from its diversion of political effort away from universalistic goals: '… multiculturalism may very well destroy the conditions for putting together a coalition in favour of across-the-board equalization of opportunities and resources'. It may, in other words, by not appealing to what groups have in common but by appealing to what differentiates them, destroy unity of action. He gives the example of money being set aside for minority cultural activities:

> This sets the stage for a struggle between ethnocultural entrepreneurs for a share of the funds, so that efforts that

> might have been devoted to more broad-based causes are dissipated in turf wars.... [T]his kind of particularistic focus will ... tend to make cultural minorities weak partners in endeavours to redistribute income from rich to poor across the board ... (Barry 2001: 325)

So for a strand of anti-racist and radical egalitarian thought, the critique is not, as mainstream anti-multiculturalists would have it, that multiculturalism has gone too far, but that it has not gone far enough: it can neither confront racism nor tackle inequality in any fundamental way.

Culture and class

Parekh's (2006) attempt to root culture in humanity's metabolic relationship with nature as a way of understanding what different cultures have in common is essentially correct. However, it remains abstract. Implied, but never made explicit or concrete, is the centrality of labour in the transformation of nature to satisfy need and therefore humanity's self-transformation. Yet without labour the relationship between the universal (what all cultures have in common) and the particular (why cultures are different) is inexplicable. Here we need to make a distinction between two aspects of labour. On the one hand, culture is the accumulation of everything that human beings have been able to learn about nature and about themselves in the long process of transforming nature and themselves through labour – which allows cultures from different periods to learn from their predecessors as the relationship to nature changes. On the other hand, culture has always been culture under the sway of a dominant class living off the labour of the exploited and oppressed. So consideration of any particular culture (the 'outside' from which we are able to evaluate it) needs to recognise this double, contradictory aspect of any culture as containing both emancipatory and oppressive elements.

When we talk about contemporary multicultural society, we need to keep this in mind. All its cultures are, to one degree or another, cultures profoundly shaped by the priorities of the capitalist mode of production, whatever their residual features either from pre-capitalist society or from societies marked by earlier phases of capitalist development. As the vast majority, whatever their cultural identity, face the need to sell their labour power in order to live they come under the sway of the dominant ideas of the system. Cultural differences, therefore, become less important – in theory. But in the process of homogenisation the remaining markers of difference are seized upon. Anti-multiculturalists use them to suggest the superiority of 'our' culture over 'theirs'. Yet versions of what is said to symbolise absolute difference can be found in 'Western' ways of life that capitalism itself has undermined in the course of historical development. So, for example, 'backward' assumptions about gender roles are often very similar to those that characterised the lives of most British people two or three generations ago – and have by no means disappeared. Capitalism by its nature continuously undermines any fixity in cultural assumptions.

Does that mean difference will eventually disappear under capitalism (or indeed that the globalisation of capitalist culture is desirable)? One obvious point is that the system perpetually resurrects difference in order to divide (the 'creation' of cultural identity has been central to internecine strife in ex-Yugoslavia and in parts of Africa and the Middle East; and to stirring up racism across the EU). But, more importantly, as far as this argument is concerned, oppressed minorities have found in adherence to their cultures 'the heart of a heartless world' (Marx 1975: 244) – something that gives meaning in a meaningless world, that mends the distortion brought into their lives by poverty and racism. Difference in this instance acts as a way of coping with alienation – not to support the right to cultural difference is to collude in the way the system operates, however much attacking cultural difference may call itself intervention in the name of women's rights or Enlightenment values.

However, the fact that capitalism imposes a shared exploitation on workers belonging to all cultures means that workers who see themselves as belonging to different cultures can also share a common resistance to exploitation. That has two effects: one is that alternatives open up within a minority culture: its conservative leadership is open to challenge from more outward looking members of the cultural group as to what is, or is not, culturally acceptable. The second is there is greater participation in the general struggles that workers wage (ethnic-minority trade-union participation is equal if not better than the average). However, crucially, the degree to which these forms of struggle engage with, and champion, the defence of multiculturalism and anti-racism, the stronger the trust that cultural minorities have that their rights are being recognised and respected.

Thinking through the class basis of culture offers a way forward in this debate. For if society is defined primarily in terms of culture (a 'white' majority culture), then what counts most is the common cultural allegiance uniting employer and worker. For multiculturalists to accept the same premise about how society is primarily defined (even though they wish to valorise minority cultures), then it is difficult to see how the dominant cultural allegiance can be modified. The only strategy is to educate whites out of their prejudices towards other cultures such that there is 'an appreciation by the white majority of the value of non-European traditions' (Callinicos 1993: 11).

However, appreciation, because unrooted in class interest, remains a purely moral affair: culture is a kind of 'fate from which those it embraces cannot escape' (Callinicos 1993: 33) The best to be hoped for is a kind of mutual acceptance in which cultural difference is inescapable. This explains why the most that can be hoped for is a new kind of Britishness: society cannot be fundamentally reorganised, there can only be a rearrangement of aspects of its structure.

Radical egalitarians, like Barry (2001), do not necessarily fare any better. 'Group rights' may well be problematic in the way multiculturalists conceptualise them. It is also problematic to assume that society really is or can be made to run on Enlightenment principles, given the fact that the reality of capitalism, with capitalists asserting their 'group right' (to exploit) and workers asserting their 'group right' (to resist) is quite at odds with the notion of its being run on an individual rights basis. So, however much the modern state might in theory be based on the idea of all citizens being equal, matters have always been different. Yet Barry appears unable to see beyond this model. At the same time, a rather different definition of a 'group' – one that relies not on culture but on the relationship to capital – provides us with the possibility of there being a class in society that has the potential to solve problems of inequality and injustice that does not depend on the existing structures of the state but on its own struggles.

We have already noted the tendency of cultures to 'leak' into one another – particularly because of the way the modern economy has developed over the last few centuries. We have also noted the way in which capitalism both annihilates cultural difference and resurrects it. Central to capitalist culture is competition – including competition between workers over jobs and resources, with cultural division serving to create racism. However, since capitalism also pulls people together, particularly in the workplace (which is the least segregated area of existence, for all its other tensions and pressures), it also creates the potential for common struggle. The unity this can create not only makes for respect for cultural difference but also enriches the prospect for cultural mixing and fusion.[8]

Conceptualising culture in ways that do not recognise its material and historical roots is mistaken. Specific cultures rise and fall, depending on the mode of production in which they come to exist. But they are not simply class-dependent – they carry a progressive element that enlarges human self-realization in its increasing ability to shape the environment to suit human needs. It is wrong, therefore, simply to see Enlightenment values one-sidedly. They are, as multiculturalists have argued, often a justification for and naturalisation of power over other cultures (humanitarian intervention – including the defence of women's rights – as a cover for imperialist barbarity). However, they are also powerful instruments of rebellion and resistance that can be flung back at the oppressor (the great slave rebellion of Toussaint L'Ouverture is unthinkable without the French Revolution).

The same point (about not being one-sided) can be made about 'minority' cultures – it is wrong to demonise them but they are not going to be any less pulled between different social forces as the 'majority' culture. Of course, therefore, oppressive relationships will exist – but no more so than in the rest of society. More crucially, it is not for the 'majority culture' to do its own form of 'humanitarian intervention' and arrogate to itself the right to bring enlightenment (as, for example, is how the vast majority of 'secular progressives', in collusion with the racist state, behave in respect of what Muslim women in France are allowed to wear on their heads in public). It will be entirely a matter for Muslim women both to choose what they wear and to fight to overcome oppression in their own communities. Only by the collective changing of material circumstances are cultures themselves likely to evolve positively.

Finally, this takes us back to the question of universalism, over which multiculturalists and radical egalitarians are at odds. An understanding of culture based on class is, this chapter has argued, a way of solving the difficulties posed by multiculturalist theory. However, it is also an answer to the argument about universalism advanced by Barry as a criticism of multiculturalism. For if culture is understand in the contradictory way suggested above, as advancing humanity's ability to shape nature to satisfy need, while at the same time being distorted by class, then Enlightenment culture, though a huge advance in terms of human emancipation, remains partial and incomplete. A true multiculturalism – one that involves both a shared emancipatory culture and respect for diversity – lies in the struggle from below to resolve that contradictory legacy.

Conclusion

For social workers it is vital that we understand the context within which we work. Social workers overwhelmingly work with the poorest, the most marginalised, the most vulnerable and the most oppressed groups in society. Yet what we are now witnessing is a significant political attack on these groups of people. In populist media and political debates there is increasing venom directed at the poor, the disabled, the young and those from minority communities – especially those from Muslim backgrounds. Britain's economic ills are blamed on the costs of supporting benefit recipients and the 'lazy' and 'workshy'. Migrant communities are targeted because they, it is suggested, come to get access to 'our' services. Muslim communities are assumed to be dominated by non-workers and benefit claimants who, furthermore, don't share 'our' way of life but instead are aggressively trying to impose 'other', 'alien' life-styles that are incompatible with traditional British norms.

The blame for this perilous position, it is claimed, is essentially the post-war settlement: its over generous, unaffordable welfare and its 'politically correct' liberal multicultural acceptance of all cultural practices (at the expense of requiring minority communities to assimilate to the dominant norms) are at the root of our present problems.

The reality, of course, as I have argued above, is very much different.

Social work is a profession that is committed to diversity, an awareness of diversity and its complexities forms part of the PCF. However, social workers do not live in a vacuum. For social work students and practitioners the danger is that the barrage of media and political attacks on minority communities – the weight of amorphous 'public opinion' – will impact upon our thinking and practices. That we will start to assume that Muslim communities are a homogeneous block dominated by ideas that are conservative, threatening and 'not modern', when all the evidence is that British Muslims have a range of attitudes and opinions that are remarkably like the varied opinions and attitudes of other Britons. That we will see communities dominated by oppressive attitudes towards women – without recognising that such oppressive attitudes towards women dominate throughout Britain and across cultures. That we will see our intervention as, partially, structured by the need to change cultural practices, rather than by offering support to vulnerable communities. Communities who have the right to celebrate their own diversity, to choose their own clothing-styles, to meet their dietary requirements as they see fit and to adapt and change their cultural practices as part of a broader struggle to liberate humanity from a range of oppressions that dominate advanced capitalist societies.

Suggested Further Reading

Modood, T. (2007) *Multiculturalism: Themes for the 21st century*, Cambridge: Polity Press.

Parekh, B. (2006) *Rethinking multiculturalism, rev. edn,* Basingstoke: Palgrave Macmillan.
Pitcher, B. (2009) *The politics of multiculturalism*, Basingstoke: Palgrave Macmillan.

Notes

[1] The shift from biology to culture should not be exaggerated: culture can be made to seem just as 'natural' ('these people are inherently backward') as 'skin colour' and anti-Muslim prejudice is more often than not dislike of brown Asian skins

[2] Eliot's own characterisation of English culture now looks quaint: 'Derby Day, Henley Regatta, Cowes, the twelth of August, a cup final, the dog races, the dart board, Wensleydale cheese, boiled cabbage cut into sections, beetroot in vinegar, nineteenth century Gothic churches, and the music of Elgar' (Eliot 1948:p31). Orwell, writing at the beginning of World War II, fared little better in selecting what he took to be '*characteristic* fragments' of English civilization – 'the clatter of clogs in the Lancashire mill towns, the to-and-fro of lorries on the Great North Road, the queues outside the Labour Exchanges, the rattle of pin-tables in the Soho pubs, the old maids biking to Holy Communion through the mists of the autumn mornings' (Orwell 1971: 75) – though the old maids were resurrected in former Prime Minister John Major's vision of tradition.

[3] Owen Jones has some interesting comments on this 'racialisation' of the working class and the concomitant tendency to view the white working class as having a culture of its own (Jones 2011: 101–4).

[4] Phillips had earlier attacked Goodhart's arguments as 'jottings from the BNP leader's weblog'. Goodhart had described himself as 'a sensitive member of the liberal elite' and claimed that *Prospect*, the magazine in which his article originally appeared as starting 'from premises that are more liberal than conservative'. The convergence between Goodhart and Phillips suggests New Labour's shift towards a very neutered multiculturalism – tolerant of diversity only provided there was not too much of it, while pursuing a hard line on immigration and welfare restructuring: a kind of anti-multicultural multiculturalism or multiculturalism for hard-nosed liberals. (Both quotations can be found in *The Guardian*, 24 February 2004.)

[5] That fact 'native' black people might express concerns about migration does not make those concerns any the less racist – all it shows is how far the dominant ideas in society can affect oppressed sections of it.

[6] In practice, this is something of a strawman argument. Really existing multiculturalists do not condone morally dubious practices justified in cultural terms. Where they do have a problem is with the claim that the really existing Western powers (as opposed to the idealised West) have the right to intervene in the name of universalist, Enlightenment values – and ignore the rights of the people within these supposedly 'backward' cultures to address such practices for themselves.

[7] Modood is not alone here. Billy Bragg has also popularised this notion of snatching the flag back from the far-right racists.

[8] Sometimes this fusion of cultures is called interculturalism, rather than multiculturalism. As long as this protects the right of communities to live fairly separate lives (the example here is not Muslim communities but certain orthodox Jewish communities), then the term seems perfectly acceptable.

EIGHT

Social work and Islamophobia: identity formation among second and third generation Muslim women in north-west England

Laura Penketh

In this chapter Laura Penketh takes up the vexed question of Muslim women's right to wear the Hijab. It seems bizarre, at one level, that the right of women to wear a headscarf has become such a 'controversial issue' in Britain and across much of Europe. However, this has become a coded issue – of Islam's apparent incompatibility with Western norms and evidence, apparently, of women's particular oppression within Islam. Based on her research with women in the north of England Penketh addresses these issues by listening to the voice of Muslim women and their perspectives on Islamophobia and racism in modern Britain.

Introduction

Social work is a profession that is committed to the values of social justice, human rights, poverty alleviation and anti-oppression (International Federation of Social Work 2007) This requires that social work academics and practitioners are aware of the roots of oppression and its various changing forms (Thompson 1993), and that they can implement these insights, acting in ways that are anti-oppressive, anti-discriminatory and just (Penketh 2000).

Yet the problem for social workers is that these requirements are often difficult to operationalise in a shifting, complex and 'messy' world. How do we combine, for example, a commitment to anti-racism, cultural awareness, and opposition to women's oppression when working with families whose country of origin and cultural practices are different to our own? How do we avoid a vapid cultural relativism or, alternatively, a crude imposition of 'Western' values and modes of living onto service users who live their lives differently to ours? These are not abstract questions but complex and sensitive issues for all practitioners. These questions are made more difficult as a result of changing socio-political contexts and the many ways in which they impact on perceptions of culture, religion and 'race'.

This has clearly been the case over the past decade with regard to understandings and perceptions of Islam in Western Europe. The launch of the 'War on Terror' by the US Government in the aftermath of the attack on the Twin Towers on 11 September 2001, led to the questioning of the presence of both Islam and the Muslim presence in 'Western' societies; a development that included interventions by media commentators, academics and politicians, as well as right-wing political fanatics on the streets.

Academic concern has been framed by Samuel Huntington's (2002) thesis that the world is entering an era of 'cultural clashes' that will produce a series of 'clashes between civilisations'. The most important (and potentially catastrophic) clash is between an egalitarian, liberal and 'civilised' West and a 'pre-enlightenment' Islamic world. Much more crudely, the author, Martin Amis, has argued:

> There is a definite urge – don't you have it? – to say 'The Muslim community will have to suffer until it gets its house in order'. What sort of suffering? Not letting them travel. Deportation – further down the road. Curtailing of freedoms. Stop-searching people who look like they're from the Middle East or Pakistan. (cited in Kennedy 2007)

The attacks on Islam and the Muslim presence in Britain have also contained a gender dimension, with a particular focus on cultural attire worn by Muslim women, such as the hijab and the niqab. Generally, in Britain, such attire is associated with the oppression and subjugation of women.

While this argument is presented in crude terms in the popular press, in the quality press it has been expressed in seemingly more reasonable and liberal terms. Will Hutton, one of the leading left-liberal journalists in Britain, wrote in *The Observer* that:

> I find the hijab offensive; it is a symbol of female oppression and relegation of women to second-class status that offends universal principles of human rights. (Hutton 2005)

A letter in *The Guardian* in 2006 from a female reader stated '... we are a secular society. Veiled and covered women are a sign of male dominance, not a sign of faith' (Guardian 2006).

In *The Independent* Deborah Orr discussed what she felt on seeing a woman wearing the niqab on the streets of London:

> [This woman was] dressed outlandishly in an outfit that proclaimed her adherence to an ancient religious code that contradicts the law of this land in its denial of equality of opportunity to women and men. ... The values these outfits imply are repulsive and insulting to me. I find these clothes to be physical manifestations of outdated traditional practices ... that oppress and victimise women, sometimes in the most degrading, cruel and barbaric of ways. (Orr 2006)

Politicians were not slow to tread similar ground. In Britain Jack Straw, while Foreign Secretary, launched an attack on women who wear the niqab (a small piece of cloth that covers the lower half of the face and mouth). He suggested it was a barrier to integration and restricted understanding between communities, arguing that communication requires being able to see the face. He said he had felt uncomfortable when trying to speak to a niqab-wearing constituent who came to his political surgery for help and advice, saying 'I felt uneasy talking to someone I couldn't see' (Straw 2006), which does raise a question as to the validity of email, texting, telephones and the radio as a medium of communication

Similar themes appeared in France. In 2004, the then Prime Minister Jean-Pierre Ruffian supported the banning of young girls wearing the hijab in school. He claimed that 'the Islamic veil in particular harms our concept of the emancipation of women' (Livingstone and Raffarian 2004). By 2007, Dutch universities and German educational establishments were also considering a ban on the hijab (Modood 2007).

Laura Bush and Cherie Blair both spoke out in favour of the war in Afghanistan in terms that linked it to the liberation of women. Laura Bush argued:

> The brutal oppression of women is a central goal of the terrorists. ... Life under the Taliban is so hard and repressive, even small displays of joy are outlawed. ... Only the terrorists and the Taliban forbid education to women. Only the terrorists and the Taliban threaten to pull out women's

> fingernails for wearing nail polish. (Bush 2001, cited in German 2007;129)

At the start of the war in Afghanistan women were portrayed as passive victims awaiting liberation. Yet, as the first phase of the war came to an end and the Taliban were cleared from central Afghanistan, clashes appeared to emerge between different groups of women. There is evidence that, on one hand, indigenous women's organisations were looking for material benefits such as healthcare, education, and poverty alleviation for themselves and their families, while women's groups linked to international non-governmental organisations (NGOs) were more concerned with removing the burqa as a symbol of women's oppression (see Povey 2007).

The thrust of the argument from academics, journalists and politicians would seem to be that Islam is a particularly oppressive religion and that Muslim women are pressurised to wear the veil (hijab) or even the niqab at the instigation of husbands, fathers and/or religious leaders. They are perceived as passive, and 'objects' rather than subjects of their own destiny.

Interviews with Muslim women

As a committed anti-racist and an academic who has worked in the field of anti-racist social work for close to 20 years (see Penketh 2000), I became increasingly concerned at these dominant depictions of Muslim communities and Muslim women. After all, if they were correct, they had major implications for the interaction and work of social workers with Muslim women and families – work that would prioritise the liberation of Muslim women from oppressive relationships. However, my engagement with the Muslim community, particularly in Preston in the north-west of England, led me to question these perspectives and focus instead on evidence of a community that was suffering from extreme levels of racism and discrimination.

As noted in the introduction, the level of poverty faced by minority communities in Britain is significantly higher than that of the indigenous population, and there is much evidence of the disproportionate levels of disadvantage that the Muslim population face. This is reflected in the higher rates of ill health and disability that Muslim males and females experience, and discrimination in the field of housing and education (*Health Statistics Quarterly* 2007; EHRC 2011).

As well as these socio-economic indicators of discrimination there is also evidence of a great increase in racist harassment and violence against the Muslim community, commonly known as 'Islamophobia'. Although the term 'Islamophobia' has been contested, the definition adopted by the Runnymede Trust (1997), which is also accepted by the European Monitoring Centre on Racism and Xenophobia, places emphasis on negative and damaging stereotypes and assumptions that portray Islam as irrational and barbaric, as well as static, unresponsive to change and inferior to Western culture. In terms of gender, Muslim culture is portrayed as inherently sexist and oppressive. The rise in Islamophobia has also resulted in the socio-religious icons of Islam attaining unprecedented prominence and provoking high levels of hostility, which has had serious consequence for women who wear the hijab. For example, Muslim women have had the hijab forcibly pulled off, and are perceived as particularly weak and oppressed when wearing it.

For many Muslims, it was the events of 11 September 2001, that signified a growth in hostility towards them. For example, Salma Yaqoob stated that:

> The reactions to the events of 9/11 and the manner in which the entire community was portrayed as extremists created a palpable sense of fear among Muslims. (Murray and German 2003: 60)

Other terrorist attacks have had similar consequences and led to increased levels of racism. For example, the bombings in London on the 7 July 2005, led to a further increase in hate-crime incidents against Muslims and mosques, and a 47-year-old Muslim male who was visiting Britain was beaten to death in Nottingham by a gang of youths shouting anti-Islamic abuse (Dodd 2005a). The Muslim Council of Britain received more than 1,000 emails containing threats and messages of hate after the bombing, and across the country levels of abuse against Muslims rose (Dodd et al 2005).

The bungled terror attacks in London's West End on 29 June 2007, and at Glasgow airport the next day led to another spate of race attacks. In one incident a London imam was repeatedly punched in the face and had fingers jammed in his eyes, and a Glasgow newsagent's was gutted after a car was driven into it. At the time, Inayat Bunglawala, spokesman for the Muslim Council of Britain said:

> There has definitely been an upsurge in prejudice against Muslims. It appears people are taking out their frustrations about the failed attacks on Muslims. Some sections of the

> media have been very active in fomenting the prejudice. (Morris 2007: 4)

There was also evidence of a shift in the focus of discrimination from 'race' to religion. As Allen (2005: 50) observed:

> The socio-religious icons of Islam, and more specifically Muslims, have attained such prominence ... that they are almost immediately recognisable – and almost entirely negative and detrimental.

As a result of rising levels of discrimination substantial numbers of Muslims spoke of their plans to leave Britain. A Radio 4 programme broadcast on the 24 April 2007, claimed that two-thirds of British Muslims were considering leaving Britain after the 7 July bombings. One woman interviewed for the programme who was moving to Abu Dhabi said that in moving, she would not have to live in dread of the next excitable media story about her faith and the ensuing rise in race-hate crimes.

These events all point to a rise in what has become known as Islamophobia, a particular type of anti-Muslim racism. It is worth noting, however, that this is a contested concept that has come under attack from a range of sources. For example, the journalist Polly Toynbee dismissed talk of Islamophobia as a mere smokescreen to deflect valid and necessary criticism, and spoke of 'the lie to this imaginary Islamophobia' (cited in Allen 2005: 62). Arguments such as this are underpinned by the notion that religious belief cannot be equated with racism that is based on the negative ascription of various social traits or behaviours associated with supposed 'biological' features of particular 'races'. However, cultural differences (real or imagined) have always played a central part in racist mythology. Take, for example, the anti-Semitism faced by Jewish immigrants in the late 19th and first part of the 20th century (Cohen et al 2002), or Margaret Thatcher's infamous 'swamping' speech in the 1970s (Penketh 1997).

Interviews with Muslim women

It was against the backdrop of rising levels of Islamophobia and the increase in hostility towards the Muslim population in Britain, that I set out to explore identity formulation among Muslim women in the context of developments such as the 'war on terror', the attacks on civil liberties and the war in Iraq. This resulted in the development of a research project, which, in 2005 and 2006, involved interviews with second and third generation Muslim women in Preston, north-west England, where I live.

While there is insufficient space to fully explore research methodology in this chapter, it is worth noting several key points related to the research. First, Preston has a population of around 130,000 with 15% from minority ethnic communities. Here, the Muslim community, at 8% is the largest. In total, 13 women were interviewed, both individually and as part of focus groups, and ages ranged from teenagers to women who were between 30 and 40 years old. A few were in education, some were in work, either full- or part-time, and a small minority were housewives. Nine of the women wore the hijab at all times, whereas the other four would wear it, when required, at cultural events such as weddings. Although two of the women were known to me personally, the remainder became involved as a result of requests for participation via various activities. For example, information was distributed at social and cultural events and via the Preston Muslim Forum website and contained information regarding the nature and purpose of the research project.

It is important to note that access to interviewees was influenced by my personal and political involvement with the Muslim community in Preston, including my contribution to Stop the War meetings and demonstrations and my participation in social and community events over several years. As a result of these experiences I established a level of trust within the community that enabled me to ask sensitive questions about women's experiences. This helped to undermine levels of fear and defensiveness that could have arisen from broader experiences of hostility and discrimination, and persistent attacks on Muslim lifestyles. I felt that the element of trust was by far the most important criteria for accessing interviewees from what could have been a 'hard to reach group', particularly as I was a white female academic asking sensitive questions about gender, culture and religion. In relation to research methodology, I drew on a mix of focus group interviews and individual semi-structured interviews.

Areas of questioning during the interviews were concerned with personal, political and cultural issues. For example: personal and educational backgrounds; the role of Muslim women within the family; the importance of religion in women's lives; their views on the wearing of the hijab; their understanding of the term Islamophobia; and their responses to national and international developments specifically affecting the Muslim population.

What follows is a summary and discussion of research findings using headings that reflect key developments impacting on the lives of Muslim women in contemporary Britain.

Experiences of discrimination in the context of rising levels of Islamophobia

This section of the chapter contains material that provides evidence of the daily experiences of racism suffered by Muslim women. These include openly racist comments and other casual remarks that reveal the misconceptions about Muslim life. The accounts of women also expose the assumption among sections of the white population that they are within their rights to make comments about cultural attire and family relationships. The responses of women interviewed revealed that these experiences were not uncommon and not unusual. What follows is a sample of responses.

Many of the women interviewed talked of an increase in discrimination associated with developments after 9/11. For example, Amina said:

> 'We usually get called Osama bin Laden and it is always worse after attacks such as 9/11 and 7/7. … Once I was in town shopping and a young teenage boy tried to pull the scarf off my head. My cousin tried to stop him and he tried to pull hers off too.'

Nafysa said:

> 'We get used to being called names such as 'paki' even when we do not wear the scarf. Even though I wear jeans and jumpers with the scarf people assume I don't know how to speak English and make rude comments.'

And Khatidga added:

> 'The first time that I experienced discrimination was when the Iraq war broke out. Comments were made to me when I was studying at University about bombs in bags. … Students told me that they were frightened of Asian men with beards and would cross the road to avoid walking past them.'

She also spoke of the impact of racism on her children at school:

> 'My kids experienced discrimination in school after the Iraq war started. Other kids started calling out "You pakis," and saying things like "Muslims are idiots." I ended up moving them from that school.'

Sufia was aware of racist comments when she was out with Muslim relatives who wore the burqa. She said 'People stare and whisper and shout things like "terrorist."'

Other women were scared of the response of others in particular situations. For example, Sabiha, spoke of a trip abroad:

> 'I went to Paris with my kids and I had nightmares for weeks before. I was scared of what would happen at the airport and there were bad scenarios in my head.'

She also spoke of a change in discriminatory attitudes:

> 'We used to be labelled "pakis" which covered a lot of people who were not white. Now we are attacked as Muslims and discrimination is Islamic-based.'

Yasmin, recalled an incident experienced by her sister:

> '... my sister was out shopping with two of her children walking beside her and her youngest in a pushchair. An elderly woman pushed her out of the way and said "You people coming over to our country and taking our benefits." My sister replied that she had never claimed benefits and that her husband has his own business and probably pays more tax than most white people.'

Nafysa spoke a friend's experience:

> 'An old white man came up to my friend in the street and said you do not need to wear that [the hijab], I can get you some help. He then gave her a telephone number which he said would help her escape from her oppression.'

Other comments regarding discrimination concerned experiences in the workplace. Sabiha said that colleagues had begun to make comments she had never encountered before, such as 'You Muslims should live like we do and adopt our way of life.' She also recalled the experience of a friend of hers, a pharmacist, who wanted to carry out some voluntary work in a high school in order to give something back to the community. However, when she went to see the head teacher she was told that she could not wear the hijab in his school as it would cause problems. Jenab who is a social worker spoke of the inference from colleagues that Muslim women who wore the hijab could not speak English, and Sadia spoke of the persistence of racist stereotypes and assumptions associated with Muslims in the school where she worked.

The accounts of women also revealed the ways in which they attempted to directly challenge overt incidents of discrimination, an important corrective to perspectives that indicate the passivity of Muslim women in the face of discrimination.

Khatidga said:

> 'I have a friend who has experienced racism especially since 7/7. She was born and bred here but wears ethnic dress. A young man called her a "fucking terrorist". She turned round and said, in a strong Lancashire accent "Who do you think you are calling a fucking terrorist?" and he was really shocked.'

A number of women also commented on generational changes. For example, Ayesha said:

> 'We are not like our parent's generation. They wanted us to blend in as best as possible and avoid trouble and there were some language barriers. Today younger people are different and will fight for their rights.'

Rehana, another teaching assistant added:

> 'Youngsters of today will fight for their rights. We, as Muslims, have done nothing wrong and we do not cause any trouble.'

These accounts reflect an anger and determination emanating from second and third generation Muslims regarding their right to live peacefully and without discrimination in contemporary Britain. They are not prepared to 'blend in' and keep a low profile. Instead, they are more willing than past generations to assert their rights in a number of ways.

Religion, oppression and the veil

One of the most notable developments since 9/11 has been the great increase in the numbers of young Muslim women wearing the hijab, and it is increasingly common in contemporary Britain to see them in such attire in public spaces and the workplace. However, this is still perceived by many as reflecting a level of weakness, passivity and subservience linked to religious oppression and family pressures, particularly from males in a household. The women interviewed were critical of such interpretations and challenged their validity, rejecting the widespread assumption that they were somehow forced to, or coerced into wearing the hijab. They also offered their own understandings as to why more women are choosing to wear cultural attire, drawing on religious and political explanations.

Nafysa said:

> 'After 9/11 my dad did not want my mum to go into town wearing the hijab as he was worried about her. I was too … I can hold my own against abuse, but my mum couldn't.'

Sufia said:

> 'All the women I know who wear the hijab are not told to do so by their husbands or fathers.'

Some women, such as Yasmin, wore the hijab in particular settings, but had other female family members who always wore it. She said:

> 'I will wear the hijab if I go to mosque or to a religious gathering out of respect. My mum always wears it and my sisters-in-law do, but two of my sisters don't.'

In terms of a re-engagement with religion, Sofia explained:

> 'There has been a rise in women wearing the hijab which I think is because of more awareness about religion. Quite a few of my aunts have taken up wearing it. … It is done according to their religion. It not only makes us happier but means we will get rewards in the hereafter.'

Amina added:

> 'I feel that covering my hair goes some way to doing what my religion requires me to do. I feel more respectable and more Muslim.'

For some, religious engagement was also linked to political developments and attacks on the Muslim community. Fatima observed:

> 'Wearing the scarf is a way of being recognised as a Muslim. More women are wearing the hijab and it is because of the way the media go on about Muslims and wars in Islamic countries. In some ways it has made us weaker, but in terms of our faith it has made us stronger … it is a way of being recognised as a Muslim.'

Amina said 'I think trying to ban the hijab is about Islam and hurting Muslims.'

There were quite strident responses from women who did not normally wear the hijab, particularly when discussing the ban on wearing it in France. Yasmin's response was:

> 'If they tried to ban the hijab here I would start wearing it in solidarity with other Muslim women. It is wrong in every sense to ban it – in terms of freedom to express your religion, personal liberty and basic human rights. Also, why should the government legislate about what a person should wear? Will they stop people having piercing or tattoos? I am sure most people would be up in arms if they could not dress as they wished.'

Khatidja said:

> 'I don't see wearing the hijab as a necessity even though it is part of my religion, but I got angry when I heard about the banning in France. For some women … you can't separate the hijab from religion. It is "part and parcel" of the religion and not optional.'

Sabiha criticised the hypocrisy inherent in the media relating to women who wear the hijab when she voiced the opinion that:

> 'If it is the perogative of white women to dress how they wish and to walk around half-naked at times, then it is my prerogative to cover myself up.'

These accounts indicate the need for a more complex understanding of the reasons why Muslim women choose to wear the hijab, and an acknowledgement of the faults and contradictions in the link between religion, oppression and wearing the veil. The women's responses undermine dominant stereotypes and assumptions regarding their subservience, and reveal that, for many, wearing the hijab is a personal choice linked to a re-exploration of the meaning of Islam in their lives.

An increase in the numbers of Muslim women wearing the hijab and re-engaging with religion also needs to be contextualised in relation to wider social and political developments impacting on the Muslim community in Britain and the global Muslim community (the Umma). Many of the women interviewed spoke of their increasing political awareness since the events of 9/11, the war in Iraq and the 'war on terror', and a few had become politically active as a result of these developments. For example, Khatidga had become a member of the Stop the War coalition and was involved in local political campaigns. She gave this account:

> 'I could not see any links between Saddam Hussein and Al Qaeda and it really angered me. I think that Muslims need to be politically involved or they will become marginalised as second class citizens and I do not want that for my children. There are very strong Muslim women who are challenging perceptions and proving that Muslim women have a brain and are articulate and not oppressed, even though they wear the hijab … I think the younger generation are becoming more aware through education and political organisations such as Stop the War, and they are getting more involved in politics.'

Amina said:

> 'My sister went to the London demonstration and I went to the one in Preston. We need to get the point across to Tony Blair that the war in Iraq is wrong.'

Yasmin said the war in Iraq had led to her being involved in politics for the first time:

> 'We have become more politicised and more Muslim women are identifying with the anti-war struggle. What is happening internationally impacts on us here as well. The language used by Bush and Blair in debates about war and terrorism affects the lives of Muslims across the world.'

Others had become more analytical about politics and levels of discrimination. For example, Sabiha said:

> 'We have to think consciously about things now. We have become more aware of national and international political developments. I have started to read about and explore the past struggles of groups such as Jews and black people in Britain and America, and making comparisons with the treatment of Muslims in contemporary society. I have also started to read about what happened in Bosnia.'

Some women had also considered historical parallels regarding discrimination, raising issues such as how black people were portrayed during the Brixton riots and how the Irish were demonised when there were bombings in Britain.

Conclusion: social work relevance

This chapter began with a definition of social work as a profession being committed to anti-oppressive practice, with a requirement that academics and practitioners understand the roots of oppression and its various changing forms. The findings from this research project are important for social work educators, trainers and practitioners in understanding the levels of discrimination and oppression that Muslim women face in contemporary society, in the context of rising levels of Islamophobia.

A key feature of Islamophobia, like all forms of racism, is its changing nature and function as new political needs emerge, and unless social workers can critically engage with and understand these developments, they are likely to fall back on simplistic and inaccurate stereotypes and assumptions that undermine effective anti-discriminatory and anti-oppressive practice with Muslim women and families.

Of course, social workers need to be aware that Muslim women, in common with other women, whether Christian, Jewish or atheist, are oppressed. However, it is damaging if Muslim women are viewed as particularly oppressed, or if Islam is seen as being uniquely predisposed to the oppression of women.

In relation to theoretical awareness it is important for social workers to engage with debates about identity and oppression. They need to be aware of external and internal pressures on identity formation, and to understand that identities are not fixed and static but 'dynamic, fluid and constantly shifting according to time and place' (Younge 2009). For example, the accounts of some women detailed above, reveal that Muslim women who move to identify primarily with Islam, do not do so from a position of increasing oppression, but as a consequence of a complex inter-play of local, national and global features such as poverty, inequality, racism and the 'war on terror'.

Of course, it is also paramount that social workers understand socio-economic factors of social exclusion and that they are aware of the disproportionate levels of poverty and disadvantage that Muslims continue to experience in Britain today. As well, it is necessary to acknowledge the ways in which British Muslims have begun to redefine the racism that they experience, from discrimination based on colour to a racism that targets them by focusing on distinctive stereotypes and that vilifies aspects of their culture. In terms of Muslim women, ethnicity and gender as well as class need to be taken seriously in exploring and analysing their lives and experiences.

These are issues that have been marginalised by the rise of Islamophobia and the demonisation of Muslims as a distinct threat to British society, and as a result there is little debate on how to improve the lives of the Muslim population, and no acknowledgement of the role of racism in contributing to their relative deprivation. In a climate of economic austerity, rising economic insecurity and unemployment, as well as 'savage' cuts to public expenditure, 'scapegoating nationalism' is a real threat as highlighted in the activities of the English Defence League and the British National Party (Ahmed 2013).

In conclusion, it is vital that social workers have a critical understanding of the impact of Islamophobia, and the ways in which it leads to discriminatory and oppressive policies and practices that impact negatively on the lives of Britain's Muslim communities. However, they should also retain a sharp focus on the ways in which poverty, disadvantage and inequality continue to blight the lives of Muslims. Social workers who are informed about these circumstances, and the changing nature of oppression, will be better placed to ensure that Muslim social workers and service users are treated in a sensitive and non-discriminatory manner, and better able to ensure that anti-racist policies and practices are firmly rooted in all aspects of social work intervention.

Suggested further reading

Abbas, T. (ed.) (2005) *Muslim communities under pressure,* London: Zed Books.

Finney, N. and Simpson, L. (2009) *Sleepwalking to segregation? Challenging myths about race and migration*, Bristol: Policy Press.

Keaton, T.D. (2006) *Muslim girls and the other France: Race, identity, politics and social exclusion*, Indianapolis: Indiana University Press.

NINE

Institutionalised Islamophobia and the 'Prevent' agenda: 'winning hearts and minds' or welfare as surveillance and control?

Michael Lavalette

In this chapter Lavalette looks at the 'Prevent' policy agenda. This policy was rolled out in the aftermath of the 7/7 bombings in London. It was an amalgam of internal security policy, social inclusion policy and a political strategy to 'win hearts and minds'. Yet it was built upon a series of worrying assumptions about Muslim communities and ill-defined definitions of 'extremism'. Teachers, probation staff and social workers were all tasked with 'soft' policing the policy agenda – raising issues for social workers around the Professional Capabilities Framework domain 2 (working in ways that are reflective of our values and ethics). With the election of the Conservative–Liberal Democrat coalition in 2010 the policy was redirected and its connection with 'social inclusion' dropped. It remains a policy framework that is 'mainstreamed' within a range of local authority measures but its rationale and its assumptions remain deeply controversial. In the aftermath of the Woolwich murder in London in May 2013 Prime Minister David Cameron, London Mayor Boris Johnson and Home Secretary Teresa May all made reference to the need to monitor and control Muslim communities and Muslim students on university campuses in a bid to stop young men (mainly) from becoming 'radicalised'. In this context 'Prevent' is being identified, once more, as a central government policy driver.

> Preventing violent extremism in the name of Islam must, first and foremost, be about winning the struggle for hearts and minds. (Department of Communities and Local Government [CLG] 2007b: 5)

Introduction

In the aftermath of the 7/7 Bombings in London the, then Labour, Government beefed up its counter-terror strategy called CONTEST (which is always written in block capitals), central to which was 'Prevent': a mechanism to engage with Muslim communities and to win 'hearts and minds', particularly the 'hearts and minds' of young Muslims who are susceptible to 'Islamic extremism' (Department of Communities and Local Government [DCLG] 2007a). As Hazel Blears (at the time Minister of State for DCLG) said in February 2009, '[It's not] because we think Muslims are violent extremists but instead it is because we know the violent extremists prey upon Muslims and especially young people' (Blears 2009). According to former Labour Home Secretary Jacqui Smith:

> [W]e are facing a rapidly evolving terror threat that spans the globe … [W]e have to work particularly hard at local level to make sure that we are tackling violent extremism before it can take root. … The police have recognised that the community needs to be at the heart of their strategy in tackling this threat. They have prioritised a partnership approach that includes working closely with schools, colleges, universities, and across communities. (Smith 2008)

In terms of delivering the 'Prevent' outcomes, the policy pursued a partnership approach with local (Muslim) communities and a range of national, local government and voluntary sector agencies to 'build capacity' and community 'robustness'. As the DCLG at the time said:

> Winning hearts and minds will take significant efforts by Muslim communities to tackle the pernicious ideology being spread by a small minority of extremists, and will mean local Muslim communities taking a leadership stance against sophisticated campaigning extremist messages. Our aim is to support that through targeted capacity building. (DCLG 2007b: 5)

Thus the Labour Government claimed that their aim was to support:

> 'legitimate' community organisations and community leaders; to support the 'Muslim voluntary sector' and to address 'social exclusion … deprivation … capacity building,

> community development and community cohesion' in the Muslim community. (Khan 2009: 8)

Yet despite the supine language there was concern that 'Prevent' actually represented something quite different: that it involved welfare workers and local communities in surveillance programmes that, in effect, identified Muslim communities as a potentially problematic presence in modern Britain. As one critic pointed out:

> The government programme ... is being used to gather intelligence about innocent people who are not suspected of involvement in terrorism. ... The information the authorities are trying to find out includes political and religious views, information on mental health, sexual activity ... and other sensitive information. ... The information can be stored until the people concerned reach the age of 100. (Dodd 2009)

An editorial in Muslim News in November 2009 suggested 'the entire premise of Prevent ...[is] to treat all Muslims as potential terrorists'. It went on:

> One of the main flaws in the Prevent agenda is that it conflates the issues of community cohesion and community service delivery with issues of intelligence gathering and counter-terrorism. (*Muslim News* 2009)

'Prevent' funding was channelled down to local authority and voluntary sector organisations and teachers, social workers and youth workers suddenly found themselves working on projects, part of whose outcome measures were linked to 'discovering' and challenging young people who were susceptible to 'extremist radicalisation'. For many frontline workers such funding created significant dilemmas over their relationship with vulnerable people in minority communities – and the expectation from a range of state institutions that they perform various 'surveillance' activities.

As a result the 'Prevent' strategy provoked fierce criticism.

In 2010 the new Conservative Home Secretary Theresa May, announced that the new coalition government would 'dismantle' 'Prevent', given the widespread loss of confidence in the policy from within the Muslim community in Britain (Travis 2010). Part of the new government's concern was also financial: 'Prevent' was costing the government £60 million and there were concerns, in the new atmosphere of austerity, that the spending couldn't be justified. Nevertheless, in June 2011, after a government review, Home Secretary Theresa May presented the coalition government's *new* 'Prevent' strategy (Home Office 2011). In the new policy the Conservative–Liberal Democrat government claim to have 'de-tangled' the counter-terror policy from Labour's failed intersection of 'counter-terror' with 'social inclusion'. Prime Minister David Cameron, for example, has claimed that 'Prevent' money will not be provided for any community organisation that cannot clearly show support for 'our' values. As he said in his 'Munich' speech:

> We should properly judge these organisations. ... Do they believe in universal human rights – including for women and people of other faiths? Do they believe in equality of all before the law? Do they believe in democracy and the right of people to elect their own government? Do they encourage integration or separation? ... Fail these tests and the presumption should be not to engage with organisations – so, no public money, no sharing of platforms with ministers at home. (Casciani 2011)

Nevertheless, there is a continuity between the last two governments over 'Prevent' that aims to stop Muslim young people being misled, misdirected and recruited by 'extremists' who exploit grievances for their own 'jihadist' endeavours. 'Prevent' seeks to work with these young people and win them to a broad commitment to British democratic protocols; to divert their energies, concerns, criticisms and enthusiasm into 'mainstream' pursuits and 'mainstream' forms of 'citizenship engagement'.

In this chapter I want to look at the background to 'Prevent', to consider its impact in the generation of 'institutionalised Islamophobia' and consider what social workers should do when confronted with project funding that has its source in the state security services.

Preventing violent extremism – 'Prevent' policy origins and background

In 2001 *The Observer* presented the findings of a major survey into 'Race in Britain' (McVeigh 2001). One of the questions asked 'Which Ethnic community has had the most positive influence on British society?' Fifty-two per cent of respondents thought the answer was 'Asians'.

Today the landscape looks very different. Muslim communities are increasingly demonised as a 'threat' to national security, as harbingers of 'terrorists' and extremists, and as communities whose religious beliefs make their presence in Britain 'suspect'. In 2005 *The Guardian* reported that:

> the use of counter-terrorism stop and search powers has increased sevenfold since the July 7 attacks on Britain, with Asian people bearing the brunt of the increase ... figures from July 7 to August 10 showed that the transport police carried out 6,747 stops under anti-terrorism laws, with the majority in London. The force recorded 2,390 stops of Asian people, 35% of the total, and 2,168 of white people, who were 32% of the total. In London Asian people comprise 12% of the population. (Dodd 2005b)

A Harris poll in 2007 found that nearly 30% of British people believed that it was impossible to be both a Muslim and a Briton and 38% thought Muslims posed a threat to national security. In 2008 the *Pew Survey of Global Attitudes* found a quarter of Britons described themselves as 'hostile towards Muslims' (Traynor 2008).

The growth of anti-Muslim racism – or Islamophobia – is one example of what Fekete (2009) calls 'xeno-racism' (see also Fekete, Chapter Two, this volume). Sivanandan (2001) describes this as a racism that is not just directed at black and Asian people from former colonies: it includes the displaced, the dispossessed and the uprooted, including poor whites, who are trying to enter 'fortress Europe'. As it includes poor white migrants, it is often passed off as 'merely' xenophobia. But Sivanandan (2001) suggests that in the way it denigrates and reifies people it bears all the marks of old racism. Thus, he argues, it is racism in substance, but 'xeno' in form.

Fekete (2009) takes Sivanandan's definition and argues that, since the launch of the 'war on terror' in the aftermath of the 9/11 bombings:

> The parameters of institutionalised xeno-racism ... have been expanded to include minority ethnic communities ... simply because they are Muslim. Since Islam now represents 'threat' to Europe, its Muslim residents, even though they are citizens, even though they may be European born, are caught up in the ever-expanding loop of xeno-racism. They do not merely threaten Europe as the 'enemy within' in the

> war on terror, their adherence to Islamic norms and values threatens the notion of Europeanness itself. (2009: 44)

The recent growth of Islamophobia in Britain is directly related to the Government's involvement in the 'war on terror'. The Preventing Violent Extremism (PVE) agenda (now normally just shortened to 'Prevent') was both a response from government to the loosely defined 'enemy within' and, at the same time, a further factor in the process of treating Britain's Muslim communities of 'suspect aliens' who are failing to integrate and assimilate into British society appropriately. Of course, by introducing legislation and policies that problematise the Muslim presence in Britain, and turn suspicion onto the whole community, the government further reinforced and fuelled all measure of crude, 'commonsense' anti-Muslim racism.

The' Prevent' programme has its roots in the CONTEST strategy that began in the aftermath of the 9/11 bombings. As the government joined George Bush's 'war on terror' CONTEST was launched as the Government's counter-terrorism strategy:

> The aim of CONTEST is to reduce the risk to the United Kingdom and its interests overseas from international terrorism ... CONTEST is one part of the first UK National Security Strategy. (HMSO 2009: 10)

The strategy is managed by the Office for Security and Counter-Terrorism (OSCT). Initially the funding attached to 'Prevent' programmes was limited. However, in the aftermath of the London bombings of July 2005 'Prevent' became much more significant.

Prior to 2005 the dominant security perspective was that the main threat from Islamists in Britain came from migrant *diaspora* communities: but the 2005 bombers were British. As Roy argued at the time:

> Britain has been astonished to discover that the terrorists responsible for the London bombings on 7 July were British citizens born there and apparently well integrated. ... The British authorities' perception of the radical Islamist activism that was flourishing in London during the 1990s ... saw it as a product of a diaspora of political refugees who want to change the regime in their countries of origin. ... [Clearly, this] was fundamentally flawed. (Roy 2005)

The London bombings provoked apprehension and fear in government circles over what was happening within Britain's Muslim communities. 'Prevent' was identified as the policy device to try and fill the surveillance and security-knowledge gap.

In 2007 DCLG established a PVE Pathfinder Fund with a budget of £6 million to support 70 priority local authorities in England. In addition £650,000 was made available through the Community Leadership Fund. In April 2008 DCLG announced £45 million funding for a three-year programme for 94 local authorities. In August 2009 this budget was increased by a further £7.5 million. The Community Leadership Fund was given £5.1million to distribute over the same three-year cycle. Other government departments also made contributions to 'Prevent' funding. As Kundnani points out:

> The total Prevent budget in 2008/09 was over £140 million. In March 2009, it was anticipated that by 2011 the total Prevent budget would have increased by a further £100 million. (2009: 12)

At the time this included monies channelled through DCLG, the Home Office's OSCT (which was providing £5.6 million of direct funding to the National Offender Management System and a further £3.5 million to the Youth Justice Board), the Police Forces, the Department of Children, Schools and Families, the Department for Business, Innovation and Skills and the Department for Culture, Media and Sport. Post 2007, therefore, the 'Prevent' agenda grew dramatically in scale and breadth. At the time the government's long-term aim was to:

> mainstream Prevent into the core business of local councils and other statutory agencies ... across services such as housing, education and social services ... into primary care trusts, mental health trusts, schools, colleges and other agencies. This means that Muslims will be permanently labelled as 'potential terrorists' in the provision of all their services and constantly under surveillance by staff delivering services.(Khan 2009: 7, 16)

It is important to recognise what this meant in practice. As part of mainstream funding in a range of services, social workers, community workers, health and education workers and a range of agencies in the voluntary sector were increasingly expected to report on their success on fulfilling 'Prevent' targets – of tracking and reporting on people who were being influenced by 'Islamic extremism'.

In March 2009 CONTEST *2* was launched, pulling together the broad panoply of 'community cohesion/counter-terrorism' projects. Delivery of the strategy was organised around four components or 'workstreams': *Pursue* – to stop terror attacks; *Protect* – to strengthen overall protection against attacks, *Prepare* – where we cannot stop an attack, to mitigate its impact; and *Prevent* – to stop people becoming terrorists or supporting violent extremism. As the government noted:

> CONTEST is intended to be a comprehensive strategy: work on Pursue and Prevent reduces the threat from terrorism; work on Protect and Prepare reduces the UK's vulnerability to attack. (HMSO 2009: 11)

CONTEST suggested, therefore, that Muslim communities were a fertile recruitment ground for Islamist extremists and that funding should be put in place to 'win the hearts and minds' of marginalised communities and 'prevent' them becoming radicalised.

'Winning hearts and minds'

> Prevent is about stopping people wanting to commit violence in the first place. Prevent is built on the idea that …we all have a role to play in stopping them. … Prevent is designed to empower communities so that they can spot when people may be at risk of being groomed by terrorists. (Blears 2009)

Initially discussion surrounding 'Prevent' seemed to acknowledge some of the social and economic roots of 'Muslim disengagement' from social and political life. The Muslim communities include some of the poorest people in Britain, proportionately over-represented among the unemployed and those working in badly paid jobs, with some of the worst health indicators, living in some of the least adequate housing, and with poorer levels of educational attainment (Abbas 2005). As Gary Younge points out:

> Two-thirds of Bangaldeshis in Britain and over half of Pakistanis live in poverty. The unemployment rate for Pakistanis is four times higher than for whites; for

> Bangladeshis it is more than five times. Among the youth it is worse. (Younge 2009)

However, these facts were given an interesting spin in the official documentation. The government suggested that 'Apologists for violent extremism both exploit and create grievances to justify terrorism.' They went on:

> Some of these grievances reflect the experiences of individuals living in this country: racism, discrimination, inequalities, lack of social mobility, under employment, the experience of criminality. A wide range of well established Government policies and measures are already addressing these issues. (HMSO 2009: 91)

The government undermined the reality of structural inequalities and racism faced by Muslim communities in Britain by suggesting that there were significant and appropriate policies in place to address such grievances. Instead the focus was to be on the difficulty of 'integrating' Muslim communities into 'British values'. However, this also indicated a significant misunderstanding of the reality of Muslim life in Britain – and the hopes, dreams and aspirations of second and third generation British Muslims. As Gest (2009) argues

> The new CONTEST strategy … effectively distinguishes Muslims from the British 'collective' [and] reinforces a sense that the government is uninterested in the welfare of Muslims. … In my field work, young Muslims tend to feel extraordinarily British and wish to be acknowledged as such. Mostly born here, they love football, hip-hop and chicken and chips. They tend to come from close families, participate in community activities, and aspire to be more prosperous and educated than the previous generation. (Gest 2009)

In many ways Britain's Muslim communities – especially in the towns and cities across the north of England – resemble those stereotypical (and contradictory) working-class communities of the immediate post-war era (German 1989; Ferguson et al 2002): extended kinship and solidarity networks, a strong sense of community, traditional gendered roles, a strong commitment to marriage and family, and, at the same time, an occasionally narrow and stultifying outlook on life (Ansari 2004).

At the heart of the 'Prevent' programme was an attempt to fill perceived deficits within Muslim communities. These relate to four particular themes: women's empowerment and citizenship (because it is assumed that Muslim women are particularly oppressed and that Islam, in particular among religions, promotes women's subservience and inequality); the development of an appropriately trained layer of British-born, English-speaking imam (because it is assumed too many imam are unable to speak English, which is a barrier to their ability to offer appropriate guidance to young Muslim men in their congregations); governance of Mosques and Madrasa (because it is assumed that Mosques are run by older, first generation migrants who can't relate to the problems of Muslim youth); and 'youth inclusion work' (because Islamic extremists are preying on vulnerable Muslim young people). What these themes revealed, however, was a confusion – or an entanglement – between aspects of the government's 'social inclusion' agenda and their 'counter-terrorism' agenda.

Further, the government's account of the 'four themes' was simplistic and unidirectional, in reality, debates about each of the four themes is more complex than the various 'Prevent papers' suggested.

The argument that children need citizenship education at Madrasa ignores the fact that this is an additional system of religious teaching and that the children also go to school (the vast majority to state comprehensives), which should provide citizenship education as part of the National Curriculum.

The suggestion that Muslim women are particularly oppressed ignores the general levels of women's oppression in society and often becomes reduced to the question of women wearing the hijab or niqab (see Penketh, Chapter Eight, this volume). Yet there are other more nuanced accounts (German 2007) that suggest that the increasing numbers of young Muslim women who wear hijab is at least a partial reflection of their assertion of their Muslim identity at a time when it is being problematised by the state and is something that is occurring within the context of the 'war on terror' and its discontents. Anyone who was on any of the large anti-war demonstrations of the first decade of the 21st century could not but notice the significant numbers of young Muslim women, wearing hijab, and assertively demanding their rights, an end to war and support for the people of Palestine, for example, a picture that does not sit easily with the suggestion that Muslim women are uniformly meek and passive (German and Murray 2005).

Imam do not run mosques. They are run by mosque committees, which are elected each year by the congregation. Of course, politics and intrigue often play a part in these elections – as they do at many community group, trade union and other locally elected committees in Britain. The committees employ (and dismiss) the imam who, after years of study, are badly paid (the average salary of an imam is somewhere between £10,000 and £12,000) and often subject to the changing whims of the committee. Imam often have to take other jobs to supplement their income, which means that they have less time to provide pastoral care to their congregation. It is these economic factors that help to explain why there are relatively few British-born imam and why many mosques employ imam from overseas (who are willing to work with the poor pay and employment conditions on offer) (Bunglawala 2007).

Nevertheless, the government's 'four themes' were reflected in the types of projects that received initial 'Prevent' funding. For example, *The Guardian* (28/1/2009) reported that funding was provided for projects in Birmingham to look at governance in mosques, citizenship studies as part of the curriculum of Islamic schools, and 'youth inclusion work'.

Given the extent and range of the projects devoted to 'winning hearts and minds', one would expect that the government was clear about how to identify the nature of the extremist threat.

Defining 'extremism'

> Somewhere out there is the Muslim that the British government seeks. Like all religious people he (the government is more likely to talk about Muslim women than to them) supports gay rights, racial equality, women's rights, tolerance and parliamentary democracy. He abhors the murder of innocent civilians without qualification – unless they are in Palestine, Afghanistan or Iraq. He wants to be treated as a regular British citizen – but not by the police, immigration or airport security. He wants the best for his children and if that means unemployment, racism and bad schools, then so be it. ... He raises his daughters to be assertive: they can wear whatever they want so long as it's not a headscarf. He believes in free speech and the right to cause offense but understands that he has neither the right to be offended nor to speak out. (Younge 2009)

Central to the entire Labour Government strategy was the need to identify vulnerable people (particularly young people) who were showing signs of 'extremism'. The obvious question to ask, therefore, is 'what is extremism?'

None of the Government documents contained any clear definition of what appropriate 'indicators of Muslim extremism' might be. On 17 February 2009 *The Guardian* published an article drawing on a leaked (early) version of the CONTEST 2 strategy. Here 'extremism' was defined – though after the leak controversy, this section was removed from the final document. In the leaked version 'extremism' was defined as being made up of the following key elements: support for a Caliphate and Sharia law; opposition to homosexuality; opposition to 'apostate regimes' in the Middle East; support for 'Muslim terror organisations' across the world; and use of the internet.

Yet these categories are open to contestation with regard to their meaning and significance; they reflect religious, cultural and political debates about the relevance and significance of these practices and beliefs for the modern world and are not simply a throw back to 'fundamental' practices and beliefs adapted to present settings.

Support for a Caliphate and Sharia law

A Caliphate is a traditional form of Islamic government for the Umma (the entire Muslim community). There is considerable debate between Muslim scholars about what this would mean in practice (Siddiqui 2008) and there is no single vision of what a Caliphate would be like. Historically, there have been several different caliphates, based in different regions of the world and working to different principles (from the first Caliphate of the Prophet Mohammed (pbuh) to the Ottoman Empire that was dissolved at the end of World War I). Muslims in Britain may (or may not) express a general, and rather abstract, preference to live under a Caliphate, but this does not mean that they all have a shared conception about what this would look like, have any intention of 'fighting' to establish such a form of government in Britain or, indeed, reject British democracy as the system under which they live. 'Support for a Caliphate' may reflect no more than an abstract commitment to a conception of what any individual thinks is the best form of governance according to the Quran. For others it may express an idealised preference for a system that offers an alternative to the poverty, inequality, alienation and racism that is the lot of many Muslims in modern Britain.

Similarly with Sharia. Most Muslims in Britain live according to (at least) some of the principles of Sharia: they eat Halal meat and avoid foods that are Haram, give Zakhat (charitable payments accounting for 2.5% of family savings and profits), undertake Islamic marriage vows, and often use banking and mortgage services that avoid accumulation of interest, for example. However, it is a significant conceptual jump to suggest that people who adopt Sharia marriage vows are therefore committed to punishment by beheading, amputation or stoning that *some* states in the Middle East (most notably Saudi Arabia, one of the British state's key allies in the region) declare derive from their reading of the Quran and the hadiths (sayings and practices) of the Prophet Mohammed (pbuh).

Opposition to homosexuality

In recent years there has been significant opposition to gay adoption and fostering from within the Catholic Church (Petre 2008). The Church of England continues to be deeply divided over questions of gay rights and gay clergy (Edemariam 2009) and the Church of Scotland has similarly found itself embroiled in debate over homosexuality (Carrell 2009). At the end of 2009, in Liverpool and London, there were large protest demonstrations against the growth in hate-crimes against gay communities in both cities (BBC 2009). *The London Evening Standard* reported in 2011 that there had been a 28% increase in homophobic hate-crime over the previous four years (Davenport 2011). All this is evidence of growing homophobia in modern Britain, but these examples are all from the majority 'non-Muslim community'. So the obvious question is 'Why is Islam being singled out as a particularly anti-gay religion?'

Opposition to 'Apostate' regimes in the Middle East

> Violent extremist ideology … regards most Governments in Muslim countries as 'un-Islamic' or apostate. (HMSO 2009: 9)

In January 2009, and then again at the end of 2012, as Israeli bombs rained down on Gaza, Europe witnessed some of its largest demonstrations in support of Palestinian rights. In Britain the demonstrators were drawn from all communities – the majority were non-Muslim. In 2009, hostility to Israel's attack was matched by hostility to the Egyptian regime of Hosni Mubarack, which refused to open the

Rafa crossing and let Gazans flee the military onslaught. Opposition to Middle Eastern governments, from large numbers of anti-war activists, remains a reflection of these governments' active support for American imperial interests, their support for the American and British 'war of terror' and the consequences of such support on the Arab peoples of the region. In other words, opposition towards many of the governments of the Middle East is a legitimate political position within the spectrum of the anti-war movement in Britain: the biggest popular social movement in British history (German and Murray 2005). It is also worth pointing out that not many of the states in the region at present (for example, Saudi Arabia, Jordan, Lebanon, Kuwait, Iraq, Afghanistan) would meet many criteria for 'democratic accountability and engagement'. Of course, from the perspective of 2012 it is now increasingly clear that Tony Blair took Britain to war in 2003 to pursue 'regime change' in Iraq because he didn't support the government of Saddam Hussein (Norton-Taylor and Hirsch 2010). So the question is, surely, 'Why are Muslims not allowed to speak out about their opposition to some – or all – of the governments of the Middle East, when British Prime Ministers [at the time] make their opinions clear to the world?'

Support for 'Muslim terror organisations' across the world

> Unresolved regional disputes and conflicts (particularly Palestine, Afghanistan, Bosnia, Chechnya, Lebanon, Kashmir and Iraq) and state fragility and failure. (HMSO 2009: 9)

In effect the Government were arguing that opposition to the war in Iraq or Afghanistan; support for the Palestinian people, especially the elected Palestinian Government under Hamas; voicing support for the Lebanese resistance (led, for example in the 2006 war, by Hezbollah); or raising support for independence for Kashmir or Chechnya, marks one out as a potential 'Jihadist'. Yet support for these issues is not confined to a minority of 'Islamist extremists', indeed they are issues with considerable 'mainstream' political support – including the support of a number (albeit small) of elected MPs in the British Parliament.

Use of the internet

> Modern technologies … facilitate terrorist propaganda, communications and terrorist operations. (HMSO 2009: 9)

There are, of course, lots of very unpleasant sites on the internet but often people do not know what a particular site is about before visiting. For example, a Google search on 'Palestinian rights' will include a vast range of, predominantly useful and interesting, sites about Palestine and the rights of Palestinian refugees. Yet who will decide if this is an appropriate site, especially as the government documents suggest that interest in/support for/knowledge of the Palestinian situation is a further 'indicator of extremism'?

In the 'Prevent' documents it was clear that indicators such as these, though ill-defined and open to conflicting interpretations, were meant to inform the judgement of police officers, teachers, social workers, community workers, welfare workers and 'community representatives' who were, in turn, expected to inform appropriate authority figures of their concerns that the children, students, clients, service users or community activists were in danger of becoming radicalised (*Panorama* 16 February 2009).

In the weeks after the publication of the leaked document there was considerable debate over the Government's failure to define 'extremism' adequately. The final CONTEST 2 document removed the 'indicators', but, by doing so, left the definitional issue open to all manner of misunderstandings. As a result, a series of woolly definitions were put in place within the 'Prevent' programme and became the basis upon which welfare workers were expected to report 'suspect' behaviour. As one social worker noted:

> Members of my YOT team felt that it was going down a slippery slope once we painted everyone with these views [anti-Western, radical political views] as terrorists. Many of my colleagues in the YOT team said most young people, whether Muslim or not, among our clients are anti-establishment and anti-system. This is because they are in the criminal justice system and are very mistrustful of adults in positions of authority … and that includes government. (cited in Khan 2009: 18)

The 'Prevent' agenda, and its contestable definitions or indicators of 'extremism', helped institutionalise suspicion of Muslim communities and of the Muslim presence in Britain. It reinforced an institutionalised Islamophobia that was increasingly expressing itself as the most acute and vicious form of racism in modern Britain.

Three case studies

The drive of government policy, and the atmosphere of Islamophobia that it helped to generate, affected people's lives. The following three examples all provide evidence of how suspicions generated from within the 'Prevent' programme and their paradigm of 'extremism' and 'extremist indicators', operated in practice.

Local authority workers are sacked

In April 2009 14 local authority workers in Preston – including a number who worked in the safeguarding unit – were suspended from their work at Lancashire County Council. The council let it be known that they were suspended for receiving and/or distributing an anti-Semitic email (Day 2009; Harvey 2009). It soon became clear that the (single) email in question had been a collage of photographs from the Israeli assault on Gaza, interspaced with broadly similar images drawn from photographs of Nazi troops in their interaction with East European Jews during World War II. The email ended by asking a question 'How can the grandchildren of the Holocaust survivors act in such a way to the people in Gaza?' The email was received during January 2009.

A campaign to defend the 14 workers included a letter of support in the local paper from a Jewish peace activist. It was pointed out that none of them had created the email, most had simply received it in their inbox, a few had passed it on to close friends (including one who only sent it to his home email address).

The campaign to reinstate the 14 workers was moderately successful: five got off, five were given warnings and four were sacked. All of them had had their emails messages for the previous two years trawled to investigate 'inappropriate use'. Of the four who were sacked one was dismissed because he had circulated an email joke about the brutality of the Pakistani police force (during the lawyers' protests in 2008) – he was himself of Pakistani origin but the email was deemed to reflect 'anti-Pakistani racism'. The other three were sacked for 'misuse' of the internet (one for purchasing an item on-line during their lunch-break). None was dismissed because of the original 'anti-Semitic' email – supporting 'international extremists' (that is, the Palestinians of Gaza) – that provoked their suspension and the investigation. Preston was one of the initial 'Prevent' pilot areas and IT (mis)use was one of the target indicators of 'extremist' activity. For many of those who were suspended and their supporters it was operationalisation of the 'Prevent' indicators that led to the initial suspensions and prompted the 'trawl for evidence' on the part of the council's IT managers.

200 children 'potential terrorists'

> The Channel programme [is] a community-based initiative which uses existing partnerships between the local police, local authority and the local community to identify those at risk from violent extremism and to support them, primarily through community-based interventions. (HMSO 2009: 13)

In March 2009 the Chief Constable of West Yorkshire told *The Independent* that 200 school children, some as young as thirteen, had been identified as 'potential terrorists' by the 'Channel Project' over the previous 18-month period (though the figure up to June 2008 'was only 10', indicating a dramatic increase in the number reported in the second half of the period). The Channel Project is run by the Association of Chief Police Officers. It

> asks teachers, parents and other community figures to be vigilant for signs that may indicate an attraction to extreme views or susceptibility to being 'groomed' by radicalisers (Hughes 2009)

The Chief Constable helpfully gives some indication of the kinds of things people are looking for, such as writing slogans supporting extremists in or on school exercise books. However, he does not indicate whether this would include slogans against the war in Iraq or support for Palestine.

The Channel Project was piloted in Lancashire and Lambeth in 2007 but was then rolled out to cover the rest of London, West Yorkshire, the Midlands, Bedfordshire, South Wales, Thames Valley, South Yorkshire, Greater Manchester, Leicestershire, Nottinghamshire and West Sussex.

Once identified the children were 'subject to a programme of intervention', including police intervention (Hughes 2009).

12 students arrested

In April 2009 12 students in the north-west of England, all of Pakistani origin and 11 with student visas, were arrested in a series of high-profile 'intelligence-led' anti-terror raids. The Prime Minister at the time, Gordon Brown, announced that the raids had been to thwart 'a very big terrorist plot' and that the 12 had been monitored 'for some time' (*The Telegraph* 22 April 2009). Despite the 'extensive monitoring', all 12 were subsequently released without any charges – though the British government then attempted to deport those without permanent British residency.

The arrest of the students coincided with the release of figures that showed that Britons of South Asian descent are far more likely to be detained in anti-terrorism raids than other ethnic groups; that seven out of eight people arrested under Britain's terror laws since 2001 have not been convicted of a terrorism offence, and that more than half of all suspects arrested in terrorism cases since 2001 have been freed without charge.

> Between 11 September 2001 and 31 March 2008, there were 1,471 arrests under terrorism offences in Britain. Of these, 521 resulted in a charge of some form, with 222 people charged with terror offences, and 118 people charged with terror-related offences, such as conspiracy to murder. (Verkaik 2009)

The same figures show that, of those arrested by anti-terror police between 2005 and 2008, 303 – or 42% – were classified as Asian, although people of South Asian ethnicity account for about 4.4% of the British population of 60 million (Stringer 2009).

In addition, police officers in England and Wales used Terrorism Act powers to stop and search 124,687 people in 2007–2008, up from 41,924 in 2006–2007 – the fourth year in a row that the numbers have increased (Sky News 2009). The 124,687 stop and searches produced 1,271 arrests, only 73 of which were for terror offences (Verkaik 2009). Samira Shackle, (2009) provided an example what this data meant to 'ordinary' young Muslims in Britain who happen to stir someone's suspicions.

> My cousins – who are Bangladeshi, but both British passport holders – were recently arrested in London on suspicion of possessing false passports. Twin brothers aged 24, they were attempting to open bank accounts at a branch where the family have banked for years. After keeping them waiting for several hours, staff called the police, who arrested them and put them in separate cells. They were fingerprinted, and forced to take a drugs test and give DNA samples. ... After three hours, during which they were not allowed to call

> their parents or a lawyer, police verified their passports with the Home Office and they were released. (Shackle 2009)

An intimidating atmosphere that targeted young Muslims – the vast majority of whom have committed no crime – was the direct result of a 'surveillance culture' that perceived Muslims in general, and Muslim young men in particular, as a potential threat and an 'enemy within'.

But the outcry that 'Prevent' generated within Muslim communities in Britain forced a government rethink. The election of the coalition government in 2010 seemed to mark a turning point in the government's 'Prevent' policies.

New government, same old surveillance?

As noted in the introduction the coalition government elected in 2010 made an early announcement that 'Prevent' would be dismantled. It was too expensive, there was not enough accountability or monitoring of projects and there was confusion over its aims and rationale – was it about community cohesion or about counter-terrorism? The government undertook a review overseen by Lord Carlile of Berriew, which produced five key principles of government strategy. First, despite earlier claims that 'Prevent' would be dismantled, it is to remain an integral part of the government's counter-terrorism strategy (Home Office 2011: 5). Second, 'Prevent' will be expanded to include other forms of terrorism, including extreme right-wing terrorism (Home Office 2011: 15) and Northern Irish terrorism (Home Office 2011: 14), nevertheless, the main focus remains on 'Islamic terrorism'. Third, 'Prevent' will be expanded in another significant way: it will now set out to counter non-violent extremism that, it was claimed, 'creates an environment that conducive to terrorism' and the popularisation of their ideas. Fourth, 'Prevent' will now draw a clear distinction between counter-terror work and 'social inclusion' work. Fifth, *new* 'Prevent' must have clear objectives and must be properly monitored to stop money being wasted. Finally, no public money will be provided for any extreme organisation who does not support the values of democracy, human rights, the rule of law and mutual respect and tolerance.

In turn these principles lead to three key objectives. So new 'Prevent' will:

1. Respond to the ideological challenge of terrorism and the threat from those who promote it:

> All terrorist groups have an ideology. Promoting that ideology, frequently on the internet, facilitates radicalisation and recruitment. Challenging ideology and disrupting the ability of terrorists to promote it is a fundamental part of Prevent. (Home Office 2011: 7)

2. Prevent people from being drawn into terrorism and ensure that they are given appropriate advice and support:

> Radicalisation is usually a process not an event. During that process it is possible to intervene to prevent vulnerable people being drawn into terrorist-related activity. (Home Office 2011: 8)

3. Work with sectors and institutions where there are risks of radicalisation that we need to address:

> A wide range of sectors in this country are helping to prevent people becoming terrorists or supporting terrorism. The way Government works with particular sectors will vary. Priority areas include education, faith, health, criminal justice and charities. (Home Office 2011: 8)

Rather than be 'dismantled' 'Prevent' has been refocused as a clear counter-terrorism strategy. At its heart is the intention to fund a series of programmes that challenge the ideological legitimacy of extremism (with a particular focus on Islamic extremism) and intervention to prevent 'vulnerable young people' from becoming radicalised. The new 'Prevent' strategy document contains the following definition of extremism:

> By extremism here we mean the active opposition to fundamental British values, including democracy, the rule of law, individual liberty and the mutual respect and tolerance of different faiths and beliefs. (Home Office 2011: 34)

This definition does not take us very far. What are fundamental British values? What do we mean by democracy? What if a law is wrong or unjust, is it okay to oppose it? Does the requirement to respect different 'faiths and beliefs' mean that Christian fundamentalist groups should now be monitored in the UK?

In addition to this 'definition' there are a list of indicators of extremism. These include a list of international 'Al-Qaida' influenced groups support for whom is suggestive of extremism – and lists both Hezbollah and Hamas. As we saw above, broad support for these organisations in the complex politics of the Middle East extends quite far in the anti-war movement in Britain and would include some elected MPs. The document includes discussion of the role of Madrassas, of theological questions and of support for a Caliphate, and the central role played by the internet in 'grooming' potential terrorists. Here the *new* 'Prevent' sounds very similar to the *old* 'Prevent'.

Furthermore, the review reveals that there has now been training for 15,000 frontline staff through the Workshop to Raise Awareness of Prevent (WRAP). This covers issues such as the history of terrorism, radicalisation as a social process, connections to other forms of extremism' (Home Office 2011: 57). Training, presumably, is based on the *old* 'Prevent' notion of extremism that is effectively continued in the *new* 'Prevent'.

Just as before, 'Prevent' has consequences for people's lives. The document looks at the growing number of young people referred via the Chanel project. Between April 2007 and December 2010, 1,120 people have been referred:

- the majority of referrals were made by education partners, the police and youth offending services;
- the majority of referrals were aged between 13 and 25;
- there were 290 referrals aged under 16, and 55 referrals aged under 12;
- 88% were referred owing to concerns around international terrorism;
- 8% were referred owing to concerns around right-wing violent extremism; and
- 4% were referred owing to concerns around other types of violent extremism.

The coalition government's 'Prevent' strategy reinforces many of the old assumptions about Muslim communities, about politics and about the 'enemy within'. It is part of a series of government reports and reviews that embed an institutional Islamophobia within British political structures. *New* 'Prevent' has disaggregated the counter-terror thrust of *Old* 'Prevent' from funding projects for 'social cohesion', but it has not reduced the requirement on front-line workers in social work, community work and education to watch and monitor the behaviours of some of their service users.

From 'red scare' to 'green peril'

There have been relatively few people arrested and charged with terror offences in Britain. Despite this there is a significant and growing government programme that aims to fund 'counter-terrorism' and does so in a way that threatens civil liberties and places welfare workers to the fore as agents of social surveillance and control.

The evidence suggests (for example, from the increase in reports under the Channel Project) that as schemes roll-out and become 'mainstreamed' more people (especially young men) will find themselves regarded with suspicion and subject to intervention. This is not because there is more 'extremist activity' but because imprecise definitions of extremism, misunderstanding of the Muslim community and their religious and cultural practices, and an atmosphere of institutionalised Islamophobia combine to target a poor, minority community who find themselves increasingly portrayed as the enemy within.

There are historical precedents to such a situation. In the early 20th century in Britain, migrant Jewish communities fleeing from pogroms in Eastern Europe found themselves targeted as anarchists, criminals and a threat to the British 'race' (Hayes 2002). In post-war America (and to a lesser extent in Britain) communists and leftists became the 'enemy within' during the Cold War. They lost their jobs, were castigated in the media and were subject to all forms of surveillance (Neale 2001). In the 1970s, as the IRA undertook their 'mainland campaign', and particularly after the Birmingham pub bombings of 1974, the Irish community came under suspicion. The Prevention of Terrorism Act became a tool of harassment as the Irish community faced intervention from the security services (Hillyard 1993)

So, in one sense, the Muslim community find themselves in a 'familiar' situation: as the British government engage in wars overseas, they target internal dissent and opposition. In the past this was the 'red scare' now it's the 'green peril'.

Conclusion: social work relevance

The 'Prevent' programme threatens the fundamental rights of British-born citizens. The complexity of addressing this issue in the modern world is identified within the PCF domain 4, as central to social work education, training and practice.

The outcomes of 'Prevent' are increasingly tied to the funding of a range of youth, community, probation and offender projects where social workers, community workers and probation officers (social workers in Scotland) will be expected to report and inform on suspect 'extremist' behaviour. The problem, as I noted above, is that the definitions are imprecise and unhelpful and the projects are likely to alienate further communities who already feel threatened and targeted.

This raises an obvious question: what should social workers do when confronted by such 'Prevent' requirements?

Individual social workers will make their decisions about their practice, about what is ethical and how they implement their social work values. Certainly the International Definition of Social Work would seem to indicate that social workers should not implement policies that infringe upon people's rights or reinforce oppression (as I have suggested 'Prevent' does). However, whatever individual decisions social workers may take, it would be wrong to advocate that individuals have to threaten their own employment by knowingly refusing to carry out 'Prevent' monitoring. Instead, what is needed is collective campaigning, through the social workers' union Unison, and via BASW, the College of Social Work and the Social Work Action Network for this regressive and damaging policy to be rescinded. 'Prevent' puts welfare workers on the front-line of a counter-terror policy, it turns them into 'soft' policers of vulnerable communities and threatens to alienate them from service users in such targeted communities. As such' Prevent' is incompatible with social work values.

Suggested further reading

Fekete, L. (2009) *A suitable enemy,* London: Pluto.

Kundnani, A. (2009) *Spooked: how not to prevent violent extremism,* Institute of Race Relations www.irr.org.uk/pdf2/spooked.pdf

Mamdani, M. (2004) *Good Muslim, bad Muslim,* New York: Pantheon Books.

Peirce, G. (2010) *Dispatches from the dark side: on torture and the death of justice,* London:, Verso.

TEN

'Street-grooming', sexual abuse and Islamophobia: an anatomy of the Rochdale abuse scandal[1]

Judith Orr

In this chapter Orr looks at the recent cases of 'street-grooming'. The purpose, primarily, is not to look at the complexities of child abuse (though, of course, this is touched upon) but the way this has become a 'moral panic' that has focused on the 'alien' culture of Pakistani Muslim men and their attitudes towards women and children in general and white women and children in particular. Recently *Guardian* columnist Joseph Harker (2013) ran a column called 'Time to face up to abuse in the white community' in which he reviewed the Jimmy Saville, Stuart Hall and north Wales children's home scandals and asked 'what is it about white people that makes them do this?' and he goes on to ask 'Is it white people's culture? Or maybe it's their religion?' His questions, of course, are sarcastic. However, they are there as a direct challenge to the politicians and media pundits who used the small number of cases where Muslim men were involved in abusing young girls as 'evidence' of the incompatibility of Muslim and Western cultures. Orr's case is that the 'grooming scandals' are an example of a racially induced moral panic. For social work students, educators and practitioners being able to unpick such 'moral panics' is vital if we are to intervene effectively and appropriately.

Introduction

Towards the end of 2012 British society was rocked by revelations from a series of sex-abuse scandals. First, the former Radio One disc jockey Jimmy Saville was revealed as a serial sex-abuser of young women in a shocking story that implicated a range of high-profile individuals and institutions in British society – from the BBC to the prison and hospital services. Then in a second set of revelations, a series of establishment figures were implicated in a terrible story about the abuse of young people in a north Wales children's home in the 1970s and 1980s. In both cases the abusers were linked to powerful elites in

British society – and in both cases there was a backlash against the accusations. There was no suggestion that the revelations raised issues about any 'abusive culture of power' at the heart of the establishment, or that the political establishment were using 'political correctness' as a cover to inhibit investigation (though Prime Minister David Cameron claimed that gay men were at risk of a 'witch hunt' if the media did not stop digging around – even though no one had made any link between the abuse cases and gay men).

However, 'cultural failings' and 'political correctness' were identified as central elements within a third sex-abuse case to be brought to trial in 2012, that of the so-called Rochdale grooming scandal. The case of nine men convicted of appalling sexual exploitation of young women in Rochdale in north-west England unleashed a tide of racism and Islamophobia. The media coverage of the case asserted that the most shocking aspect of the story was not the abuse itself, but the fact that the male abusers were Pakistani Muslims and the women they abused were white – and social workers were 'warned' that they, 'Must not let political correctness get in the way of investigating the grooming of vulnerable children' (Doyle 2012). *The Daily Mail*, for example, argued that:

> Police and social services have ... fuell[ed] a culture of silence which has allowed hundreds of young white girls to be exploited by Asian men for sex.
>
> Agencies have identified a long-term pattern of offending by gangs of men, predominantly from the British Pakistani community, who have befriended and abused hundreds of vulnerable girls aged 11 to 16. (Brooke 2011)

A number of racist and far-right organisations used the case to mobilise, supported by the tabloids whose front pages were an invitation to see all Muslim men as dangerous paedophiles. At the same time the mainstream right used the comment columns to pour out their barely concealed racism about Muslims and Pakistanis. Even the judge in the Rochdale case, Gerald Clifton, joined in, saying, 'I believe one of the factors which led to that is that they [the young women victims] were not of your community or religion' (*The Manchester Evening News* 2012).

His words are now used on British National Party (BNP) leaflets headlined 'Racist Muslim paedophilia'. Throughout the hearing the BNP, the English Defence League (EDL), and other racist and fascist organisations picketed the court. It was revealed at the end of the case that on the opening day two barristers on the defence legal team, both

Asian, were attacked outside the court. They pulled out of the case in fear for their safety and that of their families. The hearing was delayed by two weeks, the jury was discharged and new barristers were found to represent the defendants (Carter 2012).

At the end of the trial an investigation into whether jury confidentiality had been compromised had to be set up. This was after BNP leader Nick Griffin tweeted that seven of the men had been found guilty while the jury was still deliberating. The investigation concluded that there was no evidence that the jury had communicated with Griffin.

But the far-right and the tabloids are not the only ones using the issue of sexual exploitation to stoke up racism. When children's minister Tim Loughton was asked about the Rochdale case he said, 'Political correctness and racial sensitivities have in the past been an issue.' He added that the authorities still 'have to be aware of certain characteristics of various ethnic communities' (Doyle 2012).

The implication that there is something specific among Muslims or Pakistanis that makes them more likely to commit these crimes has become the common theme on the right. The first Muslim woman to serve in the cabinet, Baroness Warsi, joined the chorus in an interview in *The London Evening Standard* newspaper, saying:

> There is a small minority of Pakistani men who believe that white girls are fair game. And we have to be prepared to say that. You can only start solving a problem if you acknowledge it first. ... This small minority who see women as second-class citizens, and white women probably as third-class citizens, are to be spoken out against ... Communities have a responsibility to stand up and say: 'This is wrong; this will not be tolerated.' ... Cultural sensitivity should never be a bar to applying the law. (Murphy 2012)

Columnist Melanie Phillips in *The Daily Mail* claimed, 'The police maintain doggedly that this has nothing to do with race. What a red herring. Of course it doesn't! This is about religion and culture – an unwesternised Islamic culture which holds that non-Muslims are trash and women are worthless. And so white girls are worthless trash' (Phillips 2012).

TV historian David Starkey spoke at a conference of school heads shortly after the trial ended and proclaimed, 'If you want to look at what happens when you have no sense of common identity, look at Rochdale. ... Those men were acting within their own cultural norms.

Nobody ever explained to them that the history of women in Britain was once rather similar to that in Pakistan and it had changed' (Shepherd 2012). This is the same David Starkey who showed his commitment to women's equality when he denounced the 'feminising' of history by women historians who turned it into 'soap opera' for their 'mainly female audience' (Allen 2009).

There has not been the same denouncing of the 'cultural norms' of how women are treated when it comes to non-Muslim sex attackers. Look no further than the number of footballers in cases of alleged rape. The gross custom of footballers or their representatives cruising the shops of Manchester picking up women to have sex with even has its own term, 'harvesting'. These women are brought to clubs and hotels where they are then assumed to be willing to have sex with numbers of footballers – coined 'roasting', often while being filmed.

In a recent case Ched Evans, Welsh international and Sheffield United player, was jailed for five years for rape. The teenager he raped after he and other male friends picked her up drunk in the street had her name revealed on social media and was abused for taking the case out against him. His sister and a group of fans even tried to organise a public tribute to him as a show of support at a match after he was imprisoned (Gaskell 2012). We do not see front pages devoted to denouncing the misogynist culture of football, or calls for footballers as a collective to examine why a number of their colleagues have been accused of sex crimes. Yet all the time Muslim representatives are called upon to denounce the crimes as if in some way by nature of a shared religion they are collectively responsible.

In October 2011 the Office of the Children's Commissioner for England started a two-year project looking at the extent of child sexual exploitation. Their interim report, published in November 2012, suggested 16,500 children were at 'high risk' of exploitation and that 2,409 children had been sexually exploited during the first 12 months of their research period (Berelowitz et al 2012). However, as they emphasise: 'The vast majority of the perpetrators ... come from all ethnic groups and so do their victims – contrary to what some may wish to believe' (2012: 5). Further, Berelowitz, interviewed in *The Guardian*, suggested that while in the majority of cases the 'ethnicity of perpetrators' was not recorded (in 68% of cases this was the case), she suspected that, given the present furore there may have been 'proactive recording' of Asian males by police forces in some areas – further skewing the data (Topping 2012).

Rape and sexual abuse are horrendous crimes whoever the perpetrator. Women often feel unable or unwilling to report assaults for fear they will not be believed, their sexual history will be on trial or they will be judged culpable because of what they wore or how they behaved.

The reaction to the Rochdale case was seen through the prism of race. However, this will not bring us any nearer to understanding or stopping the problem of sexual abuse. In fact, if grooming and sexual exploitation are seen as solely a crime carried out by Pakistani men, many victims will not get the help and justice they deserve.

Racist stereotypes and women's oppression

Whatever the spin, it is not concern for women's rights but race that is driving the agenda in these debates and it is not for the first time. In January 2011, after a case in which two Asian men were convicted of rape and sexual abuse in Nottingham Crown Court, Labour MP Jack Straw declared that young Muslim men were 'fizzing and popping with testosterone' and saw young white women as 'easy meat' (*Socialist Worker* 2011).

These views reflect centuries-old racist stereotypes of black men as sexual predators, which deemed even consensual sexual relationships between a black man and a white woman an aberration. From the days of slavery through to the 20th century black men have been brutally punished for having sexual relations with white women. White slave-owners on the other hand saw raping their black slaves as perfectly normal.

With the rise of Islamophobia overt racism has been veiled in talk of 'culture'. This approach has been used by both far-right activists and mainstream politicians alike in recent years. In the Rochdale case it has served the purpose of allowing naked prejudice to be dressed up as concerned commentary. Below the screaming headlines some tried to cite academic research to legitimise the racialisation of this crime.

One study in particular was regularly quoted. The research, by the Jill Dando Institute of Crime Science at University College London (UCL), supposedly showed that Pakistani men are the main perpetrators of grooming and abusing young women. In fact, this study does no such thing. Eleanor Cockbain and Helen Brayley, who undertook the research, are concerned at how their work is being used. Cockbain said, 'The citations are correct but they have been taken out of context. Nor do they acknowledge the small sample size of the original research, which focused on just two large cases' (Vallely 2012).

The study's purpose was precisely to look at the nature of social networks of the perpetrators and victims in two cases that involved groups of Pakistani men. It explains that gangs and paedophile rings are rare and goes on to say 'Contrary to stereotypes of sinister paedophile rings, most child sex offenders act alone,' and quotes research on child sex offenders showing that "only 4 percent were involved in an organised network and 92 percent had no contact with other offenders prior to arrest (Vallely 2012).

The researchers were worried that 'limited data had been extended to characterise an entire crime type, in particular of race and gender'. They said of the cases they studied that there was no evidence that white girls were targeted by offenders, saying, 'Though the majority were white, so too were the majority of local inhabitants' (Vallely 2012).

Referring to the Rochdale case Assistant Chief Constable Steve Heywood of Greater Manchester Police was careful to point out that it was not about race, but 'adults preying on vulnerable young children'. 'It just happens that in this particular area and time, the demographics were that these were Asian men', he said. 'However, in large parts of the country we are seeing on-street grooming, child sexual exploitation happening in each of our towns and it isn't about a race issue' (BBC 2012). The police themselves have confirmed that 95% of those on the Greater Manchester sex offenders register are white.

Those who claim that statistics prove that 'street grooming' is predominantly committed by Pakistani men have difficulty in explaining how they have come to this conclusion as 'street grooming' is not a specific criminal offence. It is a term that serves to racialise the crime of sexual exploitation in the same way as the term 'mugging' in the 1970s became used to denote a crime committed by mainly young black men (Hall et al 1978; BBC 2012).

What about the women?

Amid the obsession about the race and religion of the male perpetrators less attention has been spent on their victims. The real question of Rochdale is how could the system have let down these young women. They were vulnerable, in or around the care system, and their abuse took place over a number of years. Race was not the issue that made getting justice difficult for these women. It was deep-seated prejudice that deemed their lives less worthy as young women from poor working-class backgrounds who had already had troubled lives.

The police comment said it all: they described the young women as coming from 'chaotic' or 'council house backgrounds' (BBC 2012). Being a council house tenant is obviously seen as being a problem in itself. In other words they were not from stable middle-class families.

Even when one young woman alerted the police to the abuse she was suffering as far back as 2008 the case did not get to court. At 15 she was arrested for causing a nuisance outside a kebab shop and during questioning explained that she had been having sex with a number of men based there in return for gifts of food, phone cards and vodka. She even gave the police an item of her underwear that had traces of DNA, evidence from a 59-year-old man who was eventually one of the nine convicted.

After almost a year's investigation the Crown Prosecution Service (CPS) did not take the case to court because they decided the young woman would be an 'unreliable witness' and would not be believed by a jury. These assumptions about the credibility of the young woman condemned her to yet more abuse until the case was taken up again (Martinson 2012).

This is the common experience of children and young people who report cases of sexual abuse. The CPS calculates that of the 17,000 reported cases of sexual offences involving children under 16, just under a quarter went on trial this year. Even adult women reporting rape find the legal system often judges them rather than helps them. In February of this year a report by inspectorates of police and crown prosecutors found evidence that rape cases were 'no-crimed', that is, recorded as if no crime had taken place, more often than other crimes. According to figures from different police forces around the country in 2010/2011 the volume of rape offences 'no-crimed' was 2,131, nearly 12% of the total number of recorded rape crimes. Offences of rape are 'no-crimed' four times more often than, for example, the offence of causing grievous bodily harm with intent (HMIC/HMCPSI 2012). This massages statistics that can help fulfil targets for conviction rates while burying clues that could lead to serial rapists being tracked down.

The Metropolitan Police's specialist sex-crime unit Sapphire underwent an overhaul in 2010 after two serial rapists were allowed to continue to commit crimes even after women's reports of rape. The women were simply not believed. In June 2012 the unit is once again under investigation and two officers are accused of perverting the course of justice. It has emerged that officers were closing cases and informing women that no charges were going to be brought in their case even though this had not been decided (Laville 2012).

All this shows that while a woman's experience of rape or abuse is judged by the preconceptions of a society in which women's oppression is entrenched they will not get justice.

Grooming

The horror of such cases as the Rochdale abuse is that the life experience of these young women had been so difficult that they could be 'groomed' into believing that serial abuse and rape were something they had to live with. The whole purpose of grooming is to lead a vulnerable young person into believing they are in a loving relationship. Some of the women in this case refused to give evidence to the police against men they continued to perceive as their 'boyfriends'. In some cases it took many hours of interviews and counselling for them to come to terms with the reality of the situation they were in. Such was the paucity of love and respect in their life that the experience of being groomed was perceived as being positive.

Helen Brayley, one of the researchers at UCL, wrote an advisory note on grooming for police saying, Many of the victims in our data set were either too scared or too extensively groomed to go to the police. They either believed they were in a relationship with one of the offenders and therefore did not want to get them into trouble, or they somehow felt complicit in their abuse' (Gilbert 2011).

Bea Kay is a GMB union steward in children's social care in Sheffield, training those who work with young people on issues of grooming and sexual exploitation. In an interview she told me, 'The support for young people today is pitiful. Vulnerable young people often feel worthless. An older man or group of men who pay attention to them and give them "gifts", however trivial, can make them feel valued' (Orr 2012). This means that overt physical violence is not necessarily a component of these abusive relationships. Certainly at the beginning the abuser concentrates on building up the victims to feel important, desirable and valued and to separate her or him from any networks of family or friendship that might offer an alternative.

Women of all ages in our society are encouraged to see themselves as sex objects, to see being attractive as a measure of their value. Whether it is in the numerous women's magazines with top tips for make-up, cosmetic surgery or clothes, it is assumed we are all aspiring to be sexually attractive. With the rise of raunch culture over the last decade or so we are witnessing an increasing tolerance of women's sexuality being used as a commodity in ever more crude ways.

Sex has become a valuable currency in our society – and for some women it may be their only currency. Sexual exploitation is one of the most extreme and distorted expressions of women's oppression and the alienation of human relationships. Of course, young men can also become victims, although they are the minority.

Abuse and the family

The reality is that the form of sexual abuse exposed in Rochdale is not the most common, although it receives a disproportionate amount of media coverage. The charity Barnardo's found that 'child sexual exploitation is much more likely to happen in private than in public, and this year's survey showed that street-based grooming and exploitation remains rare' (Barnardo's 2012: 6).

Despite all the media frenzy children and young people are more at risk of abuse, physical and sexual, within the family unit rather than on the street – most adult abusers are known to the victim: 'The majority of perpetrators sexually assault children known to them, with about 80 percent of offences taking place in the home of either the offender or the victim' (Grubin 1998)

The roots of women's oppression lie in the institution of the family, which Frederick Engels identified as becoming established with the rise of class society and private property (Engels 1884/1978). The role the family plays in people's lives and in wider society has gone through many profound changes. Yet it still plays an important function in modern capitalism. It is still the place where majority of the next generation are brought up. Although marriage rates have been declining, and in 2010 nearly half of all babies were born outside marriage or civil partnerships (46.8%) compared with 39.5% in 2000, the number of births registered with only one parent has been declining (Office for National Statistics 2011: 6).

Politicians, both Labour and Conservative, extol the virtues of the traditional family and the notion that any problems people suffer are their individual responsibility and not rooted in the structured inequality of society. This ideological offensive is designed to make people feel it is their responsibility to carry an extra burden when cuts mean there are fewer affordable residential homes for the elderly, or less respite care for those looking after a relative or child with disabilities (Ferguson and Lavalette 2013).

The role of the family and how children are brought up goes right to the heart of the debate over child sex-abuse and sexual exploitation. The young women who were preyed on by the men in Rochdale were on the streets and vulnerable because they had no effective network of support from a family or from the state. Social services had had contact with all the young women in the case. At least one was sent to a care home in Rochdale to escape problems experienced at home.

What happened to those young women cannot be separated from the contradictions in the nature of the family in society, contradictions that mean that families can act as a bulwark against the harshness of life under capitalism and when they break down can leave people more vulnerable. However, at the same time they can be the place where all the rotten experience of alienation and inequality is distilled and distorts relationships in the most brutal fashion.

Institutional solutions?

If the family is a frightening and dangerous place for some, what is offered by the system as an alternative can be equally problematic. Institutions for children without a family, orphanages, children's homes, poor houses, whatever the good intentions of many of those who worked in them, have historically been seen as the option of last resort.

Some, like the Christian Brothers' 'industrial' schools in Ireland, have become notorious for the brutality meted out to their young charges. Such institutions should be a refuge from suffering; instead they can be places where already damaged children and young people are vulnerable to abuse. In some cases they have enabled networks of abusers to coalesce to mutually cover up and perpetuate the crimes. The scale of child abuse that is still being revealed by victims, now adult, in the Catholic church is a good example of this. Many of those who carried out the abuse did so in the sure and certain knowledge that they would be protected because even if their victims spoke out the church would never allow itself to be exposed to the scandal (Devine 2010).

Today such institutions are no longer seen as the best way to look after children in the care of the state. However, social workers are constantly under the spotlight, particularly those dealing with child-protection cases. They are denounced for taking children from families without enough evidence, but when something goes wrong then they are criticised for not removing a child sooner. This is against a background of ever-shrinking budgets and cutbacks, which means increasing workloads on fewer staff.

Many of the young people in the up to 47 private care homes in Rochdale are not from the area and so are not the responsibility of local social services. As a Department of Education report in 2011 noted:

> almost 23,000 looked-after children in England were placed out of area, of 65,520 in total. And nearly half of those in residential care, as opposed to foster care, were not living in their local area. (Tickle 2012)

Young people are sometimes sent there from hundreds of miles away. Their local social services may have moved them to a new area to help them break from a cycle of abuse in their family or in their hometown. Sometimes their local council will have chosen to move them there due to the cheaper cost of care in the area. The high number of private homes in Rochdale is partly due to cheap housing. However, if a young person has been taken into care because of abuse, moving them into a new town may not help if nothing else is done to support the individual. Instead they can fall into a new cycle of abuse if they are left exposed.

Rochdale has its own problems; a town of just over 200,000 people, it is the tenth most deprived district in England, measuring factors such as employment, income, health and housing. It has a life expectancy below the national average and such is the inequality within the town between some wards there is a difference in life expectancy of 10 years (Rochdale BC 2011; Rochdale Online 2013).

The main high street is crowded with charity shops, pawnbrokers and cash converters. All around are reminders of the town's past as an industrial powerhouse: the imposing gothic town hall is now a grade 1 listed building. As one local youth worker put it, "We are now a manufacturing town without any manufacturing."

Such deprivation can become a breeding ground for deep-seated social problems and the government's policies will only make the situation worse – the council budget faces cuts of £125 million.

There's profit in misery

Today in Britain the majority of children's homes are run by private companies and two-thirds of fostering provision is controlled by the private sector. These companies run, primarily, for profit. There are millions to be made from looking after the most vulnerable young people in society.

> It costs between £200,000 and £300,000 a year for residential care for a child and £30 to £60,000 for foster care. ... (For comparison, it costs £30,000 to keep someone in a low-security prison for year, and £30,000 to send someone to Eton.) (Williams 2012)

The search for profit can result in low pay for workers and slackening of standards for skills and supervision.

Green Corns was the private company that ran the care home responsible for the care of the 15-year-old young woman who was one of the victims of years of sexual abuse. The company was providing 'solo care'. Solo care means that a number of staff on round the clock shifts are dedicated to looking after one young person. For this care of a single young person a council can be charged over £250,000 a year. The company had received repeated warnings from Ofsted about care standards and advice that its staff needed training in sexual-exploitation issues.

Green Corns was bought up by private equity group 3i for £26 million in 2004 and became part of the Continuum Care and Education Group. Annual operating profits reached £2.7 million. In turn Continuum was bought up by Advanced Childcare Limited (ACL), which itself had been bought by another private equity company, GI Partners, in April last year. Then managing director Alfred Foglio boasted, 'Advanced Childcare has pioneered the trend of managing children's care services on behalf of budget constrained local authorities' (GI Partners 2011).

ACL is now the largest provider of specialist children's care and education services in Britain. It reported an annual turnover of £15 million in 2010, up from £11 million a year earlier. Pre-tax profit increased to £2.6 million during that period, up from £700,000 in 2009. Most of this income is from local authority contracts for residential care. The combined company now runs 143 children's homes with 416 placements, 15 special schools and over 100 fostering placements. The company's founder, Riz Khan, expressed his high hopes for future profits: 'We would be disappointed if we cannot at least double the size of the business in the next three to five years' (GI Partners 2011). This is what privatisation of the welfare state means. Profit-driven multinationals owned by venture capitalists are put in charge of providing comfort and succour to young people damaged by the system.

Conclusion

The reaction to the Rochdale case has generated a moral panic – the perception of the danger of Pakistani men and street grooming is totally disproportionate to the reality. This is because it has not happened in a vacuum. Instead it has happened when the level of Islamophobia in British society is intensifying.

The question of child abuse and sexual exploitation is not straightforward. Sexual exploitation of children and young people is evidence of just how distorted humans and their relationships with each other can become, but we have to avoid the danger of simplistic explanations: there are multiple factors involved in such cases and when Islamophobia is added it becomes a toxic mix. However, it is vital that we challenge the dominant 'common sense' about the issue and expose the bigotry that is being whipped up to distract people from the real scandal: how the system fails people, especially the most vulnerable.

Suggested further reading

Berelowitz, S., Firmin, C., Edwards, G. and Gulyurtlu, S. (2012) *'I thought I was the only one. The only one in the world', The Office of the Children's Commissioner's Inquiry into Child Sexual Exploitation By Gangs and Groups (Interim Report)* Nov. 2012 www.childrenscommissioner.gov.uk

Cohen, S. (1972/2011) *Folk devils and moral panics* (London: Routledge).

Note

[1] I would like to thank Bea Kay, Tony Staunton, Andy Brammer, Sam O'Brien and Michael Lavalette for their helpful advice.

ELEVEN

My people?

Dave Stamp

As a result of austerity measures local councils across Britain are making a range of cuts to social and public services. These cuts are often deep – and raise questions about the viability of social work practice when there are few material resources available to meet people's needs. However, what if (or when) the cuts are disproportionately focused on projects working with minority communities – and justified because, unfortunately, these are not 'our' people? In this chapter Dave Stamp draws on his practice experience to look at the ways in which local councils are justifying cuts to services for minority communities – and asks what social workers should do when faced with such 'racist cuts'.

Introduction

In October 2010, Birmingham City Council's cabinet member for Housing, John Lines, announced the local authority's proposal to stop providing housing and support for asylum seekers, noting that in 'these difficult economic times … my people have got to come first' (Bloxham 2010).

Lines' words were an explicit articulation of a process of abjectification (Squire 2009) by which asylum seekers and other undocumented migrants are excluded from the mainstream of social welfare provision. This discourse constructs asylum seekers and other irregular migrants as 'illegal' – or, perhaps more accurately, as 'illegals', with the term becoming a noun by which those subject to immigration control are dehumanised and set apart from the rest of us. (Dauvergne 2008: 10). Quite bluntly, as the BBC reported in relation to the lives of people seeking asylum in Glasgow, 'the Government says these people should not exist' (Nye 2013). This chapter will seek to explore the implications of this imposition of illegality on both the lived experiences of those subject to immigration control, and on those professionals working to provide – or, increasingly, to deny – services and support to them.

It will draw heavily on my own experience as a practitioner working in a small, grassroots voluntary sector agency advocating on behalf of asylum seekers and other undocumented migrants in Birmingham although the opinions voiced are my own and not necessarily those of the agency itself.

Leaving vulnerable people unable to meet their needs

One consequence of this discourse is that some thousands of refused asylum seekers are left destitute due to policies that seek effectively to starve them into agreeing to return 'voluntarily' to their countries of origin. Policies and procedures that leave vulnerable people unable to meet their basic subsistence needs are justified on the basis that to do otherwise would 'act as an incentive for people to remain in the UK once they have exhausted their appeal rights',[1] irrespective of the fact that, for a great many people, the prospect of any departure from the UK is an impossibility, with ever increasing numbers of officially stateless individuals left without even the most fundamental human rights (UNHCR/Asylum Aid 2011: 25). For thousands of others, the prospect of a 'voluntary' return to countries in which war, human rights violations and abject poverty are commonplace remains a simply unthinkable prospect. Destitution is being used as a tool of public policy, in a futile attempt to persuade refused (or, to use the Home Office's more pejorative term, 'failed') asylum seekers to return to their countries of persecution.

Those fortunate enough to fit the Home Office's narrow criteria for accommodation and support find themselves surviving on a subsistence allowance set at 55% of Income Support levels, often without access to cash and instead able only to access those commodities considered 'essential' (that is, food and clothing, but not telephone or travel costs) by means of the 'Azure' swipe card, which can be used in a range of major retailers. The Government's spending review has specifically targeted asylum-support rates as a Home Office expense to be cut (Grove-White 2010). Some of the consequences of this process have been quite vividly highlighted, to both farcical and tragic effect. Cynically, the Home Secretary Theresa May, sought to woo the Conservative Party Conference by claiming, entirely falsely, that the Home Office is routinely prevented by burdensome 'human rights' considerations from exercising effective immigration control on the flimsiest of pretexts, such as 'offenders' ownership of domestic pets. As has been pointed out, the introduction of such 'complex vulgarisations' (Fiori 1965/1990:

238) into the public consciousness has the long-term effect that such ideas become a kind of commonsense 'ambient truth' (Williams 2011), to be used as evidence of the UK's 'soft touch' approach to immigrants, who, of course, are represented as a drain on scarce public resources, as 'Benefit tourists', notwithstanding the absence of any evidence on which such a claim might realistically be based (*The Independent* 2012). This toxic discourse leaves many people – and particularly many women and others who already occupy a relatively disempowered space within capitalist society irrespective of their precarious immigration status – vulnerable to exploitation and abuse.

The brutal reality of the situation is more accurately reflected in another, far less widely reported, story, that of Osman Rasul Mohammed, a refused asylum-seeker from Iraq, who took his own life following 10 years' struggle to regularise his status in the UK, during which period he had established a family life with a British citizen, with whom he had had children (BBC 2011). In this light Lena Dominelli's claim that 'immigration policy has been the major public arena in which the politics of race impinging on social work practice has been played out' (Dominelli 1988: 25) remains depressingly true – with the exacerbating fact of two and a half decades of neoliberal ideology, and an attendant scapegoating of the poor and the marginalised as responsible for society's ills. As Owen Jones has written:

> There was once a popular narrative that social problems were caused by the injustices of capitalism that, at the very least, had to be corrected. With those ideas forced out of the mainstream, it has been easy for the idea that all social problems are caused by outsiders, immigrants, to gain a foothold. (Jones 2011: 224)

This discourse has become ever more fevered in the light of the strong showing in the Eastleigh by-election by the United Kingdom Independence Party (UKIP) following which the leaders of all three mainstream political parties in the UK have become engaged in a race to the bottom. Miliband, Clegg and Cameron are all keen to demonstrate their 'toughness' on immigration, and the Prime Minister declaring – without a shred of evidence that a 'something for nothing' culture had developed within the UK's migrant communities, which he was determined to stop (*Inside Government* 2013).

Increasing numbers of public-service professionals appear to internalise this discourse, with calls for health and welfare professionals to be ever more vigilant in their scrutiny of service users' immigration statuses to help clamp down on health and welfare 'tourism'. The discourse is magnified through a lens of racist and sexist stereotypes about fecklessness and fecundity, with the consequence that respected medical professionals can write, without a trace of evidence and apparently entirely ignorant of the legalities of the situation they are describing, of 'heavily pregnant women arriving in the UK because childbirth qualifies for emergency care and the child would be British, thereby providing the mother with residency rights' (Thomas 2013).

Marginalisation of social justice

In other words, contemporary social work practice is carried out in an environment in which questions of social justice are marginalised and in which the message from the political mainstream has been unequivocally that immigration is a 'problem' in need of urgent attention, and that questions of immigration control are practical, rather than ideological. Any and every political contemporary event, no matter how complex, is explicitly linked to the 'problem' of immigration. Hence *The Daily Mail*, editorialising on the outbreak of rioting within many of England's major cities in August 2011, could proclaim – explicitly parroting the rhetoric of far-right groups such as the British National Party (BNP) – that:

> Mass immigration – imposed on Britain without any debate – has stretched schools and other social structures to breaking point and saturated the jobs market with foreign workers. (*The Daily Mail* 2011)

The asylum seeker, the refugee, the forced migrant, the 'illegal' therefore occupies a particularly charged space within the neoliberal discourse. For not only are they likely to have been the most afflicted in their country of origin by the very processes of fragmentation – war, privatisation, deregulation, fiscal austerity and marketization – which characterise the neoliberal project of 'armed globalisation' (Callinicos 2003) itself, but they also, on arrival, find themselves at the forefront of the attack by forces such as John Lines, or *The Daily Mail*'s editorial writers, who yearn for 'simpler, exclusionary times' (Dauvergne 2008:p4), before the globalisation genie escaped its bottle.

There is, in other words, a charged ideological debate underway, in which definitions of who does and who does not 'belong' are fiercely contested, so that an idealised citizen – who is invariably, in Lines', Thomas' and Cameron's image, wealthy, white, male and 'deserving' – is contrasted with an abject 'illegal' – who is 'free-riding', black, fecund, irresponsible and 'undeserving'. While John Lines would doubtless be quick to deny the existence of any relationship between 'his people' and questions of race and ethnicity, it is little short of impossible to hear the phrase as anything other than a 'dog-whistle', specifically designed to resonate with those who also identify with the image of the idealised citizen being promoted. There is, in effect, a conflict underway centring on the essential relationship between democracy, citizenship rights and culture.

From this perspective, the coalition government's relentless assault on human rights legislation can be more easily understood, since it is simply unthinkable that the rights assumed by Lines' ideal citizen might ever be in question. Rather, it is the very idea that such rights – to family life, to marriage, to a fair trial, and so on – might be assumed by those who 'should not exist'. As Steve Cohen has reminded us, immigration controls are, by definition, exclusionary and racist. Racism and justice are incompatible (Cohen 2006: 4)

Given this scorched political landscape, it is perhaps little wonder that social work in Britain today can be described as having 'lost its direction' (Social Work Action Network 2004). While it may well be the case, as the Manifesto notes, that 'many of us entered social work- and many of us still do- out of a commitment to social justice, or at the very least to bring about positive change in people's lives', there is an almost tangible sense of defeatism within the profession – frequently even before people become qualified to practice. Writing from a personal perspective, this has become apparent to me from the routine reactions of social work students participating in workshops on working with people subject to immigration control as part of a local university's social work degree course on which I teach. Here, case studies involving clients in a variety of true-to-life desperate and disempowered circumstances are discussed and potential interventions considered: ever more frequently, student feedback to these scenarios justifies the refusal of even hypothetical services with the response 'we're just social workers'.

It is true that some students are emotionally moved by the scenarios under discussion, with people regularly pledging that, if working with individuals in the desperate, destitute situations in question, they would provide money from their own pockets to help meet their immediate subsistence needs. Yet seldom is there any discussion of an engaged, collective professional response to the circumstances that leave pregnant women and other vulnerable individuals sleeping on the streets. There is, rather, an already internalised acceptance of the idea that social work as a profession can aspire to nothing other than 'supervising the deterioration of other people's lives', as the Manifesto puts it, as though an analysis of the social conditions in which social work's service users live, and the development of a practice vocabulary with which such conditions might be challenged is neither necessary nor particularly desirable.

Defeatist practice

Some of the implications of this defeatist practice on the lives of people subject to immigration control can be illustrated by the example of a young man who eventually found himself, shivering in slippers and pyjamas, in the office of the agency for which I work on a bitterly cold October day. He had been discharged onto the street from hospital, where he had spent 18 months as an inpatient, suffering from the consequences of tuberculosis and hepatitis. He was cognitively impaired as a consequence of his multiple health problems, and had restricted mobility. No plans had been made for his care and support following discharge, despite there being a clear case for an assessment of need under section 21 of the National Assistance Act – a piece of legislation passed in 1948 to replace the Poor Law, precisely to ensure that no one with insufficient national insurance contributions could go without basic subsistence support. On contacting the hospital social work team to investigate why no such assessment appeared to have been carried out, the response – perhaps predictably enough – was that no such assessment was necessary since the individual in question was 'an illegal'. Bafflingly – given that the young man in question had been medically diagnosed to have experienced brain damage – there was also a suggestion that he might be seeking to exaggerate the symptoms of his cognitive impairment in a bid to bolster his claims for leave to remain and support in the UK, in an unconscious (or not) echo of the 'scrounger' rhetoric routinely applied to recipients of disability benefits. (Clark 2012). Here, in other words, was a young man who had been expelled from humanity altogether, and to whom no professional caring responsibility could conceivably be owed (Arendt 1979: 297). He was, quite simply, not one of 'our people'.

The acceptance of a status quo in which capitalism has been stripped of its Keynesian appendages and is free to be as antisocial, antidemocratic and boorish as it wants (Klein 2007: 253), and in which the most disadvantaged, impoverished and dispossessed members of society are constructed as essentially without rights is, of course, by no means unique to the social work profession. As Paul Gilroy has noted, an integral component of the neoliberal project's privatisation of society's essential welfare services has been the 'privatisation of the mind' (Gilroy 2011), a consequence of which is the contraction of the very concept of politics itself; all three major political parties in the UK are in favour of the neoliberal economic project and of the idea, to echo Owen Jones, that the social problems caused by capitalism can only be addressed by the application of yet more capitalism. Part and parcel of this process of contraction, of reduction, has been the promotion of the concept of 'firm but fair' immigration controls, a concept by which it comes to be accepted that the UK's immigration and asylum system is designed to differentiate the 'genuine' from the 'bogus', that this is in some way a legitimate goal, and that the process by which such decisions are made is itself 'just', notwithstanding overwhelming evidence to the contrary (Amnesty International 2004), and notwithstanding the demonstrable fact of the Home Office's frequently dismal decision-making processes.

A Palestinian client of the agency for which I work, for example, was bewildered to receive a refusal letter from the Home Office, solemnly advising him that arrangements were being put in place to return him to the 'city of Lebanon', which was apparently in the independent state of Palestine and in which his parents had been resident since 1948. Plainly, no logic, knowledge or research could have informed this conclusion, which appears to have been tailored solely to fit a prior decision to refuse, to exclude.

Hand in hand with this contraction of the concept of the political has been the reduction of the concept of racism to a consideration of unpleasant and anti-social attitudes and behaviour attributed to and displayed by some groups of people – most notably the white working-class – set entirely adrift from any consideration of social power relations. By way of illustration, we might consider the very different public responses to the deaths of two black men. Stephen Lawrence, famously, was attacked and killed by a group of white men in Eltham in 1993. Two of his killers were finally convicted in 2012 following a high profile campaign led by, among others, *The Daily Mail*. Their convictions were hailed in the media as a victory for justice, with commentators such as Dan Hodges observing that

> things have changed. And it's you (Lawrence's killers) that changed them. The racism. The bile. The hate. It's still there, swirling around. But it's been driven underground, into the sewers. It's no longer striding cocksure, clad in its tacky grey and yellow trim jacket, down Eltham High Street. (Hodges 2012)

In other words, Lawrence's killers and the community from which they had risen were described as thuggish badly dressed anachronisms, 'driven underground' by a groundswell of tolerance and open-mindedness. This is an elitist discourse on which the far-right thrives, and in which white working-class communities are seen as irredeemably worthless 'chavs', devoid of any cultural merit (Jones 2011: 225), further increasing the potential alienation for members of such communities, and reducing the likelihood of their seeking to form alliances with those members of new migrant communities with whom they are likely to perceive themselves to be in competition for jobs, housing and services.

State power and control

Yet this rhetoric also deflects attention away from the relations of state power, exclusion and control that leads to the deaths of those considered surplus to the state's needs. One such, Jimmy Mubenga, was a 'failed' asylum seeker, who was killed in October 2010 by contractors employed by G4S, facilitating his 'removal' from the UK on behalf of the UK Border Agency. Witnesses report seeing the three security guards 'heavily restraining' Mubenga by forcing him down and sitting on him for as long as 45 minutes, ignoring his cries for mercy and evident struggle for breath (Lewis and Taylor 2010). While a verdict of unlawful killing was eventually reached in July 2013, no one has yet faced prosecution (Coles and Scott 2013). No high-profile media campaign, led by *The Daily Mail*, exists to bring his killers to justice, or to insist that there should be no repetition of the events that led to his death. Neither the organisations nor the individuals responsible have been denounced as worthless or barbaric or as relics of a crude, violent prehistory. Instead, the agency by which his killers were employed, G4S, has been awarded a lucrative Home Office tender to provide accommodation and support to asylum seekers (UK Border Agency 2011). Mubenga's death, and the treatment of those responsible for it, is a grim reminder of the state's willingness and ability to use the most brutal, authoritarian violence against those deemed unwanted (Cohen 2006: 14) – or, as Councillor Lines might put it, not one of 'my people' – no matter what defenders of the status quo may wish to tell themselves about contemporary attitudes to race and racism post-Lawrence.

Racism is reduced as a concept to a set of unpalatable ideas displayed by those on the margins of society, rather than a set of economic, political and ideological practices through which a dominant group exercises hegemony over a subordinate group (Hall 1980: 338). Similarly, little attention is paid to the ways in which women's disadvantaged positions within patriarchal society intersect with questions of race, ethnicity, class and impoverishment to leave women who are subject to immigration control in particularly disadvantaged circumstances. Some of the consequences of this depoliticisation, this effective disengagement with the social and political forces, which shape service users' lives, can be illustrated by the example of an individual social worker's response to a referral made on behalf of 'Sarah', a single mother with two children, aged 11 months and 5 years respectively. Sarah had entered the UK from Nigeria as a spouse, with her husband here on a five-year working visa. As such, she had no recourse to public funds, and limited legal rights in her own right. Her relationship with her husband had broken down due to domestic violence. At the point of her referral to my own agency, she had been sleeping with her two children on a friend's living room floor for three weeks. Her friend also has a husband and children. Sarah had outstayed her welcome, and had been given two days to find alternative accommodation. At the point of her referral, she was desperate and tearful, telling us that her children had not eaten for a day and that she was terrified, during the bitterly cold spell we were then experiencing, of the prospect of street homelessness for her children. As with so many of our clients, Sarah was in a 'catch 22' situation, faced with the prospect of a hostile reception as an unmarried and 'disobedient' single mother in her deeply conservative country of origin, but denied the ability to settle and build her life in the country in which her children have spent most of their lives as a consequence of immigration control.

Given the dismal circumstances in which this family was surviving, a referral was made to the appropriate local authority for an assessment of need under section 17 of the Children Act. Throughout the process, however, Sarah routinely considered herself 'judged' by the worker carrying out the assessment, who repeatedly and variously demanded to know why she had never reported domestic violence to the police, why she had 'failed' to leave her abusive partner earlier if she was genuinely in danger, why she simply did not return to him, given that she had survived the 'alleged' abuse endured to date, and why she did not arrange to return with her children to Nigeria given the impoverished circumstances in which the family was then living. Yet nowhere was there any apparent attempt to understand, explore or even acknowledge the limited options safely available to Sarah as a consequence not only of her immigration status but also as a woman disadvantaged by patriarchal systems in which her 'legal' and approved presence in the UK was entirely dependent on her relationship with a violent and abusive partner, and in which she would be met with hostility, destitution and disapproval if returning to her country of origin as an unmarried mother.

From the vantage point afforded by such depressingly common case studies, not only can the social work profession be seen to have failed in its responsibilities to 'promote social change' or to uphold 'principles of human rights and social justice', as set down in the definition of the profession used by the International Federation of Social Workers, but also it can actually be seen to be in the vanguard of a movement to reintroduce elements of the virulently racist, oppressive and xenophobic discourse challenged by academics, activists and service user groups in the 1970s and 1980s. So, while David Cameron has called for members of the public to report suspected illegal immigrants to the appropriate authorities (Travis 2011), and Home Office officials have been observed apparently illegally stopping and searching coach passengers, detaining them at will if they cannot produce proof of citizenship (Townsend 2011), the blunt fact is that local authority social workers have been charged with this duty of surveillance for years. Schedule 3 of the Nationality, Immigration and Asylum Act 2002 imposes a positive obligation on local authorities, including social workers, to inform the Home Office when a suspected relevant ineligible person applies for support and assistance under various provisions.

This is compromising in the extreme in relation to social workers' duties to act as advocates for their clients; furthermore, the fear this practice engenders serves as a barrier, to prevent some of the most vulnerable members of society from approaching social work agencies for assistance and support. Writing as a voluntary sector practitioner, I am acutely aware of the ways in which this fear can be cynically manipulated by local authority team managers seeking to corral their budgets by instructing workers explicitly to advise potential service users subject to immigration control that no assessment process can begin – and much less can any services be put in place – until the information in question has been passed to the UK Border Agency, with the hope surely being that such potential service users will withdraw from engagement, leaving vulnerable individuals, including children, cut adrift from welfare provision.

The linking of entitlement to services with the question of the individual's immigration status, and the 'gatekeeping' duty this can be seen to impose on practitioners has been described as 'collaboration' with the enforcement of immigration controls that are, by definition, exclusionary and racist. As Mynott has noted (in Ferguson et al 2005: 135) the practical implications on social work practice and on the professional's duty to act in the client's best interests of any collaboration with agencies seeking to detain or deport service users lead, ultimately, to a breach of professional duty.

This manifests itself in quite alarming ways, such as the example of the local authority social worker who contacted the advocacy agency for which I work, explaining that she had been working for some years with an unaccompanied asylum-seeking child from Afghanistan, who was about to turn 18. Her manager had been advised by Home Office representatives that the service user was due to be detained at his next reporting event, in preparation for immediate removal to Afghanistan. The Home Office had then requested that the service user's social worker actually accompany him to the reporting event, specifically to ensure his attendance at the appointment, and thereby his detention and ultimate 'removal' from the UK. The manager had acceded to this request. The worker, uncomfortable with this state of affairs, was seeking to explore whether there were any legal avenues of redress available to this young man to avoid detention and removal. Yet, commendable as this was, the option of simply refusing to escort a vulnerable young man for whom she had a duty of care to an appointment specifically designed to facilitate his removal to an active war zone appeared little short of unthinkable to this worker. Indeed, she was unprepared even to share the information about his planned imminent removal with her service user, and specifically instructed us that, if it was possible to do anything to assist the child for whom she had been entrusted with a duty of care, her name should be 'kept out of it'.

Social work values

In other words, there is a clear tension between the principles of human rights and social justice, which lie at the core of the social work profession, and the requirement that social workers should collude with, as Steve Cohen (2006: 2) has put it, the right of the state to expel or exclude people from its territory, whether by means of deportation or the denial of citizenship represented by the machinery of destitution. Social work, then, cannot be neutral. Practitioners must explicitly and consciously decide whether their allegiance is with those designated as 'illegal', or with those state authorities seeking to deny such individuals 'the right to have rights', echoing Hannah Arendt (Cohen 2006: 8); there is no half-way position. Such a critical social work practice would necessitate not only a breach with the 'common sense' assumptions of the neoliberal paradigm, but also with managerial imperatives that seek to restrict creative and liberating modes of professional expression.

Such a practice must, therefore, work from the foundation that no one is 'illegal', challenging institutional racism precisely by, as Dominelli suggested, recognising explicitly that social work is *political*, and that the practice decisions made by social workers have political ramifications on the lives of their service users. Social workers who choose to make such decisions within the paradigm of the dominant ideology, of the discourse that constructs certain individuals as 'illegal', are not acting impartially or apolitically. They are instead enforcing an oppressive status quo (Dominelli 1988: 75).

However, such practice must also be informed by a position of resistance to neoliberal managerialism, in which 'social domains, whose concern is not producing commodities in the narrower economic sense of goods for sale, come nevertheless to be organised and conceptualised in terms of commodity provision, distribution and consumption' (Fairclough 1992: 207), or what has been described as 'digital Taylorism' (Chakrabortty 2011), as a consequence of which process professionals have ever decreasing control in their workplace, particularly in relation to how decisions are made, and are instead 'the white-collar equivalent of a factory line' (Chakrabortty 2011).

The implications of this managerialism on aspects of social work practice can usefully be illustrated by an exploration of Zizek's elaboration of Lacan's concept of 'the big Other', to which many professionals subordinate their own autonomy and agency, disavowing responsibility for the impact of their actions (or inactions) on other people's lives by instead deferring ultimate responsibility for decisions made onto other, more remote, authorities: 'keep me out of it' (Fisher 2009: 49). In a sense, many professionals located within such managerial structures see themselves as having little more agency or control than the 'illegals' whose lives they may administrate, or indeed, than the passengers who sat and witnessed Jimmy Mubenga being choked to death on an aeroplane.

As Mynott has noted (in Ferguson et al 2005: 139), an engaged, oppositional practice that resists this tendency towards bureaucratic impotence cannot emerge without the independent collective organisation of social workers themselves, and the development of a form of political trade-unionism, which recognises the wider political dynamics of globalisation, and the ways in which asylum seekers, refugees and other forced migrants – the "illegals" – are in the frontline of the neoliberal onslaught, while simultaneously seeking to fight to retain the professionalism and autonomy of its members. One means by which such a political trade-unionism could inform the development of such an oppositional, non-collaborative practice is through the consideration of a 'Don't ask, don't tell' position in relation to service users' immigration status. This would see public-sector unions, such as UNISON, taking up a policy of non cooperation and non-implementation of internal immigration controls by supporting their members in refusing to ask questions relating to a service user's immigration status and by refusing to pass any such information to the Home Office. In the United States, this position has been adopted in San Francisco, which has declared itself a 'City of Refuge' and has declared that 'No department, agency, commission, officer or employee of the City and County of San Francisco shall use any City funds or resources to assist in the enforcement of federal immigration law or to gather or disseminate information regarding the immigration status of individuals in the City and County of San Francisco.' (San Francisco Administrative Code, Chapter 12H). The position, then, seeks to make city services – such as access to social care – available to all city residents, without discrimination on the basis of immigration status. Local authority service providers would not seek immigration-status-related information, and nor would local authority employees share the immigration status of those seeking to access such services with immigration enforcement authorities (San Francisco Administrative Code, Chapter 12H).

This is, of course, a position dramatically, if not diametrically, opposed to the status quo in the UK, where as we have seen social workers have become used to working in close co-operation or, indeed, collaboration with, those forces seeking to facilitate their clients' detention and removal. It would, as Mynott reminds us, be a fantasy to claim that such professionals are free agents, 'bound only by their conscience and the limits of their imagination' (in Ferguson et al 2005: 134). Social work practice is carried out in a set of given economic, political and legal conditions. Yet nor is the call for a 'Don't ask, don't tell' position hopelessly idealistic or utopian; indeed, some of these very same economic, political and legal factors under consideration can be seen to point directly to the adoption of precisely such a position.

By way of illustration, the Los Angeles Police Department – arguably not the agency to which one would automatically first turn for an example of empowering and progressive migrant justice practice – has, for the past 30 years, operated what is essentially a 'Don't ask, don't tell' policy, arguing that doing so enables appropriate policing of neighbourhoods in which there are significant volumes of undocumented migrants, for whom the fear of investigation, detention and deportation might serve as a barrier to co-operation with the police or to coming forward to testify as witnesses against crime (Kim

2008). The adoption of such a policy was a direct response to a surge of violent crimes in Los Angeles' immigrant communities that often went unreported, thereby leaving such communities vulnerable.

It is at least arguable that similar considerations can be applied to social work practice with undocumented migrants, and in particular with such practice relating to children and families. As already noted, section 17.1(a) of the Children Act 1989 places local authority social workers under a duty to 'safeguard and promote the welfare of children within their area who are in need'. Quite plainly, such a duty towards children cannot feasibly co-exist with a model of practice that seeks to collaborate with those agencies seeking to uproot them from their communities whether by the practice of detention or removal. (It should be noted that, notwithstanding the rhetoric of the Conservative-Liberal coalition government, children do continue to be detained [Barnett 2011]).

Similarly, while it may well be true that certain statutory guidelines, such as Schedule 3 of the NIA to which I have referred, encourage social workers to work in 'collaborative' and oppressive ways, it is equally true to say, as Mynott does (in Ferguson et al 2005: 136), that legal duties are open to interpretation. Bearing this in mind, it is the case that a raft of case law, particularly relating to the rights of children, enables and obliges professionals to work alongside their service users in a considerably more empowering and liberating fashion. Where the law can be used to the benefit of the marginalised and in the face of the destructive machinery of oppression, there is plainly a professional duty on the social worker committed to principles of human rights and social justice to ensure that it is so used. Examples of such legislation would include *Clue* v. *Birmingham City Council* [2011], in which it was ruled that the local authority's refusal to provide section 17 Children Act support to a destitute family awaiting the UK Border Agency's consideration of submissions requesting Leave to Remain in the UK were unlawful, or *R (VC)* v. *Newcastle* [2011] where the Court ruled that a local authority was not within its legal rights to withhold the provision of section 17 support from a refused asylum-seeking family purely on the basis that accommodation and subsistence support might otherwise be available to that family under section 4 of the Immigration and Asylum Act 1999. Social workers, therefore, have a professional responsibility to work creatively within these contradictions, precisely to uphold the principles of human rights and social justice that are at the profession's core.

Moreover, this position of non-compliance demonstrably works; internal immigration control simply cannot work without the acquiescence of welfare professionals. An example of how it is possible, acting in solidarity with the undocumented, to fight the logic of collaboration is provided by the response of social workers, supported by UNISON, under the impetus of the Sukula Family Campaign in Bolton. The Sukulas were threatened under section 9 of the Asylum and Immigration (Treatment of Claimants) Act 2004; this legislation allowed families with dependent children to be left entirely destitute, without even the provision of the meagre support packages provided to asylum seekers by the Home Office. Local authorities would be prohibited from providing any support or services to such families, other than under section 20 of the Children Act – thereby separating children from their families, and again further disadvantaging women, who overwhelmingly assume or are given the responsibility for children's welfare. The statute was 'piloted' in Bolton, where social workers refused to enforce it. The position was supported by UNISON, which undertook both nationally and locally to oppose section 9. The branch secretary of UNISON's Bolton branch vowed:

> I hope that no social worker will ever be instructed to knock on the Sukula's door to enforce the government's indefensible policy. But if it does happen, I hope that social workers will refuse to carry out the instruction. They will have the full support of Bolton Metro UNISON Branch if they do. (www.labournet.net/ukunion/0510/bolton1.html)

No child was ever taken into section 20 care due to section 9; nor was any family evicted onto the street under the legislation, which was quietly filed away and never enacted as a direct consequence of an organised and concerted programme of professional non-compliance, in solidarity with service users (Cohen 2006: 158).

There are, of course, potential pitfalls in a social work practice that actively seeks not to engage with the issue of a service user's immigration status. For one thing, given the fact of links between social entitlement and immigration status, a practitioner could conceivably fail to pick up on a service user's entitlement to public funds, and the welfare rights that would accompany such an entitlement. Such a situation, however, could potentially be avoided if the practitioner keeps mindful of the reasons for seeking such information. Put simply, is the enquiry motivated by concern for the interests of the service user, or from an impetus to collaborate with oppressive and exclusionary forces? Does the worker's action seek to collude with the machinery that seeks to oppress the service user, or is it instead motivated by a principle of solidarity with the undocumented? Again, the engaged and empathic practitioner can reflect on the fact that immigration control in and of itself creates those very factors for asylum-seeking families – poverty, isolation, precarity – which are 'normally' considered due justification for social work intervention (Grady in Hayes and Humphries 2004: 138). To seek further to increase these factors, through collusion with the processes responsible for them, cannot conceivably sit squarely with social work's core professional values.

True it is that local authorities are facing ever tighter squeezes on the budgets available to them. Yet, as Simon Cardy has written, the duty on social workers in such situations is to explore and create opportunities to work alongside their clients to help improve their life chances. Rather than colluding with the managerial discourse that insists financial considerations are of paramount importance, an engaged social work practice would entail practitioners advising their managers that 'you might control the budget but my job as a social worker is to spend it!' (Cardy 2013).

Conclusion

Social workers seeking to develop a model of practice committed to supporting the marginalised, the poor and the oppressed, as we have seen, have had their voices drowned out by those arguing for ever tighter budgetary constraints and firmer control of resources (Hayes and Humphries 2004: 218). This position has become still further entrenched by a political climate in which 'austerity' is the byword, public services are under attack, and organised labour has been weakened by three decades of neoliberal onslaught. People subject to immigration control have been firmly cast in the public imagination as 'undeserving', with the consequence that even those immigrants legally entitled to take up employment, and to claim contributory benefits, are constructed as 'a problem', in need of government intervention (Grayling 2012). Practitioners, therefore, seeking to demonstrate solidarity with those marginalised by immigration control have tough choices to make. Yet they must be made. Workers must choose compliance or defiance. There is no middle position.

An engaged, politicised social work of use to those subject to immigration control must therefore entail a re-engagement with the politics of gender, race, sexuality, disability and class, and a re-examination of the power relations that exist in the actions and motives of those state organs that seek to exclude the undocumented from the ranks of 'our people'. It requires us to focus our attention at least as much on the actions of those who contract, countenance and endorse the suffocation of deportees on aeroplanes, or the abduction of children from families, as on the actions of alienated and marginalised white youths. It requires us to locate our practice base firmly and unapologetically in the politics of the slogan 'No one is illegal'.

Suggested further reading

Athwal, H. (2010) *Driven to desperate measures (2006–2010)*, London: Institute of Race Relations.

Cohen, S. (2003) *No-one is illegal*, Manchester: Trenton.

Vickers, T. (2012) *Refugees, capitalism and the British State*, Farnham: Aldgate.

Notes

[1] Baroness Ashton of Upholland, House of Lords Official Report, *Hansard*, 7 February 2006.

TWELVE

Twenty-first century eugenics? A case study about the Merton Test

Rhetta Moran and Susan Gillett

In this chapter Moran and Gillett, both active practitioners in the asylum field, raise disturbing questions about the age-assessment test (the Merton Test) that many social workers will be asked to participate in. The PCF domain 2 is concerned with ensuring that social workers practise in an ethical way that reflects social work values. Yet Moran and Gillett suggest that the Merton Test effectively breaches social work ethical codes: it is, they suggest, a new form of eugenics. Their case is that the Merton Test has no basis in science, that questions asked are culturally insensitive, and that the test is only applied to those deemed as 'other' by institutional racist immigration and asylum laws. Given this, they argue, social workers, whose primary concern should be with safeguarding vulnerable children, should not engage in age-assessment 'tests'.

Introduction

This chapter is about exposing and resisting the institutionalised racism (as defined by Macpherson 1999) that is practised through the test known as the Merton Compliant age assessment that, through its introduction into the field of social work practice, is an indicator of the advancement of the neoliberal agenda (Harman 2007).

The Merton Compliant is the general guidance to local authorities about how to decide whether a child seeking asylum who claims to be a child, is a child. It was included in the findings of Judge Burnton in the High Court in 2003[1] and, when it is used, it is applied by practising social workers to a child who is, in conjunction, being 'processed' as an asylum seeker by a United Kingdom Border Agency (UKBA) 'caseowner'.[2]

The authors textually analyse: policy and legal case documents; the guidance accompanying one local authority's Merton Compliance assessment tool alongside the empirical content of that tool as applied to a 15-year-old boy by a local authority social worker; and anonymised extracts from the audit trail of that 'Merton Complied' case study. Through this combination of sources and method, the authors explore whether and how this test, and in particular the guidance about the 'tool' used to apply it, offers a contemporary example of a judicially and medically supported operationalisation, by social workers, of an essentialist and deeply racist statutory policy. The authors seek to demonstrate whose interests are being represented (Vickers 2012: 112; cf. Roberts 2004) by the test, and to expose why they are neither those of the child, nor of any social work practitioner whose commitment is to safeguarding the child.

Tha authors also offer some commentary about the different practices and vested interests that are revealed through their outline of some of the anti-racist interventions by a private fostering agency social worker who, working collaboratively with the child himself, his foster family and a human rights organisation, contested the test result directly in the specific case and opened up a route to justice that is still being travelled. Contrasting the actions of the two, differently located social workers helps to position this test, and the social worker's relationship to it, within the wider, neoliberal political context[3] (Harman(2007; Bone 2012), in Britain that has developed out of the Thatcher era.

In summation, the authors argue that this 'test' represents a leaf in the neoliberal book, being a re-emergence of a form of pseudoscience that can be associated with the eugenics movement (European Molecular Biology Organization [EMBO] 2001) and is, being exclusively applied to 'outsiders and through immigration law', inherently racist: it must be excised from social work practice.

The judicio-political context surrounding Merton Compliance

In 1990, when the UK ratified the United Nations Convention on the Rights of the Child (UNCRC)[4] that set out the rights of all children under the age of 18, it maintained a reservation of article 22 of the Convention. This effectively excluded children subject to immigration control from the rights enshrined within it.

In 2008, however, that reservation was lifted. Theoretically then, since 2008, the UK Government must ensure that:

> asylum seeking children, unaccompanied or accompanied, receive appropriate protection and humanitarian assistance in the enjoyment of all the rights under the UNCRC and shall be afforded the same protection as any other child

> permanently or temporarily deprived of his or her family environment. (UNCRC Article 22)

However, Merton Compliance is superseding this Article in practice. Pinder (2011) posits that a lack of central government guidance on this issue has inhibited the courts[5] from specifying precisely how a local authority should give an applicant the opportunity to enjoy all rights under the UNCRC (see further discussion at paragraph 21 of the judgment[6]). The courts have noted that some local authorities have their own published Practice Guidelines (namely Croydon and Hillingdon), as does the UKBA,[7] but that that there is 'a lacuna in respect of formalised central government guidance [for] age assessment disputes and JR [judicial review] claims' (Pinder 2011).

Forty-five per cent of all unaccompanied children are age disputed (Corria 2010) and Merton Compliant assessments are *only* undertaken when the child's age is disputed: not all children are age assessed as a matter of course. The context in which the assessment is done is therefore important. The assessments are never only intended to establish age – and correlating access to statutory provision. They are – intrinsically – assessing a child's credibility and are intended to decide whether what a child is saying is a lie or the truth. The assumption of dishonesty underpins the process and the burden of proof is placed upon the child to demonstrate beyond doubt that they are telling the truth; something they are, not surprisingly, often unable to do. This inability is then used to 'prove' their dishonesty.

However, this proof process affects not only asylum claims but also children's access to safeguarding and welfare provision and whether statutory authorities are liable to pay for those provisions. It is precisely because of this financial liability consideration that statutory and non-statutory social workers are potentially, and in our case study actually, differently located in their relationships to the child.

More generally, from our discussions with practising social workers, it does not seem unreasonable to conjecture that there may well be a correlation between negative age assessments and the Suffolk judgement,[8] which states that councils must treat homeless 16- and 17-year-olds as 'looked after'. In practice, in many councils, this 2003 law was not implemented for years and it is still left to the assessing social worker to ensure the young person understands the legislation and support to which they are eligible – including aftercare services/grant.

Further, the authors have been unable to definitively locate any form of nationally agreed curriculum content and/or externally accredited training process for assessors. Rather, anecdotal evidence suggests that

Merton Compliant assessors must volunteer to become such while recent Refugee Council research has established that would-be assessors are exposed to either two or three hours of non-standardised training and that the absence of consistency in training is compensated for through a 'learning on the job' approach (Clarke 2011: 33).

Case study

Frank (not his real name) is an orphan who lost one leg in a bomb blast in the centre of his home city. He was 16 when he phoned the mobile number of the agency family-placement social worker Margaret (not her real name) who, for the previous six months, had been responsible for supporting and supervising the foster carers in a northern conurbation with whom Frank had been placed on the very day that he arrived in the UK and claimed asylum. An injury had taken Margaret away from her caseload for six months but, on the day she returned and made her first placement visit, Margaret found Frank in his carer's hallway, surrounded by bin bags of his belongings, having been told by his local authority social worker that he was leaving the carer's home. Immediately, prompted by his appearance of destitution and isolation, Margaret gave Frank her mobile number and that of an independent human rights organisation that worked with refugees[9] and that she was aware of as being located within the centre of the conurbation: "His appearance of destitution and isolation is what prompted me to put my arm of support out to him" (direct quote from correspondence with authors). That day, Frank was taken to view a small bedsit in the attic of a large house. The foster carer immediately objected to this on the grounds of Frank's disability needs and Margaret expressed the carer's concerns to the local authority team manager who instructed the social worker to find more appropriate accommodation on a ground floor.

Thereafter, Margaret had little interaction with Frank. However, when she visited the family over the next six months and spoke with Frank about his placement experience, she always made it explicit to him that she was acting independently of his local authority social worker. On the day that Frank attended his UKBA asylum hearing alone, he phoned her. By this time, the local authority social services department, who had paid for his foster placement, were preparing to move Frank into a hostel for adults, on the grounds that – according to their Merton test result – he was now 18.

Margaret responded to Frank's call and arrived at the home of his foster family to find him, alongside distressed members of the family, waiting for the local authority social worker to arrive. Within a few days, during which time Frank remained with his foster family, Margaret had succeeded in securing agreement from the local authority that Frank be rehoused in a one-bedroomed house with a downstairs toilet, pending the outcome of his asylum appeal.

Margaret's intervention – at Frank's invitation – marked the beginning of a David and Goliath contest that is yet to be concluded.

Deconstructing guidelines[10]

The local authority 'age assessment' tool that was applied in the case study is structured into two columns. The left-hand column offers guideline statements for the assessors that relate to one of 10 specific assessment themes that are, in turn, written about in the right-hand column: physical appearance; demeanour; social history and family composition; developmental considerations; education; health and medical assessment; information from documentation and other sources, analysis of information gained; and conclusion.

The discussion in this section highlights some extracts from the guidelines for the racist ideology that they demonstrate and that is underpinned by an essentialist world view. The extracts are illustrative rather than exhaustive.

For the first, physical appearance, the guidance urges: '*It is important to consider racial differences here e.g. it is normal in some cultures…*'. In addition to the complete conflation between race and culture (Yan 2008), this guidance reduces the complexity of norm formation to a single, anodyne phrase.

But what is normal? According to whom? 'Norms' are socially and culturally constructed (Berger and Luckmann 1966: 51–5, 59–61). Being fluid and multiple, rather than fixed and monolithic, norms are further complicated through temporal, organisational patterns (Ancona et al 2001). Further, the guidelines concede that, in assessing demeanour, '*it is essential to take account of how the person presents, style, attitude and authority and relate this to the culture of the country of origin and events preceding the interview*'… but intrinsically fail to recognise that culture itself – even in a single country – is multiple (Fekete 2011).

The assessor is advised that '*Life experiences and trauma may impact on the ageing process, bear this in mind.*' In addition to the obvious limitations associated with assuming that some non-specialised individual, who has been exposed to three hours of training, can understand the full complexity of the potential life experience that any child may have presented from, and the skills to locate and assess their stories and individual experiences within this understanding, this guidance also assumes that there is a uniform experience of and ageing reaction to trauma and, therefore, a legitimate form of traumatised ageing. In fact, reactions to trauma can vary enormously (Silverman et al 2003).

'*It is useful to establish the length of time that the person has taken to arrive in the UK from the time they left their country of origin and include this in the age calculation.*' The unpredictable nature of overland travel, particularly when people are being smuggled across borders, and the range of different ways in which people through the world may conceptualise and articulate about the passage of time itself (Goody 1968), may mean that children do not know the date they left, or how many days have passed since they left their home country. Here, though, the inability to provide dates and timescales may be used to argue that the child is lying or older than they claim, as they are unable to account for periods of time.

'*The practitioner should be observing factors such as the manner in which the person copes with the assessment. Does he or she appear confident or overwhelmed?*' It is unclear whether or not appearing overwhelmed is considered an indicator of youth. However, from a child's view point, having arrived in the UK unaccompanied and with no idea of what is going to happen to them, they may well appear overwhelmed or, conversely, the confidence and tenacity that they developed in order to survive the ordeal so far may inhibit their demonstration of feeling overwhelmed. Either way, an observation of confidence in presentation – or the lack thereof – is not indicative of age. Further, the implicit assumption that age should correspond with confidence levels, once again indicates the presence of an essentialist world view that is failing to accommodate either culturally specific factors or individual personality.

'*Does what the person is describing seem age appropriate?*' In whose terms is a description perceived to be age appropriate? Is it age appropriate to have been rag picking on rubbish tips at the age of six[11] or told to shoot a fellow child soldier (Judah 2004)? If you have endured such experiences, can you even begin to talk about them in the context of proving yourself to strangers?

This last question is cursorily addressed within the guidance through the statement: '*Answering questions related to many of the above may be too painful until a relationship of trust has been established.*' It seems ridiculous to us to suggest that a relationship of trust is an option within a situation where the reason that local authority social workers are conducting an assessment in the first place is because that service itself has decided that there *is* a contest about the child's age. Given that this test is being conducted, most likely, on teenagers, it is unsafe to assume that the child will be oblivious to the fact that the starting point for the procedure is that they are currently disbelieved about their age and must overtly prove otherwise about themselves to the assessors. Even assuming that they are oblivious, how can a relationship of trust be established within a very short time frame? Trust – and especially with children who have experienced trauma and may have withdrawn into themselves – takes months to build and establish. Suggesting that it can be achieved within days and weeks is irresponsible and appears highly tokenistic.

In the authors' view, the essentialist world view that is promoted through these operational guidelines that are, in turn, suffused with racist ideas, are also creating social work parameters within which it is acceptable – even expected – to practise poorly. This assertion is reinforced by the events of 2010, when the Ombudsman ruled that Liverpool Council had used two untrained social workers to age assess a young girl from Cameroon. It was ruled that her being assessed as over 18 denied her the care that she needed for 15 months.

Following the Liverpool case, the Ombudsman ordered a review of assessments within Liverpool. A sample of 10% was reviewed (11 cases) and it was found that all were in keeping with the Merton guidance and therefore no recommendations were made. It would appear then, that the process of age assessment on which Merton guidelines are based has created a very low threshold of what is acceptable practice. When criticisms of the process are made, reviews subsequently find that the assessments are done to the required standard. This is missing the point: it is the standard/process itself that is obscene, not the fact that practitioners are, sometimes, not adhering to it.

...and the eugenics connection

Now, for a few moments, temporarily suspend the Merton Compliance from its fundamentally political purposes: to hit ever-reducing targets on the numbers of refugees allowed to stay in the UK (Bookstein 2003), coupled with advancing the neoliberal agenda that includes making swingeing reductions in public-sector spend. Let us consider whether, in the abstract, it has any scientific merit.

In the penultimate, analysis section of the guidelines it states: '*Please remember that this process is not an exact science*...'. This description is in direct reference to, originally, the 1999 Royal College of Paediatricians and Child Health (RCPCH) publication which states that '*Age determination is an inexact science* and the margin of error can sometimes be as much as 5 years either side' (authors' emphasis; Levenson and Sharma 1999: 13)

No reference to margin of error is made within the age-assessment case study at all. However, of even deeper significance is the sentence following in the RCPCH's guidelines: '*Assessment of age measures maturity, not chronological age*' (Levenson and Sharma 1999: 13). At the time, this critical distinction drawn between maturity and chronology was acknowledged by the Home Office itself .[12] Given that the stated purpose of Merton Compliance is to assess chronological age and not maturity, it is not then surprising that the fact that age assessment *cannot be* chronological has never been referred to again in the policy documents about asylum produced by either the Home Office or the Royal College of Paediatrics and Child Health (RCPCH).

By 2003, the RCPCH update on its policy is confining itself to a reproduction of its 1999 summary about age 'determination' – and abandoning the concept of age assessment altogether – as 'a complex and often inexact set of skills, where various physical, social and cultural factors all play their part, *although none provide a wholly exact or reliable indication of age, especially for older children*' (authors' emphasis;(RCPCH 2003). Even though it becomes valid, within scientific terms, to subtly alter policy position by jettisoning any further comment on age 'assessment', the RCPCH is still staying very close to its original rejection of the idea that it is possible to assess age with any degree of certainty.

However, by 2007, the RCPCH is '*accept[ing] the need for some form of assessment in some circumstances*' and, though it is still asserting that '*there is no single reliable method for making precise estimates*', it is now contributing an articulation, from a regulated, medical science body, of a '*most appropriate approach*' which involves '*a holistic evaluation, incorporating narrative accounts, physical assessment of puberty and growth and cognitive behavioural and emotional assessments*' (RCPCH 2007).

In 2011, *R (AS)* v. *London Borough of Croydon [2011] EWHC 2091 (Admin)*[13] made case law when there was a successful application for judicial review by a child, through the Official Solicitor, seeking the quashing of a local authority's age assessments, and a declaration as to the child's age. The judge quoted from the 1999 RCPCH policy statement that '*age determination was an inexact science*' but stopped a sentence short from the all-important '*Assessment of age measures maturity, not chronological age.*'[14] He then attached the 1999 RCPCH policy extract to an extract from the 2007 RCPCH policy statement, that '*the most appropriate approach is to use a holistic evaluation, incorporating narrative accounts, physical assessment of puberty and growth, and cognitive and behavioural and emotional assessments…*' (RCPCH 2007) and erroneously attributed it to the 1999 publication. This created the, false, impression that the RCPCH has endorsed age-determination processes from the beginning of its refugee children policy development. Finally, he tacked on the sentence clause '*...undertaken by social workers with relevant training*'. Thereby, the courts have most recently occluded the medical scientific opinion that this process cannot assess chronological age and, simultaneously, reinforced the legitimacy of social workers to take this 'appropriate approach'.

In their European-wide review of the age assessment procedures being used on young asylum seekers, Hjern et al found that '*Unclear guidelines and arbitrary practices may lead to alarming shortcomings in the protection of this high-risk group of children and adolescents in Europe. Medical participation, as well as non-participation, in these dubious decisions raises a number of ethical questions*' (Hjern et al 2012: 4). However, notwithstanding these misgivings, and with the aim of 'improving care', their conclusion basically tales the ideologically dominant view (Volosinov 1986: 98) that it is legitimate to attempt to determine the age of young people seeking asylum: '*To improve care for young asylum seekers with undetermined age, we suggest better legal procedures for the determination of age and a more flexible approach to chronological age.*' It is not.

To enable interventions that stop the continuation of Merton Compliance, the RCPCH should immediately restate its original – and apparently unchanged and unchallenged – view that it is not possible to scientifically assess chronological age. Children can be returned to death when their asylum claims, supported by Merton Compliance tests, are failed. The RCPCH – alongside British courts, the British government, local authorities, and British social work professional bodies and practitioners - would do well to remind itself of the EMBO's conclusion that, during the Holocaust, 'It was scientists who interpreted racial differences as the justification to murder. ... It is the responsibility of today's scientists to prevent this from happening again' (EMBO 2001: 871),

This section ends with the guideline's concluding statement '*that conclusions should always give the benefit of doubt*'. They neglect to specify to whom. However, if the benefit of doubt were given to the child, then the assessment would not occur at all: the 'process' is only enacted where a child has already been singled out, for two reasons: one, they are an 'outsider' subjected to a process that is only conducted upon people without British citizenship; two, they have, *a priori*, been placed in a group that is 'suspect' because, at some point, some one (either a UKBA official at point of entry or a local authority social worker) has introduced doubt about the child's credibility.

Analysis of case study's Merton Compliance assessment

The lead assessing social worker reassured Margaret that "we are here to protect him" (email, 4 June 2009) but their assessment process and the way in which the service proposed to treat Frank thereafter, exposes a local authority that denied its duty of care. The following, brief examination of some key failings is intended to offer a concrete example of the absurd and dangerous process.

First, a child should have the opportunity to have an appropriate adult present[15] throughout the assessment of his age, but Frank had no adult to advocate for him.

Intrinsically, that is, through doing it, the Merton Compliant age assessment is an accusation that a child is not telling the truth, and so, unsurprisingly, throughout this assessment opinions were offered about Frank's credibility. For example, when he was asked about the prominent veins in his hands, Frank replied saying that his "Dad's were like that". Rather than simply recording the answer, the assessing social worker additionally commented that 'Frank would have been 10 years old according to his claimed age when his father died.' In the analysis of information gained, the assessor's written commentary concluded: 'It is questionable if Frank was 10 by the time his father died that [sic] he had been able to observe and memorise the diminutive details of his father's physical features and use this instantly respond to a query.'

When questioned about school, Frank became confused with dates, giving two different dates for when he started school. It was therefore concluded that since Frank is a 'confident and intelligent person' this confusion had nothing to do with, for example, an assessment process that can be overwhelming, that was conducted in a language that Frank had no knowledge of, or that Frank was reliving very painful memories. The conclusion reached was that, because Frank had real as well as imagined school dates in his head, he had verbally tripped himself up in his own lies.

The language used throughout the assessment affectively manipulates the context of Frank's answers to suggest that he is older or simply lying. For example, the word 'mature' is used a lot. This has the effect – consciously or not – of coupling Frank with older rather than younger behaviours. At one point, the assessor describes 'challeng[ing]' Frank to make sense of what he is saying. Frank is not asked or invited to make sense of it, but challenged. The assessor's selection of this confrontational verb highlights both the doubt and cynicism underpinning the process and the power imbalance between Frank and the social worker.

Following the assessment, Frank was not given a copy of the document that was produced by the local authority and the decision was never explained to him by the social workers who assessed him. When asked by Frank, the lead assessor refused to discuss his conclusion or make the report available either in English or Frank's own language. Frank was told that this report would not be available to view as the report was not complete. So how could the decision about his age have been made if the report was not yet finished? Frank was informed of a new age and birthday by his asylum solicitor.

As well as introducing further confusion, the fact that his asylum solicitor was left to tell him of the decision reinforces the link between the age assessment process and the asylum process. Despite the argument that the processes associated with age assessments and asylum claims are not connected, this example clearly indicates how, through the age assessment process, social workers become co-opted into acting as quasi-immigration officials and are, as a consequence, not working in the best interests of the child.

Throughout the assessment document there is very little reference to factors that may have affected Frank's answers and behaviour. Notwithstanding our highly critical textual analysis of the assessment guidance, even within its own terms, in this case example, the assessors barely acknowledge the guidance. There is nothing in the content of what the assessors have written that suggests that they have followed the guidance. For example, throughout the assessment the social worker refers to Frank as looking 'uncomfortable and unable to sit still'. The impression conveyed is that he is anxious and the reader is left to surmise why. Later on, however, it is noted that Frank referred to being in pain because of an ill-fitting prosthetic limb. Stated as a simple fact, no connection was then made between his pain and his inability to sit still. Further, the assessor's recording of Frank's claim that he lost a limb in May of one year but did not obtain his prosthetic limb until the next year is followed by the suggestion that the time lapse between these two events is the result of lying or confusion and mixing up of dates. No alternative explanation, such as the well-documented difficulties associated with obtaining medical care in Frank's war torn home country, is even remotely entertained.

The process of age assessment was undoubtedly extremely stressful for Frank. Indeed, Frank told Margaret that meeting with the social worker who conducted it was the thing that he was most scared of. It is both disturbing and ironic that Frank would be so scared of meeting with someone who had themselves stated that their role was to 'protect' him.

In summation, in his attempts to 'protect' Frank, the assessing social worker accused him of lying, put him through the trauma and frustration of having to both relive his past and convince the social worker that he was not lying and, in conclusion, 'proved' that Frank was lying about what happened to him and as such was not entitled to the safeguards that come with being a child.

How the Merton Compliance was challenged

Ultimately, Frank contested the assessment made of his age and in court, supported by his legal team, a human rights organisation and his friends, the judge decided that the assessment was incorrect, that Frank had been telling the truth, and that he was the age he had always claimed to be. Yet the challenge only ever came to court because of a number of small actions taken by a small network of people.

In this penultimate section, the authors examine a few of these seemingly arbitrary decisions and events in order to highlight two aspects. Firstly, the way in which, if they had not all happened, Frank would have been failed by both the local authority and individual social work practitioners. Secondly, to draw out some of the practices that Margaret used and that could empower other social workers in similar situations.

In 2010, when told that he was to be moved from his foster family, Frank remembered that Margaret had given him her phone number. Despite his limited spoken English, Frank called Margaret. He understood that Margaret was a different social worker from the local authority one, and he was enabled to make that distinction through Margaret's systematic and consistent – if brief – communications with him whenever she visited his carers. He could have lost the number or she could have changed it, but as it was, she answered his call, he asked her for help and she intervened immediately.

As she did, she was fortified by the fact that she had previously recorded almost contemporaneous concerns about Frank's treatment, as evidenced within the correspondence that Margaret sent to the social worker shortly after the age assessment was conducted:

> The carer and I are concerned of the possible impact upon Frank's mental health that all this uncertainty may have. Frank … was upset by your accusations of his dishonesty during the LAC review; however I feel he was able to express himself with dignity and clarity, when he used the term 'kicked around like a football'. The carer informed

> me how Frank suffered from red blotches over his neck immediately after the meeting. He is reluctant to come out of his bedroom or leave the house, he is fearful of arrest and detainment. (email from Margaret 2009*)*

Once contacted by Frank, Margaret challenged the further attempt to move him. She later reflected on the way in which the local authority did not communicate with either the foster carer or Frank in attempts to move him and, in doing so, left him extremely confused and vulnerable:

> Today after a telephone call I find that the foster carer remains unaware of the plan for Frank. He appears to be staying over at a friend's flat who he met at college, telling the foster carer over the telephone that he has been told by your department that he is not allowed to return to the foster carers. The short notice you gave when informing Frank … impacted upon any preparation the carers were able to put in place. … As you are aware English is not Frank's first language and it is not appropriate or effective to pass on essential information regarding the plan verbally via Frank. This failure to communicate a leaving care plan with either the carers or ourselves has left the young person extremely vulnerable and his disability needs un met. (email from Margaret to local authority 2010)

Through word of mouth and on the recommendation of another practising social worker, Margaret knew about an independent human rights organisation who supported her to develop a 'thick description', in Geertz's (1975: 20) sense of inscribing social discourse that can be 'reconsulted', of the racism that she had observed. Margaret and Frank had built up a strong working relationship and with the support and guidance of the organisation, they engaged the foster family, sought advice from both a legal specialist and a welfare rights advisor, and in June 2010 they formalised a complaint which concluded as follows:

> I feel that this young man has been received an inferior level of care that has been influenced by his nationality, his asylum status and financial constrains of the local authority. As a result he has not been appropriately advocated for and misrepresented. (extract from Margaret's formal complaint 2010*)*

In that same month they presented at court, initially without a lawyer, challenged the age assessment and began the process that, so far, has resulted in the age assessment being rejected and the child being granted five years leave to remain.

The complaint against the local authority is not, as yet, concluded and any forms of civil action remain to be explored.

Empowerment in practice

When Margaret applied for, and was offered the post with, the fostering agency, she committed herself to acting in accordance with the Children Act (1989) and Human Rights Act (1998). Further, she drew upon the Working Together (Department for Education 2010) practice guidelines about the reviewing and assessment process that is intended for social workers working with looked after children. Her understanding of these guidelines combined with her practice experience fed her confidence. In turn, that self-confidence enabled her to point out deviations from these guidelines and to effectively challenge both the local authority social worker in person and the systemic failure of the local authority itself to honour its obligation to record any disagreements or disputes of the social workers' care plan, as demonstrated in an earlier section.

Margaret empowered herself through this preparedness to explicitly use the instruments intended to guide her practice *in* her practice and, with neither hesitation nor apology, expose the corresponding failure of her local authority counterpart and their management. In addition, and at the level of ideology, Margaret rejected the attempt to legitimate individuating and isolating the child that is intrinsic to the test's demand that the child bear individual responsibility for proving that they are not lying about being a child. Being conscious of the neoliberal agenda, emerging social workers must be afforded opportunities to interrogate their own practice documents and encouraged to think out loud, in collectives with their colleagues and further afield. Any radical fora – including trade-union groupings – that exist, should be encouraging young social workers to uncover the self-confidence needed to challenge management budget-led care plans, and the erosion of community in favour of individual, both as they relate to this most vulnerable group and to those other groups in the wider population being increasingly and most adversely affected by the drive to privatise, cut and individuate.

Conclusion

The Merton Test has been introduced as a device to advance the neoliberal agenda, most obviously the drive to reduce drastically public expenditure for social services. Further, the test is an example of the drive to undermine the possibilities for 'community' to advance as a core component of how human beings organise themselves, including in relation to their young. Prematurely separating the lone child from the social structures in which that young person is seeking refuge, the directive to apply the test introduces a precise pressure upon the social worker to move away from – and even abdicate - from any professional or social responsibility towards the young person.

Through textual analysis of policy and legal case documents, working age-assessment guidance, and the audit trail from a case study, the authors have exposed the institutionalised racism that is practised through the Merton Compliant age-assessment process. Furthermore, the authors have argued that it is the idea that a child can and should be age assessed – and not individual issues around practicalities and issues arising when doing so – that is absolutely unacceptable. This is because the Merton Test is premised upon an essentialist approach that assumes that there is one, uniform, homogeneous way in which children look and act, and that this can be observed, assessed and recorded.

The Merton Compliant is considered legitimate because unaccompanied asylum seeking children (UASC) are not thought to need or deserve the same protection as citizen children. They are treated differently and do not receive the same service provision, often being accommodated under section 17 of the CA1989 despite the fact that they should receive full care and support as set out under section 20. Further, there is lack of consistency about parental responsibility for UASC. It is legally possible, in theory, for the local authority not to take parental responsibility and, thereby place a child in a situation where nobody has responsibility for them. This causes practical problems in terms of consent for medical care, and so on, but also highlights the fact that there is a double standard of care for UASC and citizen children that is underpinned by the judicial and medical professions current accommodation of that double standard.

Through examination of the way in which Frank was treated by the social worker who conducted the assessment and within the asylum system, the authors have highlighted some key practice issues in an attempt convey the way in which the age assessment process – which may be seen by the social workers as just another of their many forms to complete – can both impact on the child emotionally and affect their future asylum claim.

Finally, it is hard to believe that within modern social work, a child who is without their parent(s) and has left their home country, often fleeing war or other such trauma, should be subjected to the obscenity of the accusation that they are lying about events that are – to them – very real.

The trauma and degradation inflicted by the asylum process cannot be underestimated, and it is beyond the control of the social work profession. However, when they conduct age assessments, social workers collude with the UKBA: they are actively participating in the practice of an institutionally racist policy that is designed to limit the provision and protection given to people seeking asylum. There is no place for this inherently racist policy within contemporary social work practice: Margaret's actions offers an alternative practice model. The anti oppressive values and ethics of the profession should be brought to bear inside the immediate development of a movement led by social work practitioners who actively question, challenge and intervene to end the age assessment of unaccompanied asylum seeking children.

Suggested further reading

European Molecular Biology Organization (EMBO) (2001) 'In the name of science – the role of biologists in Nazi atrocities: lessons for today's scientists', *EMBO Reports* Vol. 2, No. 10, 871 *et seq.*

Vickers, T. (2012) *Refugees, capitalism and the British state: Implications for social workers, volunteers and activists,* Farnham: Ashgate.

Volosinov, V.N. (1986) *Marxism and the philosophy of language.* Translation of *Marksizm i filosofiia iazyka* by Matejka, L. and Titunik, I.R. (1929), Massachusetts: Harvard University Press.

Notes

[1] When he judged *R and B* v. *London Borough of Merton (2003) EWHC 1689 ADMIN[2003]4 AII ER 280*) cited in 'Assessing age: UKBA guidelines on age assessing', http://tinyurl.com/pe998x3

[2] The language of slavery has recently been introduced into the administrative processes of the asylum system through the case 'owner' who uses a Processing an Asylum Application from a Child (UKBA 2009) UKBA Instruction on referring children in need (Final) (31 March 2009), www.ukba.homeoffice.gov.uk/sitecontent/documents/policyandlaw/asylumprocessguidance/specialcases/guidance/processingasylumapplication1.pdf

[3] That is, advancing market rule, cutting public expenditure for social services, deregulation, privatisation, and eliminating the concept of public good and replacing it with individual responsibility

[4] In November 1959, the UN General Assembly adopted the second Declaration of the Rights of the Child. This consisted of 10 principles and incorporated the guiding principle of working in the best interests of the child. However, this 1959 Declaration was not legally binding and was only a statement of general principles and intent. Ten years in the making, the UNCRC was adopted by the UN General Assembly in 1989, exactly 30 years after the 1959 Declaration. On 2 September 1990 it entered into force as international law.

[5] *The Court FZ, R (on the application of)* v. *London Borough of Croydon [2011] EWCA Civ 59* (01 February 2011) URL: www.bailii.org/ew/cases/EWCA/Civ/2011/59.html

[6] Para 21 In the authors' judgment, it is axiomatic that an applicant should be given a fair and proper opportunity, at a stage when a possible adverse decision is no more than provisional, to deal with important points adverse to his age case which may weigh against him. Such points are the absence of supporting documents, inconsistencies, or a provisional conclusion that he is not telling the truth with summary reasons for that provisional view. In the absence of formal central government guidance, we would not be prescriptive of the way in which this might be done, and we stand aside from requiring in every case a formal 'minded to' letter sent after the initial interview. It is accepted that these matters should not be over-judicialised. It is theoretically possible that a series of questions appropriately expressed during the course of the initial interview might fairly and successfully put the main adverse points that trouble the interviewing social workers. However, that would be a haphazard way of doing it and one that would be intrinsically likely to lead to subsequent controversy in the absence of an expensive transcript of the interview. Mr Luba agreed that fairness could be achieved in this respect if the interviewing social workers were to withdraw from the interview room at the end of the initial interview to discuss their provisional conclusions. They could record these with brief reasons in writing on a form by means of which, upon returning to the interview, they could put the adverse points that trouble them to the person whose age they are assessing, thereby giving him the opportunity to deal with them. The young person may be able to deal with points then and there or more time might be needed, for example, to obtain more documents. Either way, the interviewers could then withdraw again to consider his answers and reach their decision. This would be a

modification of the procedure adopted in this case. The authors emphasise that this suggested outline procedure is not the only way in which fairness might be achieved in this respect.

[7] See 'Asylum process guidance on assessing age', www.ukba.homeoffice.gov.uk/sitecontent/documents/policyandlaw/asylumprocessguidance/specialcases/guidance/assessing-age?view=Binary; 'Processing asylum applications from a child', www.ukba.homeoffice.gov.uk/sitecontent/documents/policyandlaw/asylumprocessguidance/specialcases/guidance/processingasylumapplication1.pdf?view=Binary; 'Conducting the asylum interview', www.ukba.homeoffice.gov.uk/sitecontent/documents/policyandlaw/asylumprocessguidance/theasyluminterview/guidance/conductingtheasyluminterview.pdf?view=Binary

[8] LAC 13 (2003) www.dh.gov.uk/en/Publicationsandstatistics/Lettersandcirculars/Localauthoritysocialservicesletters/DH_4003946

[9] Vickers (2012: 16) points out that the state uses its monopoly position in granting funding to shape even the activities that aim to oppose its policies. The human rights organisation (www.rapar.org.uk) in this case that, on principle, does not accept Home Office funding is free from such 'shaping'.

[10] Each extract is taken directly from the original form used to assess our case study example.

[11] 'The problems of street children', www.i-indiaonline.com/sc_crisis_theproblem.htm

[12] In chapter 2, section 5 of the *Asylum casework instruction handbook* (1999).

[13] www.familylawweek.co.uk/site.aspx?i=ed89977

[14] www.familylawweek.co.uk/site.aspx?i=ed89977

[15] Police and Criminal Evidence Act (*R (DPP)* v. *Stratford Youth Court* [2001] EWHC 615 (Admin) at paragraph 11; and the Home Office Guidance for Appropriate Adults.

[16] See Department for Education (2010) 'Working together to safeguard children: A guide to inter-agency working to safeguard and promote the welfare of children', www.education.gov.uk/publications/standard/publicationDetail/Page1/DCSF-00305-2010. The latest (March 2013) version

of 'Working together' should be considered for the differences in commitment to children that are expressed in comparison to the 2010 version.

THIRTEEN

The role of immigration policies in the exploitation of migrant care workers: an ethnographic exploration

Joe Greener

This chapter presents the findings of Greener's research into the migrant workers' experiences of the adult social care sector. With increasing privatisation of care in the UK, social workers working with adults will have increasing, at least formal, contact with a range of care providers and organisations. Greener's study shows that the migrant work force is often 'over skilled' for the tasks they perform. However, as a result of state legislation and a range of economic and political barriers, the workers find themselves over-worked, under-paid and often stuck in a system with no obvious escape routes. Migrant labour and racism within the social care sector creates 'institutionalised uncertainty' and Greener's chapter highlights the human costs of the UK's immigration policies on the migrant workforce.

Introduction

Demographic and social transformation in the United Kingdom (UK) in the last decade has lead to what many have described as a 'care crisis' (Age UK 2012; MacDonald and Cooper 2007). The decline of the nuclear family and the associated traditional gender roles and women's increased participation in the labour market (albeit often in the low-paying sectors) are often blamed (Yeates 2009). As well as the shift of caring from the private sphere of the family to care facilities and formal services, the UK has also experienced a growing demand for care services through a generally ageing population. The increasing demand for paid care workers coupled with the care work's status as dirty, feminised and low paying (Bubeck 2002; Hartmann 1979; Twigg

2000) has led to immigration increasingly being used to fulfil labour shortages (McGregor 2007; Moriarty 2010).

This chapter focuses on the experience of migrant care workers working in an elderly residential care home in the UK. The focus is on the how the state, through various immigration policies, is crucial in influencing the conditions of their employment and generally their life opportunities (Anderson 2010; Kemp 2004; Piore 1983), rather than focusing on the discrimination and racism experienced from colleagues and service users in the course of their employment (Aronson and Neysmith 1996; Gunaratnum and Lewis 2010; Neysmith and Aronson 1997). It contributes to wider debates regarding the role of the state in determining rights for migrant workers and theoretically understands the state as an institutional structure imperative in the continuation of racism (Hayter 2004; Miles 1982; Shelley 2007). However, rather than emphasising demographic changes or the changing role of women in contemporary society, this chapter argues that debates about the actual type of labour required by care services is often ignored. The implementation of markets for care and the increasing importance of profit and efficiency in the provision of care have led the increasingly rationalised and commercialised operators to search for cheaper labour (Williams 2010).

Immigration and the social care sector

The principle governing the last decade and a half of immigration policy in the UK is best described as the period of 'managed migration' (Flynn 2005; Anderson and Ruhs 2010). The impetus of these policies has revolved around categorising migrants on a number of different principles including asylum/refugee statues, perceived skill level and nationality. Different rights and obligations are attached to migrants on the basis of these principles. Rights include the ability to claim various welfare rights (that is, education, healthcare, unemployment benefit, and so on), the right to find employment or even simply just the right to reside within the UK territory (Flynn 2005).

Mainly, the UK system divided migrants from those from within the European Union (EU) and those from outside. In practice, it was much more complex because different immigration policies were applicable to individual nationalities. Generally, the gateways permitting entry into the UK orientated around whether an individual had emigrated from a developing or a developed country. Many migrants coming from developed countries outside of the EU had less stringent controls placed over their entry (such as those from Australia, New Zealand,

Norway or the US). Also, and as will be discussed at greater length later, different rights are attached to migrants on whether they are seen as able to contribute the UK economy.

The social care sector in the UK has become increasingly dependent on migrant workers (Cangiano et al 2009; Moriarty 2010). Historically, the sector represents a gendered segment of the labour market also with high levels of minority ethnic groups being employed. In more recent years, however, the UK care industry has employed increasing number of recently arrived immigrants. While there are recognised definitional issues in describing people as 'migrants' (Anderson 2010), it is thought that out of all care assistants and home carers 16% were foreign born in 2006 (Experian 2007: 3). Despite the financial crisis and the tightening of immigration controls, a more recent report by UNISON (2009) stated that there is no evidence that migrants employed in the public sector are beginning to return home and projections for the medium and long term indicate a continuing reliance and even an increase.

Driving immigration to the social care sector in the UK

There has been an increasing interest and awareness in recent decades of the interconnectedness of care work, both paid and unpaid, and the international movement of labour (Anderson 2000; Hondagneu-Sotelo 2007; Parreñas 2001). The locus of increasing migration into paid caring roles relates to a broad number of trends including the ageing population, the decline of the nuclear family, economic neoliberal restructuring both in the UK and in the sending developing countries, and the deliberate construction of policies that shape and control migration. Some more simplistic explanations for the increasing supply of migrant labour in caring industries point towards demographic changes. Moriarty (2010), for example, points towards an increasing demand for social care and skills shortages. Firstly, women's increasing participation in the labour market has undoubtedly led to a care gap where traditional reproductive labour stood. Coupled with this is the ageing population, which has contributed to rising demands for social care.

Yet simply referring to rising demands for social care excludes the restructuring of Western welfare systems from the discussion. The demand for migrant labour in the social care sector is not based purely on labour shortages, but it depends on the need for a particular type of 'discount' labour that British citizens are often unwilling or unable to supply. Misra et al (2006) show how neoliberal reform has resculpted the reproductive division of labour on a global scale. As care provision is increasingly supplied by private sector, profit-motivated organisation in Western states, employers have searched for cheaper workforces just as states and even households search for cheaper forms of care. Increasing spending and transforming the regulation of the UK care system could make the sector much more desirable for UK workers (Piore 1983). Improving the monetary rewards and the general status currently associated with the work would likely make employment in the area more desirable for populations that already have full UK citizenship rights. This chapter explores how policies concerned with labour immigration have systemic aims to achieve and sustain low care costs in the UK. Essentially, these policies limit the choices of alternative forms of work and create the conditions for which migrants will 'consent' to harsher forms of employment.

Anderson (2010: 307) suggests that immigration policies create an 'institutionalisation of uncertainty' for the migrants. The formation and maintenance of categories coerces and ties migrants to certain spheres of employment, such as adult social care, while others are prevented from taking any legal form of employment at all. This is experienced as a series of vulnerabilities for migrant workers. Unable to access the better forms of work due to visa restrictions migrants often find themselves with little choice but to work in the least attractive parts of the economy.

It can also be argued that the vulnerability of migrants leads to a higher compulsion to work because of a lack of access to citizenship rights. Debates around 'commodification' are relevant here. Esping-Andersen (1990) showed how the welfare state is a primary 'decommodifying' agent. Through unemployment benefits, free or subsidised healthcare, disability allowances and a host of other benefits, governments provide for citizens a degree of protection from unfettered market forces. Welfare protection allows people to subsist to a certain level regardless of their performance in labour markets. In respect of employment conditions and capital/labour relations, the provision of welfare services across society can restrict levels of exploitation (Burawoy 1983). Workers who do not have any alternative means of securing subsistence for themselves or their families are likely to accept much harsher and severe forms of employment. Capital will be in a much stronger position to impose, what Burawoy (1983) names, 'despotic' forms of employment relations.

So far then the discussion highlights two important aspects by which immigration policy can determine the exploitation of migrant workers. Firstly, immigration policies bind workers formally through visas into the low-paid segments of the overall economic system. Secondly, by denying access to welfare, both to the migrants themselves and to their wider families, immigrants' wealth and livelihood is linked exclusively to their employment.

The following section explores the employment and immigration experiences of migrants in one elderly residential care home. The data presented is based on ethnographic research conducted in 2008 in a dementia home for the elderly. The following section gives more details of both the research and where it took place.

Meadowvale[1] care home

In 2008 I embarked on an 8-month participant observation of elderly residential care work. I was employed by the residential and dementia home as a care assistant. Due to the demanding nature of the work it was impossible to write up research notes during shifts. Observations were written up immediately after but then developed in the days and weeks after. The data presented here is from conversations had with my co-workers during this 8-month period. While this may be seen as lacking the precision that a formally recorded and transcribed semi-structured interview would have there were a number of benefits. Mainly, the narratives around each of the participant's movement to the UK and the experiences of working in the care industry were built up over the weeks and months I worked with them. I was able to return ask more and more questions and flesh out the stories with further queries and clarifications.

The home employed a significant number of migrant workers. Due to the high turnover rates it is difficult to provide exact numbers of migrant workers employed at any time but it was approximately between 20 and 30. This was a sizeable proportion of the 26 to 42 workers that the home provided permanent employment to. The migrant workers who were formally employed by the home tended to fulfil care assistant, senior care assistant and domestic roles in the home. The workers were from many different countries including Poland, Ukraine, Philippines, Ghana, Congo, Nigeria, Lithuania, Mali and India. Across the UK, Cangiano et al (2009) found that 19% of all care workers and 35% of all nurses employed in the elderly care sector were migrants. Of those care workers recruited in the last year of their dataset the proportion was higher with 28% of care workers and 45% of nurses. They have also shown that in 2007/2008 the largest proportions of recent immigrants recruited into the social care sector came from Africa, Asia and Eastern Europe. The home where the research took place was fairly typical of many care facilities in the UK in its reliance on migrant workers, but how different migrant workers experience their employment remains dependent on visa status even within this one workplace. The following section will discuss the experience of individual migrant workers at Meadowvale and will explore the link between immigration status, employment opportunities and exploitation within the labour process.

Migration and care work

Since the A8 accession countries joined the EU free movement and employment of various Eastern European citizens around the rest of the EU is fairly unrestricted. Nevertheless, while immigration policy leaves workers from the EU legally free to find any sort of employment, informal processes prevented some workers from finding better jobs. The experience of Olenka[2] and Gita, two Polish women who worked in Meadowvale, shows how settling in new countries can leave workers vulnerable to exploitative employment arrangements.

Gita had been in the UK for around four years and Olenka for five. In one conversation, Gita described the reasons why she had come to the UK and how she had found work at Meadowvale. Olenka had moved to the UK slightly before Gita and had found work in a coffee shop in London. Olenka had prompted Gita's move to the UK because her manager at the coffee shop was looking for an au pair. Gita took the job as live out au pair but the arrangement had quickly gone sour. The wages, which were already low at only a £100 a week, were quickly decreased by her employers, first to £90, and then by the time she left, to only £60 a week, a wage clearly insufficient to live on in London. A contact of Olenka's had suggested she should move city to take a job in Meadowvale Cre Home, and Gita had followed her shortly after.

Despite Olenka and Gita explicitly stating that they were happy to have left Poland for England, and glad that they had moved on from London, both felt that care work was not for them. As Olenka explained, she had attended college in Poland studying history and various foreign languages. She hankered to find work in this area. Olenka and Gita complained at the long hours and low pay at Meadowvale – both often worked shift patterns in which they would have no days off for 10 days in a row.

Olenka and Gita's intertwining story of moving to the UK, working in London, and then finding work in care was one defined by a lack of opportunities. Both said that they were happy to have moved to the UK because it had offered new opportunities, new experiences and the possibility of developing language skills, but neither wanted to remain in care work. Both complained of the low pay, tough conditions and demeaning nature of the work. Indeed, both commented on separate occasions that the job was one that British people were unwilling to do because it is dirty and low paid (Stacey 2005; Twigg 2000). While Olenka and Gita's immigration status did not restrict them to any occupation or sector, both still experienced significant barriers in finding better work. They perceived a lack of language skills and qualifications to be crucial barriers to achieving success in the UK labour market. They noted that care work did have certain benefits but these benefits had to be balanced with theirgreater inability to find better paying work. Gita in particular had experienced very difficult working conditions when she arrived in the UK so while care work was a step forward for her it remained tough. Olenka stated that she wanted longer hours in order to earn a reasonable wage, but it was plainly apparent that working these long hours had taken its toll on her. Survey data gathered about Eastern European migrants working in the UK gathered by Anderson et al (2006: 63)shows that this group of workers often see a 'trade off between working below their skill level, on the one hand, and earning more money than they would have had they been in a job matching their skills in their home country'.

Near the end of my period working at Meadowvale Olenka did find new employment in a different Moonlight Care home performing secretarial and administrative tasks. She was happy with this new role as she said the money was better, the hours more sociable and there was an opportunity for future promotion. Despite the informal obstacles that reduced labour market mobility for Olenka and Gita, legally they were free to find alternative employment. For this reason, the difficulties facing Eastern European migrants in the UK labour market result from wider discrimination in society, rather than the formal political constraints suffered by those coming from Asia or Africa.

Bayani, for example, faced a series of formal policy barriers inhibiting his opportunity to find alternative work outside the care industry. He had a degree in engineering from a Manila University and had moved to the UK with the longer term goal of finding work in this area. He had been unable to get the appropriate visa to work in engineering in the UK, and his UK visa stipulated he could only work in the adult care-sector. The only possibility to move out of the care sector was to find an employer who would sponsor him for a new type of visa. He had tried contacting many companies for mechanical engineering positions but none was prepared to hire him. He said that the companies always said that they were unwilling to deal with the Home Office.

Bayani himself admitted that he had little vocation for care work. Generally, he struggled to develop a rapport and the correct manner with the residents and would quickly become forceful when attempting to complete care tasks. This meant that the manager would often give Bayani subsidiary tasks in the home such as washing dishes or cleaning.

Bayani explained that his motivations for working in the care home and staying in the UK were to support his son in Singapore. He was also sending money back to the Philippines to other family members, and this drove him to work six shifts a week when it was available.

Like Bayani, many of the non-EU migrants had taken a serious knock to their employment status during the migration process. Tala, from the Philippines, was 29 years old. A trained nurse, who had completed her qualification in Manila, she had moved to the UK about three years before I met her. Before coming to the UK she was employed in a nursing home for the elderly in Singapore. Tala had failed to get her nursing qualification recognised in Singapore or in the UK and so had been restricted to lower-grade auxiliary care-work in both countries. I asked why she had moved to the UK and she said the company had been recruiting in Singapore for positions in England. The move to the UK had been sold to her as an opportunity to acquire UK Personal Identification Registration (PIN), allowing her to take full nursing positions. The company, which owned the home, had even promised to pay for any costs associated with the training.

In fact, it is common in the UK for foreign-trained nurses to work for a period of time, ranging from a few months to a few years, as a care assistant to obtain a nursing registration (NMC 2007). Tala, unfortunately, needed to do more training in a university to acquire a PIN, and this entailed working part time for a year and roughly £3,000 in fees. Tala was frustrated at her current position because she felt she could not afford the time or the money to obtain the PIN, and so she had no choice but to continue with care-assistant work, which she felt was below her qualifications as well as being poorly paid. The travesty of this was that when she had been recruited by Moonlight Care in Singapore they had informed the prospective workers that they paid for care assistants to become nurses. Tala expressly said that she had come to the UK because of the opportunity of finding a fully qualified nursing position.

There is a growing body of evidence that forms of coercive recruitment are widespread within the elderly residential care-sector (Cangiano et al 2009; Oxfam 2009). Some might consider it too extreme to term Tala's situation as a form of trafficking. Certain media and political discourses construct 'trafficking' as a hard and fast concept – an individual has, within a conventional understandings of trafficking, either been forced into migration through threats, violence and deception or they have freely chosen to migrate. In reality, migrants often experience a range of constraints and opportunities during the migration process which vary in their degree (Anderson and O'Connell Davidson 2002; O'Connell Davidson 2006, 2010). Simultaneously, typical explanations locate the causes of trafficking as specific acts committed by 'evil' individuals. In actual fact, receiving countries have an important role in determining the extent and nature of trafficking in a given territory. Furthermore, Tala's story indicates the often hidden processes by which trafficking can operate. O'Connell Davidson (2010) argues that when trafficking is viewed as 'modern slavery' certain liberal political ideals are upheld that dichotomise and simplify the experiences into either 'free' or not. The effect of this is that many groups of migrants, who are subject to structured forms of unfreedom, such as being denied access to better paying forms of work, are categorised as free subjects justifying their exploitation. Many of the prevailing discourses on trafficking would exclude Tala's experience of migration as a form of trafficking. However, Tala's situation was obviously one of constraint, coercion and serious deception. Empty promises had been used in order to gain her qualified and skilled labour at a poorer rate of pay with clear benefits for the employer.

While immigration status obviously restricts, constrains and compels individuals into particular segments of the labour market, it is also crucial for structuring the employment experience. The pressure to work long hours also relates to a different aspect of immigration policy and the rights it fails to provide to care workers. Rosin's story exemplifies how it is welfare rights, not only labour market immobility that obliges workers to work much longer hours. Rosin was a migrant who had come to the UK from Congo eight years before I worked with her. The care job that she had originally taken had been in a different city and she talked about this previous employment very positively. Although it had been for the same company she had been working with adults with learning disabilities, rather than elderly residents. The staffing levels had been much better, time had been built into the shift to sit and talk to the residents and regular trips out of the home with the residents, including holidays, had all been part of Rosin's previous job.

She moved to Meadowvale after I had been working there for about three months. Moonlight Care had transferred Rosin, on her request, to Meadowvale because she wished to move cities to help care for her aunt. Her aunt lived in the local area and was suffering with cancer. Rosin looked after her aunt every second night in turn with her cousin, who also lived in the local area. However, Rosin's familial obligations were not restricted to those living in the UK, and she sent a large proportion of her salary to Congo. Rosin's sister had been killed in an industrial accident in Kinshasa many years ago, so Rosin was supporting her deceased sister's daughter as well as her own son who had remained in Congo. Recently, her mother had also been involved in a car accident and so Rosin was paying for her healthcare as well. This forced Rosin into a situation where she needed to work between five and six 12-hour shifts a week to earn sufficient money to support her family in Congo and herself. Just after I left my employment at the home Rosin informed me that she had fainted during a shift due, she said, to being 'tired and stressed'. Despite the obvious pressures coercing Rosin into care work, and to working such long hours, she maintained that she would not want to work outside the care sector. She could have found alternative work and her visa did not restrict from doing this, but she felt she had a deep vocation for care work. She did, however, often complain at having to work such long hours. Due to the low pay and the burden of financially supporting her family in Congo she had to live at her aunt's and her cousin's houses. She often complained at this saying that she wanted her own space. Rosin therefore spent virtually no wages on herself – the vast majority of it was sent to Africa.

Rosin's situation draws attention to an important aspect of immigration policy. Rosin had obtained the right to remain in the UK, which brought no restrictions to her visa status, and she had actually professed a desire to engage in care work. However, another aspect of Rosin's situation was similar to Bayani's – both were sending large amounts of money to support family members abroad. Rosin often talked of her strong desire to have her son, her sister's daughter and her mother with her in the England but the UK Border Agency prevented it. She often commented to me that if her son and daughter were in the UK she would be able to work far fewer hours. As a result of the minimal welfare protection offered by the Congolese government and the denial of the UK state to allow her family to enter, Rosin was forced into working extremely long hours in order to be able to send sufficient money to pay for the care of her mother and the education of her other dependents. The state was crucial in constructing Rosin's insecurity by rejecting visa's for her family members.

The logics of immigration controls

The role of the state through immigration controls clearly contextualised the employment conditions of the migrant care workers. As Joppke (1999) notes, citizenship is about ascribing particular rights to specific groups and as such these policies by their very nature are also exclusionary. As he explains, immigration policies in more recent decades have 'thus revealed citizenship in a new, post-Marshallian light, as a legal status and identity that excludes rather than includes people' (1999: 630). The institutional practices of the UK state, and indeed most if not all Western developed states, can be understood in terms of various logics that not only help secure private capital a cheap labour force but also serve to maintain lower costs across the care sector. The vulnerability experienced by the participants in this study reveals how these processes affect individual migrant workers. Furthermore, and speaking for the wider aims of this book, the continuing importance of immigration policies in contextualising the experiences of migrants, it will be argued, can and should be understood as a part of a continuing historical legacy of racism.

The structures of racism are historically malleable. Fekete's (2004, 2005; see also Cole 2009) influential analysis of the rise of 'xeno-racism' across Europe explains powerful political trends towards new forms of discrimination against various groups, although especially those emigrating from Islamic countries, on the grounds that they are culturally incompatible with European values and customs. This newer racism orientates around imagined cultural differences begging less to assumptions based on biological categories. However, whatever the constructed rationality behind forms of racism it serves to legitimate legal frameworks governing immigration. The definition of groups as 'other' has specific economic advantages for both the state and capital. Kemp (2004) explains how seemingly contradictory processes guide immigration policies in many nation states. On the one hand:

> the increasing demand for and recruitment of a cheap and docile labour force in the guise of migrant men and women' is clearly visible in many Western states, but on the other these states tend to solidify the 'social and political barriers aimed at preventing their incorporation as legitimate members of the community. (Kemp 2004: 268)

This empowerment, in the right to find employment and to access the territory, with the simultaneous denial of certain rights such as the access to a career ladder or certain welfare benefits/services is a policy materialisation of the deeper needs of the welfare state. The state has a definite role in the transmission and reproduction of racist ideas (Carter et al 1987; Miles 1982). Racialisation refers to the process by which certain populations within a given territory are constructed as a separate 'race' group who are believed to culturally and socially defy the prevailing norms of that given nation state. The historical specificity of how particular ethnic groups are constructed distinctively at different periods elucidates how ideas around 'race' often underlie the exploitation of certain groups. When groups are visualised as not belonging or not fitting into a national community, the general public will support policies that allow for their exploitation.

Miles (1982) explores how different nationalities have been 'racialised' distinctly in certain periods. So, for instance, the Irish in England were constructed as less than human, criminal and degenerate for long periods prior to any large-scale immigration from further afield (Pearson 1983). Immigration controls, according to Miles, are tantamount to system-wide forms of indentured labour. It is proposed by Miles that racialisation serves the needs of the capitalist state not only by providing cheap labour but also by simultaneously dividing the working class. Workers will not blame employers or governments for declining pay and conditions – they will see immigrants as those threatening their status.

So the state places migrants in a hierarchy in regards to the privileges they can claim but is it sensible to talk about this as a form of racism? This racism might be somewhat obscured by the fact that it does not appear to discriminate on the basis of skin colour. It does clearly, nevertheless, discriminate on the basis nationality, and as argued below, can be understood effectively a proxy for skin colour.

Hayter's (2005) interprets immigration policies as part of a longer historical legacy that produces and sustains the disadvantage of certain groups in contemporary society. These different ethnic groups are hierarchically positioned to each other in terms of their respective economic and social resources. Those from Eastern Europe are generally found to take jobs of lower status than in their country of origin (Anderson et al 2006) but, as was shown, workers from Africa and Asia were further constrained in the labour market and accordingly their experiences of employment often even shoddier. Workers from 'black' countries experienced fewer opportunities to exit employment due to immigration controls that bound them to the adult social care sector and even to a particular employer:

> As in many countries, controls have discriminated between black and white immigrants ... so as to stop the former and encourage the latter. To some extent this racism has a material base. It may suit employers and the state. ... It divides the workforce and provides employers with exploitable labour (Hayter 2000: 165)

Conclusions

The experiences of the migrants in this chapter are directly related to immigration policies that create, in very real ways, particular disadvantages and discriminations for many migrant workers. Firstly, workers such as Olenka and Gita found it considerably easier to move out of care work or to obtain promotions.

Secondly, even for those who had obtained British citizenship certain processes drove them to work longer hours. Workers' families were often left in countries that offered fewer social protections than the UK state, driving these workers to send significant money back to support their loved ones. Workers such as Rosin and Banyani were then forced to work as many hours as possible in order to support themselves in the UK as well as their family members abroad. Esping-Andersen (1990) classic account of the relationships between welfare sates and capitalism emphasises the 'decommodifying' function of social policies. Various assistance programmes offered by states assure that all citizens achieve a certain level of income regardless of an individual's performance in the labour market. When this protection is absent, as is the case for migrant workers, whose citizenship arrangements mean they or they families are not entitled to various welfare rights, then they are more likely to accept arduous forms of employment with poor remuneration (Burawoy 1983). We can then see that even if migrants are formally free to search for new forms of employment, such as Rosin in this study, they may feel compelled to work longer and harder in order to support family abroad.

The processes that underpin the creation and preservation of the various categories of migrant bring very real benefits for the UK state and private employers. Racism at a structural level continues to impact hard on the employment and general life experiences of migrant workers in the social care sector. Piore (1983), in his classic study challenging the then dominant understanding of migration in economics, describes how demand for certain types of labour in developed states underpins the migration process. It is not, as conventionally understood, simply a result of immigration policies.

Think-tanks such as Migration Watch or various political parties, most notably the United Kingdom Independence Party (UKIP), see the level and extent of migration to the country as altogether reliant on border controls – getting tough on migrants results in lower immigration levels. Labour markets, and the requirements of capital and labour shortages are left out of the story.

While the policy terrain for immigration has changed to a degree since this research took place, it seems that the demand for certain forms of labour in the social care sector will persist. Increasing privatisation and decreasing funding in various health and social care sectors means the structural need for a 'skilled' but cheap and exploitable workforce is likely to persist. Changes to benefit systems may enforce more UK citizens into less desirable segments of the labour market, but as observed, it seems that the industry may well continue to remain dependent on migrant labour. The care work sector continues to rely on an immigrant workforce, particularly in the lowest paid and most difficult positions. Proper scrutiny of the contradictions of immigration policies needs to continue, and analytical and theoretical comprehension of how migration is being used to serve the needs of the neoliberal welfare state and secure an inexpensive, vulnerable source of labour that provides frontline care work, remains important.

Suggested further reading

Hayter, T. (2000) *Open borders: the case against immigration controls*, London: Pluto Press.

McGregor, J. (2007) 'Joining the BBC (British Bottom Cleaners)': Zimbabwean migrants and the UK care industry', *Journal of Ethnic and Migration Studies* 33, 801–24.

Williams, F. (2010) 'Migration and care: themes, concepts and challenges', *Social Policy and Society* 9: 3, 385–96.

Notes

[1] Meadowvale is a pseudonym – the real name of the home is not disclosed.

[2] All names used are pseudonyms.

CONCLUSION

Race, racism and social work today: some concluding thoughts

Laura Penketh and Michael Lavalette

The aim of the book has been to re-open debates about issues of 'race' and racism in modern Britain, and the relevance for those of us involved in social work education, training and practice. Racism is a deeply entrenched social problem, built into the structure of modern capitalist societies, but this does not mean that it is static and unchanging. At different moments in time the rhetoric of racism targets specific minority ethnic groups in particular ways: black and Asian communities, (white) East European migrants, members of the Roma community, Asylum seekers or members of the Muslim community, for example. Over the last 10–15 years the most visible form of racism has been the rise of Islamophobia, with increasing levels of racism directed against the Muslim community in Britain and across Europe. To say this, is not to deny or denigrate the racism felt by other minority communities, but it is to recognise the particular forms of institutional racism and violence that manifests itself in the form of physical and verbal attacks on Muslims and in the nature of political and media debates that are increasingly framed in terms of a perceived 'problematic Muslim presence' in Britain and Europe that demands some form of political action. What that action should be remains open to contestation.

As we were finishing the book issues of 'race', racism, Islamophobia and multiculturalism once again gained high levels of political, media and public attention with the brutal and horrific killing of soldier Lee Rigby in Woolwich, in London on 22 May 2013. This led to a questioning once again, of the place of Islam and the role of migration and multiculturalism within modern Britain. In the days following the attack there was little space for rational discussion, or attempts to understand why such terrible events might take place; or even to compare the horror in Woolwich with the (far less publicised) murder of 75-year-old Mohammed Saleem killed in Birmingham while on his way home from evening prayers on 29 April 2013. According to family and friends, this was a vicious racist killing of a man whose family had previously received threats from the far-right English Defence League

(BBC 2013). Even in a simple way Mr Saleem's killing highlights the way in which media priorities can shape debate and understandings of social problems (something that Orr addresses in Chapter Ten on media portrayals of 'grooming').

In the furore over the death of Lee Rigby there was no discussion of the role of Britain in the wars in Afghanistan, Iraq or Syria and how this might create some of the conditions that produce events that the scholar Chalmers Johnson (2000) described as 'blowback'. Johnson notes that this term was originally coined by the Central Intelligence Agency (CIA) to refer to the unintended consequences of imperial interventions and policies. Johnson argues that 'Terrorism by definition strikes at the innocent in order to draw attention to the sins of the invulnerable' (2000: 33). Rather than irrational events, terrorist attacks, however horrific, can only be fully understood as part of a broader understanding of global geo-political actions and counter-activities. Neither was there much discussion of racism and Islamophobia, or the impact of poverty and inequality in creating the conditions of alienation that may lead some people to undertake such murderous acts. The need to understand the social and political contexts of events, policies and their impact is something that each of the authors in the book has emphasised – and the Woolwich murder cannot be understood without appropriate context.

Rather than an attempt to understand what may have prompted the Woolwich attack, we got knee-jerk political responses. Home Secretary Theresa May and Prime Minister David Cameron talked about the need to combat the recruitment of young men to extremist politics and the need to reconsider and reactivate the 'Prevent' agenda. Yet the 'Prevent' agenda (as discussed by Lavalette in Chapter Nine) is built on a series of misunderstandings and imprecise definitions that have failed to produce the outcomes the Government intends while, at the same time, further threatening the civil liberties of large numbers of young Muslim men and women.

In terms of interpretation, former Prime Minister Tony Blair used the events to suggest that there was something wrong, and aggressive, about some forms of Islam. He argued:

> [T]here is a problem within Islam – from the adherents of an ideology that is a strain within Islam. ... But I am afraid this strain is not the province of a few extremists. It has at its heart a view about religion and about the interaction between religion and politics that is not compatible with pluralistic, liberal, open-minded societies. ... On the one side,

> there are Islamists who have this exclusivist and reactionary world view. They are a significant minority, loud and well organised. On the other are the modern-minded, those who hated the old oppression by corrupt dictators and who hate the new oppression by religious fanatics. (Blair 2013)

Blair, of course, was the Prime Minister who sent British troops into Afghanistan and Iraq leading to the deaths of hundreds of thousands of men, women and children (according to a report published in *The Lancet* 'at least 116,903 Iraqi non-combatants' were killed between 2003 and 2011 in Iraq alone [David Blair 2013]); was in control when allies of British troops tortured Iraqis in Abu Ghraib prison; and was in charge while depleted uranium weapons were used in Iraq. In his most recent role as Middle East Envoy he has watched illegal Israeli settlements continue their expansion on Palestinian land. One is tempted to ask whether there is, within Blair's politics, a strand of Christian fundamentalism that is harmful to our pluralistic way of life. Of course, no politician or media commentator would dream of posing the question in this way, so why is it acceptable to pose such a question of Islam?

The terms in which the murder of Lee Rigby was framed in the media and within political debate created a space which far-right extremists were not slow to try and occupy. As Miles and Phizacklea (1984) noted, in the post-Second World War era politicians have gradually pulled each other further to the right on questions of 'race' and racism and, in the process, they have allowed parties of the far-right a 'legitimacy' that they hardly deserve. In the aftermath of Blair's *Mail on Sunday* article the English Defence League (EDL) released a statement noting that 'on this issue' they agreed with Blair. Mainstream politicians questioning multiculturalism and aspects within Islam opened the door to the far-right.

The EDL, on the evening of the murder, appeared on the streets of Woolwich fighting with police and terrorising people from minority ethnic backgrounds (Sky News 2013). The British National Party (BNP) argued that because one of the accused had been born into an African Christian family the problem was not just Islam but migration per se. According to Wright et al (2013) in the 48 hours after the Woolwich murder there was a sharp increase in Islamophobic attacks, including:

> attacks on mosques, assaults, racial abuse and anti-Muslim graffiti. An improvised petrol bomb was thrown at a mosque

> in Milton Keynes during Friday prayers, while attacks ... [were] reported in Gillingham, Braintree, Bolton and Cambridge.

In the days after the murder a Mosque in Grimsby was petrol-bombed (Malik and Quinn 2013), an Islamic centre in Muswell Hill, London was burned to the ground with nearby walls daubed with the initials EDL (Taylor et al 2013), and an Islamic school six miles from Woolwich was set alight (Weaver 2013). In the days after the murder of Lee Rigby 11 Mosques in Britain were attacked according to the Faith Matters project (http://faith-matters.org/), while the website Tell Mama UK (http://tellmamauk.org/) reported a significant increase in hate attacks; and the Metropolitan police reported an eight-fold increase in Islamophobic attacks in London in the three weeks after the murder (Tahir 2013).

Yet amid the horror of rising levels of racism and violent racist political action, there were some seeds of hope. The EDL tried to latch their organisation onto the charity Help for Heroes, but were rebuked by the organisers who distanced themselves from the EDL (Press Association 2013) – as did the family of Lee Rigby who appealed for calm and spoke out against violent reprisals against minority communities (Gardner 2013). Further, on the first weekend of June 2013 the BNP called a national march in London; they were out-mobilised by anti-fascist activists who blocked their path and, rather humiliatingly, the BNP had to abandon their plans. The same day the EDL intended to have marches and protests in over 30 towns and cities across Britain – in the vast majority of cases anti-racist counter-demonstrations dwarfed the EDL events. Despite the tone of media reporting and the political framing of the events it was clear that there was a large constituency of people willing and able to actively consider anti-racist responses to the far-right mobilisations and to the tone of dominant political discourse. The importance of a political response to growing levels of racism was further reinforced by a poll carried out by YouGov and reported in *The Observer* on Sunday 9 June, which indicated that opposition to immigration and the presence of migrant communities in Britain drops when respondents are told about the benefits of migration (Townsend 2013). The conclusion was that misinformation in the media and within mainstream political discourse is generating racist tensions but that this is not inevitable and can be countered by debate and political action.

The events of the summer of 2013, therefore, have emphasised the shifting terrain of the politics of 'race' in modern Britain – but they do not indicate that there has been an irreversible or fundamental turn towards the politics of the far-right. For those of us working and studying in social work – and especially those of us committed to a social work rooted in anti-racism and the promotion of social justice - it is important that we are able to think about and address these issues in a clear and consistent manner, and that we are not cowed into silence in the face of racist outbursts by politicians, media pundits or far-right street-fighting gangs.

It is important that social work professionals have a critical and theoretical understanding of debates concerned with 'race' and racism, and that they are aware of: historical analyses that focus on the 'roots of racism'; political ideologies that reinforce racist ideas; and the nature of structural and institutional inequality. Without such understandings, social workers will struggle to intervene in a knowledgeable, informed and sensitive manner when working with minority ethnic groups.

Racism is very often focused on those who are perceived to come from a different, 'inferior', race – defined in terms of either phenotypical (external physical features) and/or genotypical (genetic variables) characteristics. The world's leading biologists have long-since asserted that it is impossible to divide the world's population into discrete, permanent biological subtypes, or 'races', but the scientific evidence has not stopped racist attacks and racial harassment that occur against groups on the basis of perceived physical differences such as skin colour.

However, skin colour is not always the defining feature when explaining and understanding the manifestation of racism in society against particular groups. In the early nineteenth century in Britain the Irish community faced violence, harassment and racist oppression despite being white (Miles and Phizacklea 1984), and Poles, Romanians and Bulgarians are targeted in similar ways today (Fekete 2009). Anti-Jewish racism, or anti-Semitism, anti-Roma racism and anti-Muslim racism, or Islamophobia, may contain a 'racialised' component, but they also focus on the supposed 'alien cultures' of minority ethnic groups. Cultural racism is no less significant than biological racism in provoking racist attacks and oppressive measures (Visran 2002; Ansari 2004; Richardson 2013).

Over the last decade there has also been a revival of far-right agitation across much of Europe. In Hungary and Greece openly fascist organisations target migrants and Roma, Muslim and Jewish communities; in France and Denmark far-right organisations are polling well in national and local elections, and in England the right-wing populist and anti-immigration party the United Kingdom Independence Party (UKIP), obtained close to a quarter of the popular vote in the 2013 local government elections. This is evidence that the political climate is shifting in a problematic and dangerous way regarding the treatment of minority ethnic communities, and that social and political perceptions are hardening against the presence of these groups across Europe. In these circumstances it is important that, as social workers, we are able to cast a critical gaze on the dominant debates that – though often heavily 'coded' – shift the terrain of debate onto the perceived failings of minority communities. Take, for example, the recent assault on multiculturalism (see Jenkins, Chapter Seven). In the 1970s and 1980s critical theorists of 'race' pointed out the failings of 'multicultural' approaches to addressing racism, but the recent debates have been set by politicians on the populist right who have attacked multiculturalism to highlight the perceived failings of the post-war welfare state, of post-war migration and the 'failure' of minority communities to 'assimilate' (that is, to adopt uncritically assumed British cultural 'norms').

In the face of these challenges, the role of social workers working with minority ethnic groups becomes more urgent, the challenges greater, and the need for a vibrant and engaged anti-racist social work environment more critical.

Chapters One and Twoby Singh and by Fekete provide the background to assess the changing politics of 'race construction' in modern Britain. Singh's chapter traces the history of 'anti-racist social work'. The anti-racist movement in social work developed out of the social movement campaigns against racism and the far-right in the late 1960s and 1970s (the various monitoring projects, Rock Against Racism, the Anti-Nazi League and various community campaigns such as the New Cross Massacre Action Committee). These various strands of the anti-racist movement created a space where issues of racism and migration gained a hearing within the trade union and labour movement, and from there within the 'municipal left' Labour Party project of the 1980s. Yet the defeat and marginalisation of many of these campaigns in the late 1980s had an impact within social work and, Sing argues, the focus on anti-racism shifted to anti-oppression and on to a concern with difference and diversity – and with this shift the focus on the structural and institutional basis of racism was marginalised.

Fekete presents her work on what she, and others at the Institute of Race Relations and within the journal *Race and Class*, term the rise of 'xeno-racism'. Fekete's point is that the politics of race is never static, but shifts according to a mix of political, economic and social factors. The most virulent form of racism in the present period is one that targets migrants (who may, or may not, be black), Asylum seekers and, in particular, the Muslim communities across Europe. Often the advocates of discriminatory politics will claim that 'they are not racist' but are, instead, concerned about 'our' culture, 'our' people in the face of austerity and labour shortages and 'our' culture. There's is hostility to the 'other' – but not necessarily to 'other races'. This is xeno-racism. Of course, as she points out, xeno-racism may utilise a (slightly) different language, but it looks remarkably like older forms of racism: it targets minorities, it is deeply divisive, it is often violent and it is deeply discriminatory against, often, vulnerable people and communities.

Chapter Three by Williams looks to reassert our anti-racist practice and to think about the networks of support – comprised of academics, practitioners and service users - that are necessary to reinvigorate anti-racist practice and support those engaged in such work. Too often those engaged in meaningful anti-oppressive practice can find themselves isolated within agencies and communities and be under immense pressure to conform, not to 'rock the boat' or get caught up in 'politically correct posturing'. We need to consider how we support those committed to anti-racist practice and we, collectively, can challenge oppressive practices and structures both in the workplace and in our communities standing alongside community activists and service users.

Harrison and Burke in Chapter Four address the recent development of 'cultural competencies' as a requirement of a non-stigmatising social work practice. Clearly all social workers should be culturally aware and appropriately competent to address the needs of minority communities, but these approaches tend to focus on the interaction between practitioners and individuals – at the expense of a focus on the institutional and structural determinants of racist practice. Anti-racist practice was always based on a firm footing on the structural location of racism within modern unequal and racist societies.

Chapters Five and Six by Levine and Urh address issues that have not figured prominently within anti-racist social work debates: anti-Semitism (Levine) and anti-Roma racism (Urh). Both of these forms of racism are among the oldest racisms, though, interestingly, both are based on perceived cultural, as well as 'racial', differences. Both Levine and Urh trace the history of these racisms and address the rising levels of anti-Roma racism and anti-Semitism across Europe in the face of austerity, crisis and the rise of the far-right. Both chapters also offer an initial consideration of how these themes can be embedded within anti-racist social work practice.

The editors' own chapters look at differing aspects of the rise of Islamophobia in Britain. Penketh in Chapter Eight presents the findings of her ongoing research with Muslim women in the North of England. One of the claims often made – in the media, by politicians and by various 'liberal commentators' – is that Islam is a particularly 'backward' religion and this is notable in its treatment of women. Muslim women, like their non-Muslim sisters, suffer from oppression in modern society. Women – no matter their religious beliefs, or the colour of their skin – are objectified and sexualised in numerous ways in society; are the victims of gender violence; are poorer, earn less and face 'glass ceilings' in the work place; are the providers of the majority of domestic labour, and have overwhelming responsibility for child-care and the provision of care for sick and elderly relatives. Yet Muslim women, especially if they wear the Hijab or Niqab, are portrayed as passive and docile, under the control of their male relatives and with little or no agency. Penketh's chapter, based on interviews with Muslim women, gives voice to this community and argues for a far more nuanced understanding of the position of Muslim women.

Lavalette in Chapter Nine undertakes a policy analysis of the 'Prevent' agenda. Prevent was introduced by New Labour, has continued under the coalition government in a more marginal way – but seems likely to re-emerge as a result of the Woolwich murder. 'Prevent', argues Lavalette, was based on a number of misunderstandings of the Muslim community and a range of ill-defined concepts and theories that targeted young (mainly) Muslim men (mainly). However, as 'Prevent' was 'mainstreamed' its targets and priorities increasingly became embedded within the work of community workers, probation staff and social workers. In a profession defined by its commitment to civil and human rights, equality and social justice, how should practitioners address the dilemmas posed by being required to participate in state surveillance and soft policing?

Orr's challenging Chapter Ten looks at the ways in which 'street grooming' has become a 'racialised crime' in many parts of the media. The evidence simply does not support the claim that street grooming of vulnerable young white girls is a crime perpetuated by gangs of Pakistani men. Yet this claim – which harks back to earlier racist myths about sexually aggressive black men – has gained prominence in Britain over the last few years.

Moral panics, racialised crimes, state surveillance and soft policing are all themes raised in Chapter Eleven by Stamp and in Chapter Twelve by Moran and Gillett. Stamp looks at what social workers can and should do when faced with local politicians and local interests that argue that, in the face of crisis and austerity, we need to look after 'our people' first. Stamp argues that social work is based on universal values of equality and justice and that notions of 'our people' are incompatible with the requirement to meet all people's human needs. Moran and Gillett pose similar questions in their analysis of age-assessment practices with unaccompanied asylum-seeking children. The use of the Merton Test, they argue, breaches social work codes of ethics and poses the question 'what should ethically driven social workers do when asked to age assess?'

Finally, Greener in Chapter Thirteen looks at another aspect of the migrant labour question. He examines the exploitation of poor migrant workers within the care sector by increasingly powerful multinational service providers. Vulnerable as a result of state policy and heightened levels of racism these workers are providing essential care to a range of people with special needs. The welfare state that was built after World War II was often staffed by black and Asian workers drawn into the labour market to perform the jobs indigenous white labour no longer wanted. Greener emphasises that this process continues apace within the marketised service sector of the neoliberal welfare state.

The content of this book has, therefore, sought to reassert the necessity for a more radical approach to social work intervention that draws on anti-racist theories and practices, and suggests that, apart from some excellent work around issues of asylum and immigration, social work has not kept up with the shifting dynamics of 'race' and racism in Britain and other parts of Europe. In particular, social work needs to critically assess the implications of the 'new racism' or 'xeno-racism', and its impact on the lives and experiences of minority ethnic communities.

The issues that are critically explored in the book also contribute in an informed and meaningful way to the new social work 'Professional Capabilities Framework' (PCF) introduced in England and developed by the College of Social Work. The PCF outlines the knowledge, skills and values required of social workers in England, and is structured around a series of nine domains whose aims are to inform, educate and guide social workers throughout their careers. As well as focusing on practice the PCF reinforces the requirement that those in the profession develop and reflect on their knowledge base.

Here, there are key recommendations that reflect the importance of working sensitively with minority ethnic communities. The emphasis on 'diversity', is underpinned by the requirement that social workers understand that diversity characterises and shapes human experiences, and is critical to the formation of identity. Social workers need to have respect for those with different values and cultures, and wherever possible, challenge the oppression, marginalisation and alienation that minority ethnic groups face. The PCF is also concerned that social workers uphold principles of social justice and have a critical understanding of the effects of economic inequality and oppression on the lives of service users.

The content of this book is not always prescriptive about practice, but it is hoped that the ideas and arguments that it offers can contribute to a more critical and reflective analysis regarding 'race' and racism, and that this understanding contributes to more sensitive, informed and anti-racist methods of social work intervention.

Bibliography

Abbas, T (2005) (ed) *Muslim Britain: Communities under pressure*, London: Zed Books

Abbott, D (2011) Interview with Sky News, 9 August

ADSS (Association of Directors of Social Services) (1978) *Multi racial Britain, A social services response*. London: Commission for Racial Equality

Age UK (2012) *Care in crisis 2012,* Age UK, London

Ahmad, A (2007) Islam, Islamisms and the West, in L Panitch and C Leys (eds) *Socialist register 2008: Global flashpoints, reactions to imperialism and neoliberalism*, http://socialistregister.com/index.php/srv/article/view/5872/2768

Ahmed S (2006) The nonperformativity of antiracism, *Meridians: feminism, race and transnationalism*, 7(1) 104-126

Ahmed, S (2012) *On being included: Racism and diversity in institutional life.* Durham and London: Duke University Press

Ahmed S and Swan E (2006) Doing diversity (introduction), *Policy futures in education*, 4 (2) 96-100

Ahmed, T (2013) The rise of Islamophobia, in B Richardson (ed) *Say it loud: Marxism and the fight against racism*, London: Bookmarks

Akhtar, P (2005) (Re)turn to religion and radical Islam, in Tahir Abbas, *Muslim Britain*: *Communities under pressure* (Zed Books)

Ali, S (2011) 30 Years on: the Bradford Twelve, *Just Plain Sense* podcast, 12 July, http://blog.plain-sense.co.uk/2011/07/30-years-on-bradford-twelve.html

Ali, T (1981) Why I'm joining the Labour Party, *Socialist Review* (December) www.marxists.org/archive/harman/1981/12/ali.htm

Allen, C (2005) From race to religion: the new face of discrimination in T Abbas (ed) *Muslim Britain (communities under pressure)*, London: Zed Books Ltd

Allen, V (2009) Women turn history into a bizarre soap opera, says Starkey, *Daily Mail*, 31 March, www.dailymail.co.uk/news/article-1166125/Women-turn-history-bizarre-soap-opera-says-Starkey.html

Alleyne B (2002) *Radicals against race: Black activism and cultural politics.* Oxford, Berg

Amnesty International (2004) *Get it right. How Home Office decision making fails refugees*, London: Amnesty

Ancona, D, Goodman, P, Lawrence, B, Tushman, M (2001) Time: a new research lens, *Academy of Management Review*, 26, 4, 645-63, www.globalsepri.org/UploadPhotos/200891217359210.pdf

Anderson, B and O'Connell Davidson, J (2002) *Trafficking – a demand led problem?* Stockholm: Save the Children Sweden

Anderson, B (2000) Doing the dirty work? The global politics of domestic labour. Zed Books, London

Anderson, B (2010) Migration, immigration controls and the fashioning of precarious workers. *Work, Employment & Society*, 24, 300–17

Anderson, B, O'Connell Davidson, J (2004) *Trafficking – a demand led problem? Part 1: review of evidence and debates,* Save the Children Sweden, Stockholm

Anderson, B, Ruhs, M (2010) Who needs them? A framework for the analysis of staff shortages, immigration, and public policy, in: M Ruhs, B Anderson (eds) *Who needs migrant workers? Labour shortages, immigration, and public policy*, Oxford University Press, Oxford/New York

Anderson, B, Ruhs, M. Rogaly, B and Spencer, S (2006) *Fair enough? Central and East European migrants in low-wage employment in the UK.* York: Joseph Rowntree Foundation.

Ansari, H (2004) *'The infidel within': Muslims in Britain since 1800,* London: Hurst

Anti-Defamation League (2001) "What is anti-semitism" www.adl.org/hate-patrol/antisemitism.asp

Arendt, H (1985) The origins of totalitarianism, San Diego, Harcourt

Aronson, J, Neysmith, SM (1996) 'YOURE NOT JUST IN THERE TO DO THE WORK': depersonalizing policies and the exploitation of home care workers, *Labor, Gender & Society* 10, 59–77

Athwal, A (2010) Gazza Protesters Defence Campaign Launched IRR News 12 March 2010

Aymer C (2010) Conference Paper, SWAN Conference Liverpool Hope University

Back L (2004) Ivory towers? The academy and racism in I Law, D Phillips and L Turney (eds) *Institutional racism in higher education.* Stoke on Trent, Trentham Books

Bailey, R and Brake, M (1975) *Radical social work*, London: Edward Arnold

Bale, A. (2010) 'Antisemitism: a very short introduction', Book Review, *Journal of Modern Jewish Studies*, 9:3, 431-432

Ball, J, Milmo, D and Ferguson, B (2012) Half of UK's young black males are unemployed, *The Guardian*, 9 March, www.guardian.co.uk/society/2012/mar/09/half-uk-young-black-men-unemployed

Barany, ZD (2002) *The East European gypsies: regime change, marginality, and ethnopolitics*, Cambridge, New York: Cambridge University Press.

Barker, M (1981) *The new racism*, London: Junction Books

Barker, M and Beezer, A (1983) "The language of racism: An examination of Lord Scarman's report on the British riots" International Socialism 18 (Winter)

Barn, R (1993) Black children in the public care system, BT Batsford Ltd, London in association with British Agencies for Adoption and Fostering

Barnardo's (2012) Cutting them free, www.barnardos.org.uk/cuttingthemfree.pdf

Barnett, A (2011) Official lying in the UK. What child detention reveals about how we are governed, Open Democracy, www.opendemocracy.net/ourkingdom/anthony-barnett/official-lying-in-uk-what-child-detention-reveals-about-how-we-are-governed

Barry, B (2001) *Culture and equality*, London: Polity

BBC (2000) http://news.bbc.co.uk/I/hi/uk_politics/706718.stm

BBC (2009) Vigil for victims of hate crime 30 October 2009 http://news.bbc.co.uk/1/hi/england/london/8333530.stm

BBC (2012) Rochdale grooming trial: Split views on race issue, 8 May, www.bbc.co.uk/news/uk-england-manchester-17996245

BBC (2013) Daughter of murdered Mohammed Saleem criticises police, www.bbc.co.uk/news/uk-england-birmingham-22665571

BBC News (2005) *Iranian leader denies Holocaust*, http://news.bbc.co.uk/1/hi/world/middle_east/4527142.stm

BBC News (2013) Local elections: Nigel Farage hails UKIPs remarkable results, www.bbc.co.uk/news/uk-politics-22382098

BBC (2011) *Nottingham asylum seeker fell from balcony after taunts*

BBC News on-line (20/8/2012) Austria Freedom Party condemned for Nazi-like cartoon, www.bbc.co.uk/news/world-europe-19324613

Beller, S (2007) *Antisemitism: A very short introduction*, New York, Oxford University Press

Berelowitz, S, Firmin, C, Edwards, G and Gulyurtlu, S (2012) *'I thought I was the only one. The only one in the world.' Office of the Children's Commissioner's Inquiry into Child Sexual Exploitation in Gangs and Groups* (Interim Report) www.childrenscommissioner.gov.uk/content/publications/content_636

Berger, PL and Luckmann, T (1966) *The social construction of reality: A Treatise in the sociology of knowledge*, Garden City, New York: Anchor Books

Berman, G and Paradies, Y (2010) Racism, disadvantage and multi-culturalism towards effective anti-racist praxis. *Ethnic and Racial Studies*, 33, 2, 214-32

Berry, TR, Mizelle, ND (eds) *From oppression to grace: Women of color and their dilemmas within the academy,* Stylus Publishing, Sterling Virginia

Bhabha, HK (1994) *The location of culture.* London: Routledge

Bhabha, J and Finch, N (2006) *Seeking Asylum Alone: Unaccompanied and Separated Children and Refugee Protection in the UK,* Human Rights at Harvard.

Bhatti-Sinclair, K (2011) *Anti-Racist Practice in Social Work,* Basingstoke, Palgrave Macmillan

Blair, D (2013) Iraq war 10 years on: at least 116,000 civilians killed *The Telegraph,* 15 March, www.telegraph.co.uk/news/worldnews/middleeast/iraq/9932214/Iraq-war-10-years-on-at-least-116000-civilians-killed.html

Blair, T (2013) The ideology behind Lee Rigbys murder is profound and dangerous, why dont we admit it? Tony Blair launches a brave assault on Muslim extremism after Woolwich attack *Mail On Sunday* 2 June, www.dailymail.co.uk/debate/article-2334560/The-ideology-Lee-Rigbys-murder-profound-dangerous-Why-dont-admit--Tony-Blair-launches-brave-assault-Muslim-extremism-Woolwich-attack.html

Blears, H (2009) Many voices: understanding the debate about preventing violent extremism, Talk presented to the LSE 25 Feb, www.communities.gov.uk/speeches/corporate/manyvoices

Bloxham, A (2010) Birmingham stops accepting asylum seekers, *Daily Telegraph*

Bone, JD (2012) The neoliberal phoenix: the big society or business as usual, *Sociological Research Online,* 17 (2) 16, www.socresonline.org.uk/17/2/16.html

Bonnet, A (2000) A*nti-Racism.* London Routledge.

Bookstein A (2003) *Beyond the headlines: an agenda for action to protect civilians in neglected conflict.* Oxfam International: Oxfam Campaign reports

Boyd, J (2011) *Child poverty and deprivation in the British Jewish community,* Institute for Jewish Policy Research, London.

Braverman, M (2012) Answer to Rosenfeld: Jewish History, Anti-Semtism and the challenge to Zionism, www.jewishconscience.org/7.html

Brindle, D (2011) Black people still face mental health inequalities, *The Guardian,* 6 April, www.guardian.co.uk/society/joepublic/2011/apr/06/black-people-face-mental-health-inequality

Brittain, V (2009) Besieged in Britain, *Race & Class,* 50, 3, January-March.

Brittain, V (2010) *The meaning of waiting: Tales from the war on terror,* Oberon

Brooke, C (2011) Top detective blasts culture of silence that allows Asian sex gangs to groom white girls... because police and social services fear being branded racist, *Daily Mail,* 5 January www.dailymail.co.uk/news/article-1344218/Asian-sex-gangs-Culture-silence-allows-grooming-white-girls-fear-racist.html

Bryan B, Dadzie S, Scafe S (1985) The heart of the race. London: Virago

Bubeck, DG (2002) Justice and the labor of care, in: EF Kittay, EK Feder (eds) *The subject of care: Feminist perspectives on dependency.* Rowman and Littlefield, Oxford

Bunglawala, I (2007) Vacancy for an imam, *The Guardian,* 5 June www.guardian.co.uk/commentisfree/2007/jun/05/vacancyforanimam

Burawoy, M (1983) Between the labor process and the state: the changing face of factory regimes under advanced capitalism. *American Sociological Review*, 48: 5, pp 587-605.

Burke, B and Harrison, P (2009) Anti-oppressive approaches, in R Adams, L Dominelli, M Payne (eds) *Critical practice in social work*, 2nd edn, Palgrave Macmillan

Burke, B, and Harrison, P (2000) Race and Racism in Social Work, in M Davies (ed) *The Blackwell encyclopaedia of social work* (pp 282-283). Oxford: Blackwell Publishers Ltd

Butt J and Davey B (1997) The experience of black workers in the social care workforce. *Social Policy Review* 9, 141-61

Byrd, RP, Cole, JB, Guy-Sheftall, B (eds) (2009) *I am your sister, Collected and unpublished writings of Audre Lorde*, Oxford University Press

Cageprisoners (2010) *The Horn of Africa inquisition: the latest profile in the war on terror*, pdf report available at www.cageprisoners.com/our-work/reports/item/108-the-horn-of-africa-inquisition-the-latest-profile-in-the-war-on-terror.

Callinicos, A (1989) *Against postmodernism: A Marxist critique*, Cambridge, Polity

Callinicos, A (2003) *An anticapitalist manifesto,* London: Polity

Callinicos, A (1993) *Race and class*, London: Bookmarks

Cameron, D (2011a) Speech on radicalisation and Islamic extremism, Munich, 5 February, www.newstatesman.com/blogs/the-staggers/2011/02/terrorism-islam-ideology

Cameron, D (2011b) Prime Minister's press statement, 9 August

Cameron, D (2011c) PM's speech at Munich Security Conference, 5 February, www.number10.gov.uk/news/speeches-and-transcripts/2011/02/pms-speech-at-munich-security-conference-60293

Cangiano, A, Shutes, I, Spencer, S, and Leeson, G (2009) *Migrant care workers in ageing societies: Research findings in the United Kingdom.* Oxford: Compas.

Cantle, T (2001) *Community cohesion: A report of the independent review team*, London: Home Office, www.homeoffice.gov.uk/docs/community_cohesion.pdf

Cantle,T (2008) *Community cohesion:A new framework for race and diversity* [rev.] Palgrave Macmillan

Cardy, S (2013) How should social workers support children and families facing destitution and cuts to their benefits? Social Work Action Network www.socialworkfuture.org/articles-and-analysis/articles/306-how-should-social-workers-support-children-in-poverty

Carrell, S (2009) Gay ministers appointment divides Church of Scotland *The Guardian* 24 May 2009 www.guardian.co.uk/uk/2009/may/24/scotland-aberdeen-gay-priest-protestant

Carter, B, Harris, C, Joshi, S (1987) *The 1951-55 Conservative government and the racialisation of Black immigration*, Coventry: Centre for Research in Ethnic Relations

Carter, H (2012) Rochdale gang of guilty exploiting girls, *The Guardian*, 8 May, www.guardian.co.uk/uk/2012/may/08/rochdale-gang-guilty-exploiting-girls

Carter, R, andVirdee, S (2008) Racism and the sociological imagination. *British Journal of Sociology*, 59, 4, 661-79

Casiani, D (2011) Preventing violent extremism:A failed policy?, BBC News, 7 June, www.bbc.co.uk/news/uk-13686586

Castle, S (1992) Cut out the 'ologies' and 'isms', social workers told, *The Independent*, 13 December, www.independent.co.uk/news/uk/cut-out-the-ologies-and-isms-social-workers-told-1563382.html

CCETSW (Central Council for Education and Training in Social Work) (1991a) Anti-racist social work education, Northern Curriculum Development Project, Leeds: CCETSW

CCETSW (1991b) *One small step towards racial justice: The teaching of anti-racism in Diploma in Social Work Programme*. London: CCETSW

Chakrabortty, A (2011) How British workers are losing the power to think, *The Guardian*

Channer, Y and Doel, M (2009). Beyond qualification: experiences of black social workers on a post-qualifying course, *Social Work Education*, 28 (4) 396-412

Cheetham J (ed) (1981) *Social and community work in a multi racial society*. London: Sage

Cheetham, J, Mayor, B, Walter, Loney, M (eds) (1982) *Social and community work in a multiracial society*.London: UK: Harper and Row.

Chorley, Matt (2012) Problem families told 'Stop blaming others', *Independent on Sunday*, 10 June, http://policing.oxfordjournals.org/content/5/2/144.full

Clark, L (2012) Why doesn't Iain Duncan Smith trust a doctor's opinion? *The Independent*, 18 May, http://blogs.independent.co.uk/2012/05/17/why-doesnt-iain-duncan-smith-trust-a-doctors-decision/

Clarke S (2011) Young lives in limbo: The protection of age disputed young people in Wales. Cardiff: The Welsh Refugee Council

Clifford, D and Burke, B (2009) Anti-oppressive ethics and values in social work. Basingstoke: Palgrave Macmillan

Clifford, D (1998) Social assessment theory and practice: A multidisciplinary framework. Aldershot. Ashgate Arena.

Cohen, S, Humphries, B and Mynott, E (2002) *From immigration to welfare controls*. London: Routledge.

Cohen, S (2006) *Standing on the shoulders of fascism,* Stoke on Trent: Trentham

Cohn-Sherbok, D (2002) *Anti-Semitism,* Stroud: Sutton Publishing.

Cole, M (2009) A plethora of suitable enemies: British racism at the dawn of the twenty-first century, *Ethnic and Racial Studies* 32, 1671–85

Coles, D and Scott M (2013) Jimmy Mubenga's unlawful killing was a death waiting to happen, *The Guardian*, 9 July, www.theguardian.com/commentisfree/2013/jul/09/jimmy-mubenga-unlawful-killing-death-waiting-happen

Copsey, N (2011) *The English Defence League: Challenging our country and our values on social inclusion, fairness and equality,* Faith Matters

Corria, S (2010) Not home alone: unaccompanied asylum seeking children and the culture of disbelief. www.thenewlondoners.co.uk/news-a-features/98-immigration/350-not-home-alone

Crenshaw, K (1989) Demarginalizing the intersection of race and sex: a black feminist critique of antidiscrimination doctrine, feminist theory and antiracist politics. *The University of Chicago Legal Forum. Feminism in the Law: Theory, Practice and Criticism*, 139-67

Crenshaw, K (1991) Mapping the margins: intersectionality, identity politics, and violence against women of color, *Stanford Law Review*, 43, 6, 1241-99

CST (Community Security Trust) (2010) Antisemitic Incidents Report 2010, www.thecst.org.uk

Cudworth, D (2008) There is a little more than just delivering the stuff: policy, pedagogy and the education of Gypsy/Traveller children. *Critical Social Policy*, 28(3): 361-77

Dabydeen D, Gilmore J and Jones C (eds) (2008) *The Oxford Companion to Black British History*. Oxford, Oxford University Press

Daily Mail (2011) A broken society that needs a strong leader

Dalrymple, J and Burke, B (2000) Anti-oppressive Practice in Davies, M (ed.), *The Blackwell Encyclopaedia of Social Work*. Oxford: Blackwell.

Dauvergne, C (2008) *Making people illegal,* New York: Cambridge University Press

Davenport, J (2011) Huge rise in anti-gay attacks sparks call to fight hate crime *London Evening Standard* 10 Feb www.standard.co.uk/news/huge-rise-in-antigay-attacks-sparks-call-to-fight-hate-crime-6565675.html

Davis, R (2010) Specialist team earns trust of travellers. *Community Care*, 10 June, 20-21.

Day, A (2009) Racist e-mail investigation slammed as 'extreme' *Lancashire Evening Post*, 13 April

De Gale (1991) Black students' views of existing CQSW courses and CSS schemes, in *Setting the context for change*, Leeds, CCETSW Northern Curriculum Development Project

De Souza P (1991) A review of the experiences of black students in social work training, in *One small step toward racial justice,* London: CCETSW

Denney., D (1983) Some dominant perspectives in the literature relating to multi-racial society. *British Journal of Social Work.*

Department for Communities and Local Government (2007a) *Preventing violent extremism – winning hearts and minds*, London: DCLG,

Department for Education (2010) *Working together to safeguard children: A guide to inter-agency working to safeguard and promote the welfare of children 2010*, www.education.gov.uk/publications/standard/publicationDetail/Page1/DCSF-00305-2010.

Department of Communities and Local Government (2007b) *Preventing Violent Extremism Pathfinder Fund: Guidance note for government offices and local authorities in England*, London: DCLG

Derrington, C, Kendall, S (2007) Challenges and barriers to secondary education: the experiences of young Gypsy/Traveller students in English secondary schools. *Social Policy & Society*, 7 (1): 119-128.

Devine, K (2010) Turmoil in the Catholic Church, *Socialist Review* (May) www.socialistreview.org.uk/article.php?articlenumber=11257

Devore, W, Schlesinger, EG (1999) *Ethnic-sensitive social work practice.* Boston: Allyn and Bacon, cop.

Dodd, V (2005a) Islamophobia blamed for attack *The Guardian* 31 July

Dodd, V (2005b) Asian men targeted in stop and search, *The Guardian* 17 August

Dodd, V (2007) Only 1 in 400 anti-terror stop and searches leads to arrest, *The Guardian* 31 Oct

Dodd, V (2009) Government anti-terrorism strategy spies on innocent *The Guardian* (16 October)

Dodd, V, Taylor, M and Branigan, T (2005) The evil people who planned and carried out this want to divide us as people, *The Guardian* 8 July

Dominelli, L (2008) *Anti-Racist Social Work* (3rd edn) Basingstoke, Palgrave Macmillan

Dominelli, L (2007) Multi-ethnic Europe: diversity and the challenges of race, racism, ethnicity and nationalism, in D Zaviršek, J Zorn, L Rihter, S Žnidarec Demšar (eds) *Ethnicity in Eastern Europe. A challenge for social work education.* Ljubljana: University of Ljubljana, Faculty of social work (19-38).

Dominelli, L (1988) *Anti-racist social work: A challenge for white practitioners and educators.* London: Macmillan

Douglas, B (2012) Social workers tried to 'colour match' our beautiful baby like a pot of Dulux paint: white foster parents describe their bitter battle to keep little Sasha, *Daily Mail*, 25 November, www.dailymail.co.uk/news/article-2238075/Social-workers-tried-colour-match-beautiful-baby-like-pot-Dulux-paint-Foster-parents-say-happiness-tempered-memory-bitter-battle-Sasha.html

Doyle, J (2012a) Don't let PC brigade bury ethnic links to sex gangs, warns children's minister, *Daily Mail*, 3 July, www.dailymail.co.uk/news/article-2168365/Tim-Loughton-Political-correctness-way-police-social workers-investigating-child-sex-abuse.html

Doyle, J (2012b) Who'll take the blame over rape gangs? Not a single social worker sacked over teenage grooming scandal, *Daily Mail*, 28 September, www.dailymail.co.uk/news/article-2209724/Wholl-blame-Not-single-social-worker-sacked-teenage-grooming-scandal.html

Driver, E and Droisen, A (eds) (1989) *Child sexual abuse. Feminist perspectives,* Basingstoke, MacMillan Education

Du Bois, W E B (1903) *The souls of black folk* Chicago: AC McClurg & Co, www.bartleby.com/114/

Economist, The (2012) United against Jobbik, 8 December, www.economist.com/news/europe/21567961-politicians-all-stripes-rally-protest-against-marton-gyongyosis-speech-united-against-jobbik

Edemariam A (2009) Gay US bishop attacks treatment of gay and lesbian clergy by Church of England *The Guardian* 28 August

EHRC (Equality and Human Rights Commission) (2011) How fair is Britain? Equality, Human Rights and Good Relations in 2010, The First Triennial Review Presented To Parliament Pursuant To Section 12 of the Equality Act 2006. (Equality and Human Rights Commission, London) www.equalityhumanrights.com/uploaded_files/triennial_review/how_fair_is_britain_-_complete_report.pdf

Eliot, TS (1948) *Notes towards a definition of culture*, London: Faber and Faber

Ely, P and Denny, D (1987) *Social work in a multi-racial society*. Aldershot: Gower Publishing Company Ltd.

Engels, F (1884/1978) *The origins of the family, private property and the state*, Beijing: Foreign Language Press

Equality Challenge Unit (2011) The experience of black and minority ethnic staff in higher education in England. London: ECU www.ecu.ac.uk

Erfani-Ghettani, R (2011) From portrayal to reality: examining the record of the EDL, IRR News Service Online, 8 December

ERRC (European Roma Rights Centre) (2003) Roma Rights 1-2, 2003: Anti-discrimination law, www.errc.org/article/roma-rights-1-2-2003-anti-discrimination-law/1395

Esping-Andersen, G (1990) *The three worlds of welfare capitalism*. Cambridge: Polity Press

Esping-Andersen, G (1987) Citizenship and socialism: de-commodification and solidarity in the welfare state, in *Stagnation and renewal in social policy: The rise and fall of policy regimes*, New York: ME Sharpe

EUMC (European Union Monitoring Centre on Racism and Xenophobia) (2005) Working Definition of Antisemitism, www.european-forum-on-antisemitism.org/working-definition-of-antisemitism/

European Union (2010) *Ethnic minority and Roma women in Europe: A case for gender equality?* http://ec.europa.eu/social/main.jsp?catId=738&langId=en&pubId=492&type=2&furtherPubs=no

European Molecular Biology Organization (EMBO) (2001) *In the name of science – the role of biologists in Nazi atrocities: Lessons for today's scientists*, EMBO Reports, 2 No 10

Experian (2007) *Overseas workers in the UK social care, children and young people sector: A report for skills for care and development* London: Skills for Care and Development

Fairclough N (1992) *Discourse and social change*, London: Polity

Fawcett, B and Featherstone, B (1995) Power, difference and social work: an exploration, in *Issues in Social Work Education*, Autumn 1995, vol. 15, 1: 3–20

Fear, J (2007) *Under the radar: Dog-whistle politics in Australia*, The Australia Institute

Featherstone, B, Fawcett, B (1995) Oh no! not more isms: Feminism, postmodernism, poststructuralism and social work education. *Social Work Education*, 14, 3, 25-43

Fekete, L (2004) Anti-Muslim racism and the European security state, *Race & Class*, 46, 3–29

Fekete, L (2005) The deportation machine: Europe, asylum and human rights, *Race & Class* 47, 64–78

Fekete, L (2009) *A suitable enemy: Racism, migration and Islamophobia in Europe*, London: Pluto

Fekete, L (2011) in Mahamdallie, H, (2011) *Defending multiculturalism: A guide for the movement*, London: Bookmarks

Fekete, L (2011) Understanding the European-wide assault on multiculturalism, in H Mahamdallie (ed) *Defending multiculturalism. A guide for the movement.* London: Bookmarks: 38-52.

Fekete, L, Webber, F (2010) Foreign nationals, enemy penology and the criminal justice system, *Race & Class*, 51, 4

Ferguson, I, Lavalette, M (1999) Social work, postmodernism, and marxism, *European Journal of Social Work*, 2,1, 27-40

Ferguson, I, Lavalette, M (2004) Beyond power discourse: alienation and social work, *British Journal of Social Work*, 34, 3, 297-312

Ferguson, I, Lavalette, M (2013b) *The crisis in adult social care*, Bristol, Policy Press

Ferguson, I, Lavalette, M (2013a) Critical and radical social work: an introduction, *Critical and Radical Social Work*, 1, 1, 3-14

Ferguson, I, Lavalette, M, Mooney, G (2002) *Rethinking welfare: A critical perspective*, London: Sage

Ferguson, L, Lavalette, M, Whitmore, E (2005) *Globalisation, global justice and social work*, London: Routledge

Ferguson, I, Woodward, R (2009) *Radical social work in practice. Making a difference*, Bristol: Policy Press

Fieldhouse, DK (2006) *Western imperialism in the Middle East 1914-1958*, New York, Oxford University Press.

Finkelstein, NG (2003) *The Holocaust industry*, 2nd ed, London: Verso

Financial Times (2012) Greece grapples with shadow of Golden Dawn, www.ft.com/cms/s/0/7f797fde-f778-11e1-ba54-00144feabdc0.html#axzz2SFALrXWP

Finney, N and Simpson, L (2009) *Sleepwalking to segregation? Challenging myths about race and migration*, Bristol, Policy Press
Fiori, G. (1965/1990) *Antonio Gramsci: Life of a revolutionary,* London: Verso
Fisher, M (2009) *Capitalist realism: Is there no alternative?* Ropley: Zero
Fishman, WJ (2004) *East End Jewish radicals*, Nottingham, Five Leaves Publications
Flynn, D (2005) New borders, new management: the dilemmas of modern immigration policy, *Ethnic and Racial Studies,* 28: 3, 463-90
Fonseca, I (2007) *Bury me standing: The gypsies and their journey* (orig. Pokoplji me pokončno: Romi in njihovo potovanje) Ljubljana: Sanje.
Fook, J (2012) *Social work: A critical approach to practice*, 2nd edn, London: Sage
France 24 News online (2012) www.france24.com/en/20090325-le-pen-repeats-slur-nazi-gas-chambers-were-detail-
Fryer, P (1984) *Staying power: The history of black people in Britain*, London: Pluto
Fukyama, F (1992) *The end of history and the last man*, London: Penguin
Gardner, C (2013) Woolwich: protest marches as suspect questioned *The Scotsman* 2 June www.scotsman.com/the-scotsman/uk/woolwich-protest-marches-as-suspect-questioned-1-2951204
Gaskell, S (2012) Bid for public show of support for Ched Evans at Sheffield United falls flat, Wales Online, 28 April, www.walesonline.co.uk/news/wales-news/2012/04/28/bid-for-public-show-of-support-for-ched-evans-at-sheffield-united-falls-flat-91466-30861200/
Geertz, C (1975) Thick description: towards an interpretive theory of culture, in C Geertz, *The interpretation of cultures*. London: Hutchinson and Company
German, L (1989) *Sex, class and socialism*, London: Bookmarks
German, L (2007) *Material girls: Women, men and work*, London: Bookmarks
German, L and Murray, A (2005) *Stop the war: The story of Britain's biggest mass movement,* London: Bookmarks
Gest, J (2009) A bad trade off, *The Guardian* 25 March, www.guardian.co.uk/commentisfree/belief/2009/mar/25/islam-religion1
GI Partners (2011) GI partners expands specialist care and education portfolio with the acquisition of advanced childcare, 18 March, www.gipartners.com/news/gi-partners-expands-specialist-care-and-education-portfolio-with-the-acquisition-of-advanced-ch
Gilbert, H (2011) Tackling trafficking, *Police Magazine* (February) www.polfed.org/09_Tackling_Trafficking_Feb11.pdf

Gilroy, P (1980) Managing the underclass: a further note on the sociology of race relations in britain in *Race and Class,* 22(1) 47-62

Gilroy P (1987) *There ain't no Black in the Union Jack: The cultural politics of race and nation*, London: Routledge

Gilroy, P (1990) The end of anti-racism, *Journal of Ethnic and Migration Studies*, 17, 1, 71-83

Gilroy, P (2000) *Against race: Imagining political culture beyond the color line.* Cambridge. The Belknap Press of Harvard University Press

Gilroy, P (2011) Paul Gilroy speaks on the riots, August, Tottenham, North London, http://dreamofsafety.blogspot.com/2011/08/paul-gilroy-speaks-on-riots-august-2011.html

Gold, Nora (1996). Putting antisemitism on the anti-racism agenda in North American schools of social work. *Journal of Social Work Education*, 32(1), 77-89

Goodhart, D (2004) Discomfort of strangers, *Guardian*, 24 February

Goody, J (1968) Time: social organization, in DL Sills (1999) (ed) *International Encyclopedia of Social Sciences* 16, 30–42, New York: Macmillan

Gove, M (2011) Michael Gove slackens rules on use of physical force in schools, Speech delivered at Durand Academy, Stockwell, south London, *The Guardian* 1 September, www.theguardian.com/politics/2011/sep/01/michael-gove-physical-force-schools

Graham, D and Boyd, J (2010) *Committed, concerned and conciliatory: The attitudes of Jews in Britain towards Israel, Initial findings from the 2010 Israel Survey*, London: Institute for Jewish Policy Research

Graham, M (1999) The African-centred worldview: developing a paradigm in social work, *British Journal of Social Work*, 29, 4, 251-76

Graham, M (2000) Honouring social work principles: exploring connections between anti-racist social work and African-centred worldviews. *Social Work Education*, 19, 5, 423-6

Grahame, M (2009). Reframing black perspectives in social work: new directions? *Social Work Education*, 28, 3, 268-80

Gramsci A (1971) *Selections from the prison notebooks of Antonio Gramsci.* London: Lawrence and Wishart

Grandjean, G, Lewis, P and Taylor, M (2012) Staff deporting foreigners out of UK 'loutish and aggressive', *The Guardian*, 13 April, www.theguardian.com/uk/2012/apr/13/staff-deporting-foreigners-loutish

Grayling, C (2012) Labour didn't care who landed in Britain, *Daily Telegraph*

Green, A (2010) *Moses Montefiore, Jewish liberator, imperial hero.* Harvard University Press, London

Grove-White, R (2010) How will the savage government spending cuts affect migrants? *Migrant Rights Network,* www.migrantsrights.org.uk/blog/2010/10/how-will-savage-government-spending-cuts-affect-migrants

Grubin, D (1998) *Sex offending against children: Understanding the risk* (Home Office)

GSCC (2010) *Annual Report 2010* www.gscc.org.uk

Guardian, The (2006) Letters to the editor, 16 May.

Guardian, The (2012) Alexandra Topping and Vikram Dodd, 4 January, Doreen Lawrence: Britain still blighted by racism, www.theguardian.com/uk/2012/jan/03/doreen-lawrence-britain-blighted-racism

Guardian, The (2009a) Anti-terror code 'would alienate most muslims', 17 February, www.guardian.co.uk/politics/feb/17/counterterrorism-strategy-muslims

Guardian, The (2009b) Catholic church in Ireland covered up child abuse, says report, 26 November, www.guardian.co.uk/world/2009/nov/26/catholic-church-ireland-child-abuse

Guardian, The (2012) Workless families: a convenient untruth, 3 February, www.theguardian.com/commentisfree/2012/feb/02/workless-families-convenient-truth-editorial

Guardian, The (2013) Far-right food rally raises tensions in Athens, 2 May

Guitierrez, G. Fredricksen, K, Soifer, S (1999) Perspectives of social work faculty on diversity and societal oppression content: results from a national survey, *Journal of Social Work Education*, 35, 3

Gunaratnam, Y, Lewis, G (2001) Racialising emotional labour and emotionalising racialised labour: anger, fear and shame in social welfare. *Journal of Social Work Practice* 15, 131–48

Guy, W (1998) Ways of looking at Roma: the case of Czechoslovakia (1975), in D Tong (ed) *Gypsies*, New York/London: Garland Publishing, Inc

Hain, P (2011) Preface to Mahamdallie (ed)

Haker, J (2013) Time to face up to abuse in the white community *The Guardian* 7 May 2013

Hall, S 1980 Race, articulation and societies structured in social dominance, in *Sociological theories, race and colonialism*, 305-45, Paris: UNESCO

Hall S and Jacques M (1991) *New times: The changing face of politics in the 1990s* London: Lawrence and Wishart

Hall, S, Critcher, C, Jefferson, T, Clarke, J (1978) *Policing the crisis: Mugging the state and law and order*, Basingstoke: Palgrave Macmillan

Hall, S, Critcher, C, Jefferson, T, Clarke, J, Roberts, B (1978) *Policing the crisis: Mugging, the state and law and order.* London: MacMillan Education

Hancock, I (1988) The development of Romani linguistics, in MA Jazayery, W Winter (eds) *Languages and culture: Studies in honor of Edgar C Plome*, Berlin, New York, Amsterdam: Mouton de Gruyter

Harker, J (2011) For black Britons, this is not the 80s revisited. It's worse, *The Guardian* 11 August www.guardian.co.uk/commentisfree/2011/aug/11/black-britons-80s-mps-media?INTCMP=SRCH

Harker, J (2013) It's time to face up to the problem of sexual abuse in the white community, *The Guardian*, 6 May, www.theguardian.com/commentisfree/2013/may/06/sexual-abuse-in-white-community

Harman C (2007) Theorizing neoliberalism, in *International Socialism. A quarterly journal of socialist theory.* Issue 117, www.isj.org.uk/index.php4?s=contents&issue=117

Harman, C (1981) The summer of 1981: a post-riot analysis, *International Socialism 14* (autumn) www.marxists.org/archive/harman/1981/xx/riots.html

Harris, J (2003) *The social work business*, London: Routledge

Hartmann, HI (1979) The unhappy marriage of Marxism and feminism: towards a more progressive union, *Capital & Class* 3, 1–33

Harvey, D (2005) *A brief history of neoliberalism.* Oxford: Oxford University Press

Harvey, S (2009) Worker 'not told reason for suspension', *Lancashire Evening Post*, 16 April

Hayes, D (2002)From aliens to asylum seekers: a history of immigration controls and welfare in Britain, in S Cohen, B Humphries, E Mynott (eds) *From immigration controls to welfare controls*, London: Routledge

Hayes, D and Humphries, B (2004) *Social work, immigration and asylum,* London: Jessica Kingsley

Hayes, D (2012) Social work with asylum seekers and refugees, in A Worsley, A Olsen, T Mann, E Mason-Whitehead (eds) *Key concepts in social work practice*, London: Sage.

Hayter, T (2000) *Open borders: The case against immigration controls*, London: Pluto Press

Hayter, T (2004) *Open borders the case against immigration controls,* 2nd edition, Pluto Press, London; Sterling, Va.

Health Statistics Quarterly (2007) Inequalities in health: Expectations in England and Wales – small area analysis from the 2001 Census. London: Office for National Statistics.

Hellig, J (2003) *The Holocaust and Antisemitism,* Oxford, Oneworld Publications

Hill, Collins, P (2009) *Black feminist thought: Knowledge, consciousness, and the politics of empowerment*, London: Routledge
Hill, JD (2009) Beyond blood identities: post humanity in the twenty-first century, Lexington Books
Hillyard, P (1993) *Suspect community*, London: Pluto
Hiro, DH (1992) *Black British White British*, London: Paladin
Hjern A, Brendler-Lindqvist M, Norredam M (2012) Age assessment of young asylum seekers. *Acta Paediatrica*, vol 101, no 1, 4–7, January
HMIC/HMCPSI (Her Majesty's Inspectorate of Constabulary/Her Majesty's Crown Prosecution Service Inspectorate) (2012) *Forging the links: Rape investigation and prosecution*, www.hmcpsi.gov.uk/documents/reports/CJJI_THM/BOTJ/forging_the_links_rape_investigation_and_prosecution_20120228.pdf
Hodges, D (2012) Your arrogant racism is part of London's past: an open letter to Stephen Lawrence's killers. *Daily Telegraph*
Holloway, Lester (2012) Britain's Obama moment 25 years ago demands reflection (27 May) http://cllrlesterholloway.wordpress.com/2012/05/27/britains-obama-moment-25-years-ago-demands-reflection/
Home Office (1998) *Fairer, faster and firmer: A modern approach to immigration and asylum*, Cmnd 4018, London: TSO
Home Office (1999) *Asylum casework instructions.* London: Home Office
Home Office (2009) *Pursue, prevent, protect, prepare: The United Kingdom's strategy for countering international terrorism: Annual report*, Cm 7547, London: TSO
Home Office (2011) *Prevent strategy*, Cm 8092, London: TSO, www.homeoffice.gov.uk/publications/counter-terrorism/prevent/prevent-strategy/prevent-strategy-review?view=Binary
Hondagneu-Sotelo, P (2007) *Doméstica : Immigrant workers cleaning and caring in the shadows of affluence.* University of California Press, Berkeley
hooks, b. (1989) *Talking back: Thinking feminist, thinking black.* Boston: South End Press
hooks, b. (1991) *Yearnings: Race, gender, and cultural politics.* London: Turnaround
hooks, b. (1992) *Black Looks: Race and Representation*, London: Turnaround
hooks., b. (1994) *Teaching to transgress: Education as the practice of freedom*, Routledge, London.
Horton, G. (2013) Advocating for Palestinian children in the face of the Israeli occupation, *Critical and Radical Social Work*, 1,1, 111-15,

Hough, A 2012, Hundreds of members of the local Sikh community protesting outside a Luton police station, *Daily Telegraph* (30 May) www.telegraph.co.uk/news/uknews/crime/9299139/Luton-local-Sikh-community-protesting-over-sex-attack-police-failures.html

Hughes, M (2009) Police identify 200 children as potential terrorists *The Independent* 28 March www.independent.co.uk/news/uk/crime/police-identify-200-children-as-potential-terrorists-1656027.html

Hugman, R (2013) Culture Values and Ethics in Social Work: Embracing Diversity. Abingdon Routledge

Humphries, B (2004) An unacceptable role for social work: implementing immigration policy. *British Journal of Social Work* 34 93-107

Humphries, B, Wimmer, HP, Seale, A, Stokes, I (1993) *Improving practice teaching and learning: Anti-racist social work education*. Leeds, Northern Curriculum Development Project, CCETSW

Hunter S, Swan E (2007a) Oscillating politics and shifting agencies: equalities and diversity work and actor network theory. *Equal Opportunities International*, 26 (5) 402-19

Hunter S, Swan E (2007b) The politics of equality: professionals, states and activists. *Equal Opportunities International*, 26(5) 377-86

Huntington, SP (1993) The clash of civilizations?, *Foreign Affairs*, 72, 3, Summer

Huntington, SP (2002) *The clash of civilisations and the remaking of the world order,* New York, WW Norton and Co. Ltd

Husband, C (1991) 'Race', conflictual politics and anti-racist social work: lessons from the past for action in the 90s, in *Setting the context of change: Anti-racist social work education*. Leeds: CCETSW Northern Curriculum Development Project

Husband, C (1995) The morally active practitioner and the ethics of anti-racist social work, in R Hugman, D Smith (eds) *Ethical issues in social work*, London: Routledge

Hutchinson-Rees M (1989) And for those of us who are black? Black politics in social work, in M Langan and P Lee (eds) *Radical Social Work Today*, London: Unwin Hyman

Hutton, W (2005) A gagging order too far, *The Observer*, 19 June www.theguardian.com/politics/2005/jun/19/religion.race

Independent, The (2012) A shameful spinning of the facts on immigration, (lead article) 12 January www.independent.co.uk/voices/editorials/leading-article-a-shameful-spinning-of-the-facts-on-immigration-6292556.html

Institute of Race Relations (1993) *Resource directory on 'race' and racism in social work,* London: Institute of Race Relations

Inside Government (2013) Immigration speech by the Prime Minister, www.gov.uk/government/news/immigration-speech-by-the-prime-minister] 25/03/13

International Federation of Social Work (2007) Definition of social work, www.ifsw.org/en/p38000208.html

International Federation of Social Work (2012) Statement of ethical principles, http://ifsw.org/policies/statement-of-ethical-principles/

Inter-parliamentary Coalition for Combating Antisemitism (ICCA) (2011) About the ICCA http://archive.is/35YI

IRR (Institute of Race Relations) (2002) IRR expresses concern at excessive sentencing of Bradford rioters, press release, 5 July, www.irr.org.uk/news/irr-expresses-concern-over-excessive-sentencing-of-bradford-rioters/

IRR (2010) *Accelerated removals: A study of the human cost of EU deportation policies, 2009-2010*, IRR Briefing Paper No. 4, October 2010

IRR (2011) *Breivik, the conspiracy theory and the Oslo massacre,* Briefing Paper No. 5

Israel National News online (2012) Greece's Golden Dawn leader denies Holocaust gas chambers, 15 May, www.israelnationalnews.com/News/News.aspx/155826

James, SM, Busia, PA (1993) *Theorising black feminisms*, Routledge

John, G (2011) 30 Years after the New Cross fire: challenging racism today, *Socialist Worker*, 10 September, www.socialistworker.co.uk/art.php?id=26904

Johnson, C (2000) *Blowback: The costs and consequences of American empire*, New York: Sphere

Jones, C (1993) Distortion and Demonisation: The Right and Antiracist Social Work, in *Social Work Education*, 12, 9-16

Jones, CP (2002) Levels of racism. A theoretical framework and a gardener's tale, in T La Veist (ed) *Race, ethnicity and health*, 311-18

Jones, O (2011) *Chavs: The demonisation of the working class,* London: Verso

Joppke, C (1999) How immigration is changing citizenship: a comparative view. *Ethnic and Racial Studies* 22, 629–652

Jordan, J (1989) *Moving towards home.* London: Virago

Judah T (2004) Child soldiers, sex slaves, and cannibalism at gunpoint: the horrors of Uganda's north. *The Independent*, 23 October, www.independent.co.uk/news/world/africa/child-soldiers-sex-slaves-and-cannibalism-at-gunpoint-the-horrors-of-ugandas-north-6159396.html

Julius, A (2010) *Trials of the diaspora. A history of Anti-Semitism in England,* New York, Oxford University Press

Judt, T (2003) Israel: The alternative, *New York Review of Books*, 23 October

Keating, F (2000) Anti-racist perspectives: what are the gains for social work? *Social Work Education,* 77-87

Kemp, A (2004) Labour migration and racialisation: labour market mechanisms and labour migration control policies in Israel, *Social Identities*, 10, 267–292

Kennedy, M (2007) Enough says Amis in Eagleton feud, *The Guardian* 13 October www.theguardian.com/uk/2007/oct/13/highereducation.islam

Khan, D (2011) Never on our own: the experience of uniting a community against the EDL, in Hassan Mahamdallie (ed) *Defending Multiculturalism* (Bookmarks)

Khan, K (2009) PreventingViolent Extremism (PVE): A response from the Muslim community (An-Nisa Society)

Khosravi, S (2010) *Illegal Traveller: an auto-ethnography of borders*, Palgrave Macmillan,

Kim, K (2008) Policy Prohibiting LAPD from Asking About Immigration Status Affirmed. *New American Media*

Klein, N (2007) *The Shock Doctrine,* London: Penguin

Klopčič, V (2007) The situation of Roma in SLovenia: Roma and Gadže. (orig. *Položaj Romov v Sloveniji: Romi in Gadže).* Ljubljana: Inštitut za narodnostna vprašanja

Klopčič, V (ed) (1991) *Razprave in gradivo 25 (Romi na Slovenskem).* Ljubljana: Inštitut za narodnostna vprašanja.

Kundnani, A (2001) *From Oldham to Bradford: The violence of the violated* (Institute of Race Relations) www.irr.org.uk/news/from-oldham-to-bradford-the-violence-of-the-violated/

Kundnani, A (2007) *The end of tolerance: Racism in 21st century Britain,* London: Pluto Press

Kundnani, A (2009) *Spooked: How not to prevent violent extremism* Institute of Race Relations www.irr.org.uk/pdf2/spooked.pdf

La Rose, J (2011) *The New Cross Massacre story: Interviews with John La Rose*, London: New Beacon Books and GPI

Laird, SE (2008) *Anti-oppressive social work: A guide for developing cultural competence.* Los Angeles: Sage

Lammy, D (2011) *Out of the ashes* (Guardian Books)

Lammy, D (2012) Interview with LBC Radio, 29 January

Lancashire Evening Post (2009) Council worker sacked over racist emails, 7 July

Lavalette, M (ed) (2011) *Radical social work today*. Bristol: Policy Press

Lavile, S (2012) Met police urge rape victims to come forward as new detective arrested, *The Guardian*, 8 June

Leather, A (2012) The Bradford riots: responses to a rebellion, *International Socialism*, 136, Autumn

Lentin, A (2000) Race, racism and anti-racism: challenging contemporary classifications. *Social Identities*, 91-106

Lentin, A (2004) Multiculturalism or Anti-racism? Open Democracy Net, at, www.opendemocracy.net/debates/article-1-111-2073.jsp#

Lentin, A and Titley, G (2011) *The crises of multiculturalism: Racism in a neoliberal age*. London: Zed Books

Leonard, P (1997) *Postmodern welfare: Reconstructing and emancipatory project,* London: Sage

Levenson R and Sharma A (1999) *The health of refugee children. Guidelines for paediatricians*. London: Royal College of Paediatrics and Child Health, November, www.rcpch.ac.uk/what-we-do/rcpch-publications/publications-list-date/publications-list-date

Lewis G (1996) Situated voices: Black women's experience and social work, *Feminist Review* No. 53, Summer, 24-56

Lewis G (2000) *Race, Gender and Social Welfare: Encounters in a post Colonial society*. Cambridge, Polity Press

Lewis, P (2012) Black fireman says he was abused and tasered by Met, *The Guardian*, 19 April, www.theguardian.com/uk/2012/apr/19/metropolitan-police-accused-racism-firefighter

Lewis, P and Taylor M (2010) BA flight 77 passengers haunted by last cries of dying man, *The Guardian*

Livingstone, K and Raffarian, JP (2004) 'You've made a big mistake', *The Guardian*, 13 March, www.theguardian.com/world/2004/mar/13/religion.france

Longerich, P (2010) *Holocaust. The Nazi Persecution and Murder of the Jews*, New York, Oxford University Press

Lorde, A (1984) Sister Outsider. New York: The Crossing Press

Luccasen, L (1998) Harmful tramps: police professionalization and gypsies in Germany, 1700–1945, in L Lucassen, W Willems, A Cottaar (eds) *Gypsies and other itinerant groups: A socio-historical approach,* London: Palgrave Macmillan

Macdonald, A, Cooper, B (2007) Long-term care and dementia services: an impending crisis. *Age and Ageing* 36, 16–22

Maček, J (2001) Silenced genocide (orig. Zamolčani genocid), *Zaveza*, 11, 4, 13-24.

MacIntyre, D (1993) Major on crime: 'Condemn more, understand less', *The Independent*, 21 February, www.independent.co.uk/news/major-on-crime-condemn-more-understand-less-1474470.html

Macpherson, W (1999) *The Stephen Lawrence Inquiry: Report of an inquiry by Sir William Macpherson of Cluny*, London: HMSO

Mahamdallie, H (2002) Racism: myths and realities, *International Socialism 95* (Summer) http://pubs.socialistreviewindex.org.uk/isj95/mahamdallie.htm

Mahamdallie, H (2007) Muslim working class struggles, *International Socialism 113* (winter) www.isj.org.uk/?id=288

Mahamdallie, H (ed) (2011) *Defending multiculturalism*, London: Bookmarks

Mahamdallie, H (2012) Rochdale: media distortion will put women in danger and will only benefit racists, *Socialist Worker*, 19 May www.socialistworker.co.uk/art.php?id=28457

Mair, H (2012) Social workers 'at rock bottom' over issue of race and adoption, *The Guardian*, 6 November, www.guardian.co.uk/society/2012/nov/06/social workers-morale-rock-bottom?intcmp=239

Malik, K (1998) Race, pluralism and the meaning of difference, Kenanmalik.com, chapter 2, www.kenanmalik.com/chapters/new_formations3.htm

Malik, S and Quinn, B (2013) Grimsby mosque targeted with petrol bombs, *The Guardian*, 27 May, www.guardian.co.uk/uk/2013/may/27/grimsby-mosque-petrol-bombs?INTCMP=SRCH

Manchester Evening News (2012) You preyed on girls because they were not part of your community or religion, says judge as he jails Rochdale sex gang for 77 years 9 May, http://menmedia.co.uk/manchestereveningnews/news/crime/s/1493276_you-preyed-on-girls-because-they-were-not-part-of-your-community-or-religion-says-judge-as-he-jails-rochdale-sex-gang-for-77-years

Martinson, J (2012) Why the Rochdale grooming trial wasn't about race, *The Guardian*, 9 May, www.guardian.co.uk/society/2012/may/09/rochdale-grooming-trial-race

Marx, K (1975) *Early writings* (Harmondsworth)

Maxime, J (1986) Some psychological models of black self-concept, in, S Ahmed, J Cheetham and J Small (eds) *Social work with black children and their families.* London: Batsford/BAAF

May, T (2011) *Home Secretary speech on the riots*, House of Commons, 11 August 2011, www.homeoffice.gov.uk/media-centre/speeches/riots-speech

McGregor, J (2007) Joining the BBC (British Bottom Cleaners): Zimbabwean migrants and the UK care industry. *Journal of Ethnic and Migration Studies* 33, 801–24

McKibbin, R (2013) Anything but benevolent, *London Review of Books*, 35, 8

McLaughlin, K (2007) The equality chameleon: reflections on social identity, passing and groupism, *Social Policy and Society*, 6(1) 69-79

McShane, D (2007) *The new anti-Semitism*, www.washingtonpost.com/wp-dyn/content/article/2007/09/03/AR2007090300719.html

McVeigh, T (2001) Race split in Britain exposed by survey, Race In Britain Special Report, *The Observer*, 25 November, www.theguardian.com/politics/2001/nov/25/race.observerpolitics

McVeigh, T (2012) Rotherham council holds inquiry after taking UKIP couple's foster children, *The Observer*, 25 November, www.guardian.co.uk/uk/2012/nov/25/rotherham-council-ukip-foster

Mehmood, T (2003) *While there is light*, Comma Press

Miles, R (1982) *Racism and migrant labour*, London/Boston: Routledge & Kegan Paul

Miles, R and Phizacklea, A (1984) *White man's country*, London: Pluto

Mills, N (branch secretary) (2005) Bolton Social Workers and Section 9 of the Asylum and Immigration Act, UNISON Bolton Metro Branch, www.labournet.net/ukunion/0510/bolton1.html

Mind (2011) Inexcusable racial inequalities unchanged in six years, www.mind.org.uk/news/show/4819

Mirza, HS (ed) (1997) *Black British feminisms: A reader*, Routledge, London/New York

Mirza, HS (2006) Transcendence over diversity: black women in the academy. *Policy Futures in Education* 4(2) 101-113

Misra, J, Woodring, J, Merz, SN (2006) The globalization of care work: neoliberal economic restructuring and migration policy. *Globalizations* 3, 317–32

Modood, T (2003) Muslims and the politics of difference, *Political Quarterly*

Modood, T (2007) *Multiculturalism (Themes for the 21st century)* Cambridge: Polity Press

Moriarty, J (2010) Competing with myths: migrant labour in social care, in M Ruhs and B Anderson (eds) *Who needs migrant workers? Labour shortages, immigration, and public policy*. Oxford University Press, Oxford

Morris, N (2007) Imam attacked as anti-Muslim violence grows *The Independent* 14 August

Morrison, J (2000) *The trafficking and smuggling of refugees: The endgame in European asylum policy*, UNHCR, July

Morrison, T (1990) *The bluest eye*. London: Picador

Moss, V (2012) UKIP: Rotherham council poised for u-turn over removal of foster children from couple, *Sunday Mirror*, 25 November, www.mirror.co.uk/news/uk-news/ukip-rotherham-council-poised-for-u-turn-1455647

Mozgovaya, N (2011) Obama tells Jews: 'Never again' is not just a phrase, but a principled cause, *Haaretz*, 28 January, www.haaretz.com/jewish-world/obama-tells-jews-never-again-is-not-just-a-phrase-but-a-principled-cause-1.339697

Muir, H (2010) Racism and school exclusions', *The Guardian*, 22 January, www.guardian.co.uk/uk/2010/jan/22/racism-school-exclusions-hugh-muir

Muir, H (2011) Diary *The Guardian* 12 September

Muir, H (2012) Social workers 'at rock bottom' over issue of race and adoption, *The Guardian*, 6 November, www.theguardian.com/society/2012/nov/06/social-workers-morale-rock-bottom

Mullaly, B (1997) *Structural social work: Ideology, theory and practice*. Oxford: Oxford University Press

Mullalay, B (2001) Confronting the politics of despair: toward the reconstruction of progressive social work in a global economy and post modern age. *Social Work Education*, 20, 3, 303-20

Mullaly, B (2006) *The new structural social work: Ideology, theory and practice*. Oxford: Oxford University Press.

Murphy, J (2012) Baroness Warsi: Some Pakistani men think young white girls are fair game for sex abuse, *London Evening Standard*, 18 May

Murray, A, German, L (2003) *Stop the war: The story of Britain's biggest mass movement*, London: Bookmarks

Muslim News (2009) McCarthyism style surveillance, 24 November, www.muslimnews.co.uk/paper/index.php?article=4362

National Statistics (2011) www.statistics.gov.uk

Neale, J (2001) *The American War: Vietnam 1960-1975*, London: Bookmarks

Neysmith, SM, Aronson, J (1997) Working conditions in home care: negotiating race and class boundaries in gendered work. *International Journal of Health Services* 27, 479–99

NMC (2007) *Registering as a nurse or midwife in the United Kingdom: For applicants from outside the European Economic Area*. London: NMC.

Norfolk, Suffolk and Cambridgeshire Strategic Health Authority (2003) *Independent Inquiry into the death of David Bennett*, Cambridge: Norfolk, Suffolk and Cambridgeshire Strategic Health Authority

Norton-Taylor, R, Hirsch, A (2010) Chilcot inquiry casts new doubts on Iraq war *The Guardian* 12 January

Nye, C (2013) Glasgow's destitute asylum seekers: the people who don't exist, www.bbc.co.uk/news/uk-scotland-21835432

O'Connell Davidson, J (2006) Will the real sex slave please stand up? *Feminist Review* 83, 4–22

O'Connell Davidson, J (2010) New slavery, old binaries: human trafficking and the borders of freedom. *Global Networks* 10, 244–261

O'Hagan, K (2001) *Cultural competence in the caring professions*, Jessica Kingsley Publishers, UK

Office for National Statistics (2011) Births and deaths in England and Wales, *Statistical Bulletin*

Okely, J (1996) *Own or other culture*. London/New York: Routledge

Okitikpi, T and Aymer, C (2010) *Key concepts in anti-discriminatory social work*, London: Sage

Orr, D (2006) Why the sight of veiled women offends me, *The Independent*, 8 July, www.independent.co.uk/voices/commentators/deborah-orr/deborah-orr-why-the-sight-of-veiled-women-offends-me-407100.html

Orr, J 2012, Rochdale sex abuse is nothing to do with race, *Socialist Worker* (19 May) www.socialistworker.co.uk/art.php?id=28456

Orwell, G (1971) *The collected essays, journalism and letters of George Orwell, volume 2, My country right or left*, 1940-1943 (Penguin)

OSI (Open Society Institute) (2001, 2002) *EU Accession Monitoring Program (2001, 2002): Monitoring the EU accession process: Minority protection*, Budapest: OSI

Ottolenghi, E (2003) Anti-Zionism is anti-semitism – behind much criticism of Israel is a thinly veiled hatred of Jews, *The Guardian* 29 November, www.theguardian.com/world/2003/nov/29/comment

Panorama (2009) Muslim First – British Second, BBC 16 February 2009

Papadopoulos, I, Tilki, M, Lees, S (2004) Promoting cultural competence in healthcare through a research based intervention in the UK, *Diversity in Health and Social Care*, 1, 107–15

Pappe, I (2006) *The ethnic cleansing of Palestine*, London: Oneworld.

Parekh, B (2006) *Rethinking multiculturalism*, rev. edn, Basingstoke: Palgrave Macmillan.

Parekh Report, The (2000) *The future of multi-ethnic Britain* London: Profile

Parreñas, RS (2001) *Servants of globalization*, Palo Alto, CA: Stanford University Press

Patel N (1995) In search of the Holy Grail, in R Hugman and D Smith (eds) *Ethical issues in social work*, London: Routledge

Patel N (2002) The campaign against anti-racism in social work, in DR Tomlinson and W Trew (eds) *Equalising opportunities, minimising oppression: A critical review of anti-discriminatory policies in health and social welfare*. London: Routledge

Paxman, J (2011) *Empire: What ruling the world did to the British*. London: Penguin Viking
Paxton, RO (2005) *The anatomy of fascism*, London: Penguin
Peirce, G (2007) Britain's own Guantanamo, *The Guardian*, 21 December, www.theguardian.com/commentisfree/2007/dec/21/humanrights.uksecurity
Peirce, G (2010) *Dispatches fro*
m the dark side: On torture and the death of justice, London: Verso
Pearson, G (1983) *Hooligan: A history of respectable fears*, London: Macmillan
Penketh, L (1997) Racism and social welfare, in M Lavalette and A Pratt (eds) *Social policy: A conceptual and theoretical introduction* London: Sage
Penketh, L (2000) *Tackling institutional racism: Anti-racist policies and social work education and training*, Bristol, Policy Press
Pennie, P, Best, F (1990) *How the black family is pathologised by the social services system*, Association of Black Social Workers and Allied Professionals
Perera, S (2002) 'What is a camp...?', *Borderlands* ejournal, vol. 1, no. 1 (2002).
Petre, J (2008) Catholic adoption agency to defy gay rights law *Mail on Sunday* 8 June www.mailonsunday.co.uk/news/article-1024956/Catholic-adoption-agency-defy-gay-rights-law.html
Phillips, M (2012) The Rochdale sex ring shows the horrific consequences of Britain's Islamophobia witch-hunt, *Daily Mail*, 9 May, www.dailymail.co.uk/debate/article-2141930/The-Rochdale-sex-ring-shows-horrific-consequences-Britains-Islamophobia-witch-hunt.html
Phillips, T (2005) Speech to Manchester Council for Community Relations, 22 September
Phillips, T 2005, After 7/7: sleepwalking to segregation, Speech to Manchester Council for Community Relations, 22 September, www.humanities.manchester.ac.uk/socialchange/research/social-change/summer-workshops/documents/sleepwalking.pdf
Pilditch, D (2011) 'Gangsta salute for "fallen soldier" Mark Duggan who sparked riot' Daily Express 10 September 2011, www.express.co.uk/news/uk/270299/Gangsta-salute-for-fallen-soldier-Mark-Duggan-who-sparked-riot.
Pinder, S (2011) Age assessment disputes and JR claims, www.freemovement.org.uk/2011/03/18/age-assessment-disputes-and-jr-claims/

Pink D (1991) Black students' views of existing CQSW courses and CSS schemes, in CCETSW *Setting the context for change*, Leeds, CCETSW Northern Curriculum Development Project

Pinker R (1999) 'Social work and adoption: a case of mistaken identities' in Philpot, T (ed) *Political Correctness and Social Work*, London: IEA

Piore, MJ (1983) *Birds of passage: Migrant labor and industrial societies.* Cambridge: Cambridge University Press

Pitcher, B (2009) *The politics of multiculturalism*, Palgrave Macmillan

Piterberg, G (2008) *The returns of Zionism: Myths, politics and scholarship in Israel*, Verso, London

Poinasamy, K and Fooks, L (2009) *Who cares? How best to protect UK care workers employed through agencies and gangmasters from exploitation,* Oxfam Briefing Papers, London: Oxfam

Policy and Guidelines for the Education of Traveller, Gypsy and Roma Children in Haringey. www.haringey.gov.uk/policy_and_guidelines.pdf

Povey, ER (2007) *Afghan women: Identity and invasion*, London: Zed Books Ltd

Prasad, Y (2010) Nazis and police provoked the Bradford riot of 2001, *Socialist Worker*, 14 August, www.socialistworker.co.uk/art.php?id=22063

Press Association (2013) Help for Heroes rejects EDL donation cash *The Guardian* 28 May www.guardian.co.uk/society/2013/may/27/help-for-heroes-english-defence-league

Prevatt-Goldstein B (2002) Catch 22 – black workers' role in equal opportunities for black service users, *British Journal of Social Work* 32: 765-78

Prynne, M (2012) 'Fury at bonkers council decision to take foster kids from UKIP couple' *The Sun* 25 November 2012 www.thesun.co.uk/sol/homepage/news/4663893/Fury-at-bonkers-council-decision-to-take-foster-kids-from-UKIP-couple.html

Punwar N (2004) *Space invaders: Race, gender and bodies out of place.* Oxford, Berg

Ramamurthy, A (2006) The politics of Britain's Asian youth movements, *Race and Class*, 48(2)

Ramamurthy, A (2007) Kala Tara: A history of the Asian youth movements in Britain in the 1970s and 1980s, www.tandana.org/kalatara2000.pdf

Ramdin, R (1987) *The Making of the Black Working Class in Britain* (Aldershot, Wildwood House)

Rapley, J (2004) *Globalization and inequality: Neoliberalism's downward spiral*, Boulder, Lynne Rinner Publishers

Reed, CA (1994) The omission of anti-Semitism in anti-racism, *Canadian Woman Studies*, vol. 14, no. 2

Renton, D (2006) *When we touched the sky*, London New Clarion Press

Reuters (2011) The Great Debate UK: The racial wealth gap: not just an American problem, http://blogs.reuters.com/great-debate-uk/2011/04/08/the-racial-wealth-gap-not-just-an-american-problem

Richardson, B (ed) *Say it loud: Marxism and the fight against racism*, London: Bookmarks

Roberts JM (2004) What's social about social capital?, *British Journal of Politics and International Relations* 6(4) 471-93

Robinson, L (1997) Nigrescence, in M Davies (ed) *The Blackwell companion to social work*. Oxford, Blackwell

Rochdale Borough Council (2011) Rochdale Borough Child and Family Poverty Strategy 2011, www.rochdale.gov.uk/pdf/2012-03-20-Poverty-Strategy.pdf

Rochdale Online (2013) End Child Poverty, www.rochdaleonline.co.uk/news-features/2/news/78047/child-poverty-in-rochdale

Rojek, C, Peacock, G and Collins, S (1989) *Social work and received ideas*, London: Routledge

Rorke, B, Wilkens, A (eds) (2006) *Roma inclusion. Lessons learned from OSI's Roma programming.* Budapest: OSI, www.soros.org/initiatives/roma/articles_publications/publications/inclusion_20060605

Rose, J (2004) *The myths of Zionism*, London: Pluto Press

Rosenfeld, A (2007) *'Progressive' Jewish thought and the new anti-Semitism*, American Jewish Committee, www.ajc.org/atf/cf/%7B42D75369-D582-4380-8395-D25925B85EAF%7D/PROGRESSIVE_JEWISH_THOUGHT.PDF

Roy, O (2005) Britain: Home grown terrorists, *Le Monde Diplomatique* August, http://mondediplo.com/2005/08/05terror

Royal College of Paediatrics and Child Health (2003) Assessment of the age of refugee children, www.rcpch.ac.uk/what-we-do/rcpch-publications/publications-list-title/publications-list-title

Royal College of Paediatrics and Child Health (2007) Xrays and asylum seeking children, Policy statement, 19 November, www.rcpch.ac.uk/child-health/standards-care/position-statements/position-statements

Runnymede Trust (1997) *Islamophobia: A challenge for us all* (Summary). London: Runnymede trust.

Said, EW (1996) *Orientalism: Postcolonial studies* (orig. *Orientalizem: zahodnjaški pogledi na Orient*). Ljubljana: Studia Humanitatis.

San Francisco Administrative Code, Chapter 12H www.sfgsa.org/index.aspx?page=1069

Sand, S (2009) *The invention of the Jewish people*, Verso

Save the Children (2012) Born equal how reducing inequality could give our children a better future, Save the Children, www.savethechildren.org.uk/sites/default/files/images/Born_Equal.pdf

Sayce, L (2000) *From psychiatric patient to citizen. Overcoming discrimination and social exclusion.* Palgrave.

Scottish Council of Jewish Communities (Scojec) (2012) Being Jewish in Scotland, Interim Project Report, www.scojec.org/news/2012/12iii_bjis_interim_report/interim_report.pdf

Sebag Montefiore, S (2011) *Jerusalem: The biography*, Weidenfield & Nicholson, London

Shackle, S (2009) Since when was it OK to target Asians? *The Guardian*, 2 September

Shepherd, J (2012) Starkey makes cultural link to gang jailed for sexually exploiting girls, *The Guardian*, 10 May, www.guardian.co.uk/culture/2012/may/10/starkey-comment-gang-sexually-exploiting-girls

Short, G (1991) Combating anti-Semitism: A dilemma for anti-racist education, *British Journal of Education Studies*, vol. XXXIX, no 1, 0007-1005

Shukra, K (1998) *The changing pattern of black politics in Britain*, Pluto

Siddiqui, A (2008) Who needs a caliphate? *The Guardian*, 27 February

Šiftar, V (1970) Gypsies (orig. *Cigani),* Murska Sobota: Pomurska založba

Silverman W, Ortiz C, Viswesvaran C, Burns B, Kolko D, Putnam F, Amaya-Jackson L (2003) Evidence-based psychosocial treatments for children and adolescents exposed to traumatic events, *Journal of Clinical Child and Adolescent Psychology*, 37, 1, 156-83

Singh G (1992) Race and social work from black pathology to black perspectives, Master's Dissertation, University of Bradford, Race Relations Research Unit

Singh, G (1994) Anti-racist social work: political correctness or political change, *Social Work Education*, 13, 5, 26-9

Singh, G (1996) Anti-racist and black perspectives in practice teaching, *Social Work Education*, 15, 2, 35-56

Singh, G (2006) Anti-racist social work and postmodernism, in M, Todd and M Farrar (eds) Teaching 'race' in social sciences – new contexts, new approaches,, London: C-CSP

Singh, G and Cowden, S (2011) Multiculturalism's new faultlines: religious fundamentalisms and public policy. *Critical Social Policy* 32(3) 343-64

Sivanandan, A (1982) *A different hunger*, London: Pluto

Sivanandan, A (1990) *Communities of resistance*, London: Verso
Sivanandan A (1991) Black struggles against racism, in CCETSW *Setting the context for change*, Leeds, CCETSW Northern Curriculum Development Project
Sivanandan, A (2001) Notes in *IRR European Race Bulletin* 37, June
Sivanandan, A (2002) The contours of global racism, Speech delivered at the conference Crossing Borders: TheLegacy of the Commonwealth Immigrants Act 1962, London Metropolitan University, 26 November, www.irr.org.uk/2002/november/ak000007.html
Sivanandan, A (2006) Race, terror and civil society, *Race and Class*, 46 (3) 1-8
Sivanandan, A (2008) *Catching history on the wing: Race, culture and globalisation*, London: Pluto Press
Sky News (2009) Police use of stop and search powers soar, 30 April, http://news.sky.com/skynews/Home/UK-News/Anti-Terror-Legislation-Sees-Police-Use-Of-Stop-And-Search-Laws-Treble-In-England-And-Wales/Article/200904415272529?f=rss
Sky News (2013) Woolwich: EDL protests as mosques targeted http://news.sky.com/story/1094547/woolwich-edl-protests-as-mosques-targeted
Smith, D and Greenfields, M (2012) Housed gypsies and travellers in the UK: work, exclusion and adaptation, *Race & Class*, 53, 3
Smith, J (2008) Home Secretary's speech at the Conference on Preventing Violent Extremism, 10 December, Home Office Press Office http://press.homeoffice.gov.uk/Speeches/hs-speech-violent-extremism
Smith, R (2008) *Social work and power*. Basingstoke. Palgrave Macmillan
Social Work Action Network (2004) Social Work and Social Justice: a Manifesto for a New Engaged Practice www.socialworkfuture.org/about-swan/national-organisation/manifesto
Social Work Action Network (2011) "Defend Norbert Ferencz" www.socialworkfuture.org/articles-and-analysis/international-articles/245-vote-for-norbert-ferencz
Social Work Action Network (2004) Social work and social justice: a manifesto for a new engaged practice, *Social Work Education*, 19, 1, 77-87
Socialist Worker (2011) Jack Straw opens door to racism again, 15 January, www.socialistworker.co.uk/art.php?id=23571
Soifer, S (1991) Infusing content about Jews and about Antisemitism into the curricula, *Journal of Social Work Education*, 27, 2
Solomos, J (1988) *Black youth, racism and the state* (Cambridge, CUP)

Squire,V (2009) *The exclusionary politics of asylum,* Basingstoke: Palgrave Macmillan

Stacey, CL (2005) Finding dignity in dirty work: the constraints and rewards of low-wage home care labour,*Sociology of Health and Illness* 27, 831–54

Stewart, M (1997) *The time of the Gypsies.* Boulder, Oxford: Westview Press

Straw, J (2006) 'I felt uneasy talking to someone I couldn't see', *The Guardian*, 6 October, www.theguardian.com/commentisfree/2006/oct/06/politics.uk

Stringer, D (2009) UK: Most terrorism suspects freed *The Guardian* 13 May, www.guardian.co.uk/world/feedarticle/8505429

Štrukelj, P (2004) *Tisočletne podobe nemirnih nomadov: zgodovina in kultura Romov v Sloveniji (A thousand years of images of restless Nomads: History and culture of roma in Slovenia)*. Ljubljana: Družina

Stubbs, P (1985) The employment of black social workers: from ethnic sensitivity to anti-racism. *Critical Social Policy*, issue 12, 85, 6-27

Tablet (2012) Meet Europe's new fascists, www.tabletmag.com/jewish-news-and-politics/96716/meet-europes-new-fascists

Tabloid Watch (2011) 'The "gangsta salute" that wasn't', 8 December, http://tabloid-watch.blogspot.co.uk/2011/12/gangsta-salute-that-wasnt.html

Tahir, T (2013) Sharp rise in attacks on Muslims in the wake of Lee Rigby murder, senior police officer says, *Metro*, 10 June, http://metro.co.uk/2013/06/10/sharp-rise-in-attacks-on-muslims-in-the-wake-of-lee-rigby-murder-senior-police-officer-says-3835209/

Taylor, D and Muir, H (2010) 'Border staff humiliate and trick asylum seekers - whistle blower', *The Guardian*, 2 February, www.theguardian.com/uk/2010/feb/02/border-staff-asylum-seekers-whistleblower

Taylor, K (2001) *In search of refuge: Freedom to roam: The Roma and the EU*, www.story-index1.htm

Taylor, M, Meikle, J and Dodd, V (2013) Islamic centre fire: police investigate graffiti link to EDL, *The Guardian*, 6 June, www.guardian.co.uk/uk/2013/jun/05/police-edl-link-blaze-islamic-centre?INTCMP=SRCH

Tedam, P (2013) Developing cultural competence in A Bartoli (ed) *Anti-racism in social work practice*, Critical Publishing Ltd

Telegraph, The (2009) 12 arrested in North West terrorist raids all released without charge, 22 April, www.telegraph.co.uk/news/newstopics/politics/lawandorder/5199690/12-arrested-in-North-West-terrorist-raids-all-released-without-charge.html

Thatcher, M (1978) TV interview for Granada *World in Action* ('Rather swamped') 27 January, Margaret Thatcher Foundation, www.margaretthatcher.org/document/103485

Thomas, JM (2013) Free-riding foreigners: the next NHS scandal, *The Spectator*, 23 February, www.spectator.co.uk/features/8847831/the-next-nhs-scandal/

Thompson, N (1993) Somewhere over the rainbow: universality and diversity in social policy, in N Manning and R Page (eds) *Social Policy Review*, 4

Thompson, N (2001) *Anti-discriminatory practice.* London: Palgrave Macmillan.

Thompson, N (2011) *Promoting equality: Working with diversity and difference.* 3rd edn. Basingstoke, Palgrave MacMillan

Thompson, N (2012) *Anti-discriminatory practice: Equality, diversity and social justice*, (5th edn) Basingstoke, Palgrave Macmillan

Tickle, L (2012) Looked-after children: care should be in the community, *The Guardian,* 24 October www.guardian.co.uk/social-care-network/2012/oct/24/looked-after-children-care-in-community?INTCMP=SRCH

Topping, A (2012) Children's Commissioner defends child sex abuse report, *The Guardian,* 21 November www.guardian.co.uk/society/2012/nov/21/children-commissioner-defends-sex-abuse-report

Townsend, M (2010) 'Black people are 26 times more likely than whites to face stop and search' *The Observer* 17 October www.theguardian.com/uk/2010/oct/17/stop-and-search-race-figures

Townsend, M (2011) 'UK Border Agency Officials 'illegally targetting' bus passengers, *The Observer*, 5 November, www.theguardian.com/uk/2011/nov/05/border-agency-targeting-bus-passengers

Townsend, M (2013) Immigration opposition falls when told about benefits, survey shows, *The Observer* 8 June, www.theguardian.com/uk/2013/jun/08/immigration-opposition-falls-benefits-survey

Travis, A (2010) Ministers dismantle £60m programme to prevent violent extremism, *The Guardian,* 13 July www.guardian.co.uk/politics/2010/jul/13/ministers-dismantle-programme-prevent-violent-extremism

Travis, A (2011) 'David Cameron launches immigration crackdown', The Guardian 10 October www.theguardian.com/uk/2011/ct/10/david-cameron-immigration-crackdown

Traynor, I (2008) Antisemitism and Islamophobia rising across Europe, survey finds *The Guardian*, 18 September

Twigg, J (2000) Carework as a form of bodywork. *Ageing and Society* 20, 389–411

UK Border Agency (2011) COMPASS: Working with migrants from outside the EU, www.ukba.homeoffice.gov.uk/aboutus/workingwithus/workingwithasylum/compassprogramme

UNHCR and Asylum Aid (2011) *Mapping statelessness in the United Kingdom,* London: United Nations High Commissioner for Refugees

Unison (2009) *Unison Migrant Workers Participation Project: Evaluation report.* Unison, London

Urh, Š (2011) Ethnic sensitivity: a challenge for social work. *International social work,* 54, no 4, 471-484.

Urh, Š (2013) *Culturally competent social work: Ethnic sensitivity and antiracist perspective in social work for efficient working with members of ethnic minorities and for working in multicultural environment* (orig. *Kulturno kompetentno socialno delo. Etnična občutljivost in antirasistična perspektiva v socialnem delu za učinkovito delo s pripadniki etničnih manjšin in za učinkovito delo v večkulturnem okolju*). Ljubljana: Fakulteta za socialno delo (in print)

Urh, Š. (2009) Etnično občutljivo socialno delo z Romi (orig. Ethnically sensitive social work with Roma) doctoral dissertation. Ljubljana: Faculty of Social Work

Vallely, P (2012) Child sex grooming: the Asian question, *The Independent,* 10 May, www.independent.co.uk/news/uk/crime/child-sex-grooming-the-asian-question-7729068.html

Varsa, E (2005) Class, ethnicity and gender – structures of differentiation in state socialist employment and welfare politics, 1960-1980. The issue of women's employment and the introduction of the first maternity leave regulation, in V K Shilde, S D Schulte (eds) *Need and care: Glimpses into the beginnings of Eastern Europe's professional welfare.* Barbara Budruch Publishers, 197-220

Verkaik, R (2009) Just one in eight terror arrests ends with guilty verdict, admits Home Office *The Independent,* 14 May, www.independent.co.uk/news/uk/home-news/just-one-in-eight-terror-arrests-ends-with-guilty-verdict-admits-home-office-1684580.html

Vickers T (2012) *Refugees, capitalism and the British state. Implications for social workers, volunteers and activists.* Surrey: Ashgate

Visran, R (2002) *Asians in Britain: 400 years of history,*London: Pluto

Volosinov, VN (1986) *Marxism and the philosophy of language.* Translation of *Marksizm i filosofiia iazyka* by Matejka, L, Titunik, IR (1929) Massechusetts: Harvard University Press

Weaver M (2013) Islamic boarding school fire in Bromley treated as suspicious by police, *The Guardian*, 9 June www.guardian.co.uk/uk/2013/jun/09/islamic-boarding-school-fire-bromley-suspicious?INTCMP=SRCH

Weinstock, N (1979) *Zionism: False Messiah*, London: Ink Links Ltd.

Widgery, D (1986) *Beating time: Riot n' race n' rock n' roll*, London: Chatto

Willems, W (1998) Ethnicity as a death trap: the history of Gypsy studies, in L Lucassen, W Willems, A Cottaar (eds) *Gypsies and other itinerant groups: A socio-historical approach*, London: Macmillan

Williams C and Short C (1997) *Working with difference*, Cardiff, Care Council for Wales. www.ccw.org

Williams C and Johnson M (2010) *Race and ethnicity in a welfare society*. Open University Press

Williams, C (1999) Connecting anti-racist and anti-oppressive theory and practice: retrenchment or reappraisal? *British Journal of Social Work*. 29, 211-230

Williams, F (1996) Racism and social policy: a critique of welfare theory, in, D Taylor (ed) *Critical social policy: A reader*, London: Sage

Williams, F (2010) Migration and care: themes, concepts and challenges. *Social Policy and Society*. 9, 3, 385-396

Williams, Z (2012) Who profits from being in care? It's not the children, *The Guardian* 31 October www.guardian.co.uk/commentisfree/2012/oct/31/who-profits-from-being-in-care?INTCMP=SRCH

Williams, Z (2011) A strategic cat fib, Theresa May? It's all in the service of myth making, *The Guardian*

Wistrich R (1991) *Antisemitism: The longest hatred*, London: Thames Methuen

Wright, O, Morris, N and Legge, J (2013) EDL marches on Newcastle as attacks on Muslims increase tenfold in the wake of Woolwich machete attack which killed Drummer Lee Rigby *The Independent* 25 May, http://tinyurl.com/php3nq9

Yan MC (2008) Exploring cultural tensions in cross-cultural social work practice, *Social Work*, 53(4), 317-28. www.scie-socialcareonline.org.uk/profile.asp?guid=8766f054-51c3-490b-a799-7e65bf253eec

Yaqoob, S (2003) Global and local echoes of the anti-war movement: a British Muslim perspective, *International Socialism 100* (Autumn) http://pubs.socialistreviewindex.org.uk/isj100/yaqoob.htm

Yeates, N (2009) *Globalizing care economies and migrant workers: Explorations*. Basingstoke: Palgrave Macmillian

Yezza, H (2008)'Britain's terror laws have left me and my family shattered', *The Guardian*, 18 August, www.theguardian.com/commentisfree/2008/aug/18/terrorism.civilliberties

Younge, G (2009a) Where will we find the perfect Muslim for monocultural Britain? *The Guardian* 30 March

Younge, G (2009b) 'I've changed my mind about racism', *The Guardian* 28 December, www.theguardian.com/commentisfree/2009/dec/28/goodbye-noughties-race-relations

Zaviršek, D (2000) *Handicap as a cultural trauma* (orig. *Hendikep kot kulturna travma).* Ljubljana: Založba/*cf

Zimmermann, M (1999) The national socialist solution of the gypsy question, in U Herbert (ed) *National socialist extermination policies. Contemporary German perspectives and controversies.* New York: Berghahn Books, 186–209

Index

A

B

C

I

J

K

Z